THE POSSIBILITY OF POLITICS

THE POSSIBILITY
OF POLITICS

*A study in the political economy of
the welfare state*

STEIN RINGEN

CLARENDON PRESS · OXFORD
1987

Oxford University Press, Walton Street, Oxford OX2 6DP
Oxford New York Toronto
Delhi Bombay Calcutta Madras Karachi
Petaling Jaya Singapore Hong Kong Tokyo
Nairobi Dar es Salaam Cape Town
Melbourne Auckland
and associated companies in
Beirut Berlin Ibadan Nicosia

Oxford is a trade mark of Oxford University Press

Published in the United States
by Oxford University Press, New York

British Library Cataloguing in Publication Data
Ringen, Stein
The possibility of politics:
a study in the political economy of the welfare state.
1. Great Britain—Social policy
I. Title
361.6'1'0941   HN385.5
ISBN 0-19-828574-4

Library of Congress Cataloging in Publication Data
Ringen, Stein.
The possibility of politics.
Includes index.
1. Social choice. 2. Welfare state. 3. Income distribution-Government
policy. I. Title.
HB846.8.R56 1987   361.6'5   86-28472
ISBN 0-19-828574-4

Set by Computerised Typesetting Services Ltd, Finchley, London
Printed in Great Britain
at the University Printing House, Oxford
by David Stanford
Printer to the University

Preface

Things do not always turn out as intended. The harder we try the more we fail. The best way to solve a problem is to ignore it. Our ability to do what we think best is limited by the intrinsic tendency for things to go wrong. These are commonplace devilries which many will recognize from their daily experience. Yet simple as they are, observations such as these have always intrigued and inspired those who have wanted to understand human activity and the workings of society. Why is it, if we want something, so difficult to do what it takes, even when this is within our power?

In this book a modern method for trying to resolve the age-old dilemma of intention and achievement is discussed: that of politics. This is a case of trying extremely hard and the opposite strategy of hoping that problems will solve themselves. Is it a realistic idea that a large number of people—a population—can get together, set themselves common goals, and try to reach these goals through collective action? Or must we accept that events have a way of deciding on their own and resign ourselves to playing the game of life with the cards we happen to be given by some invisible hand? For some decades there has been much optimism about the potentiality of politics; it appeared to have elevated our societies to a level of rationality wherefrom we could boast that what we want we can also have. But recently, many have come to see us as overtaken again by the dilemma we have wanted to escape; we have tried too hard, and instead of order we have confusion of a different kind.

The politics analysed are those of welfare state reform. Reformism is a cheerful ideology. It is not as optimistic as *laissez-faire*, which is the belief that things work themselves out for the best on their own, but much more optimistic than the revolutionary call for all or nothing. Granted that politics are necessary, the reformist says that a little is enough. We can limit ourselves to cautious and piecemeal interventions and still have reason in society. This is a sympathetic idea well worth taking in earnest. It is attractive to all who see beauty in economizing, to all who mistrust absolute power, and to all who fear the costs of strong political interventions, such as infringements of freedom. Yet for many, notably among academic writers, it is repulsive—some half-cocked approach which is neither hither nor thither. The extremes—Let the market rule! Don't just reform society, change it! — appear to have more appeal to the intellectual mind. I intend to take reformism seriously and to see if the experience of reform has proved to be as bad as the coalition of romantics left and right will have it.

The welfare state is reform on a grand scale. It is an attempt to change the circumstances individuals and families live under without basically changing society. No less; no wonder it is controversial. If the welfare state works, reform works.

Today's intense debate over the welfare state has become part of a larger debate over politics and has thereby grown increasingly general. In response to this movement from a concern with its practicalities to its principle, social scientists have taken up a study of the welfare state as such, to which tradition the present book belongs. By saying that this is a study of the welfare state as such, I mean that my concern is with the whole of the welfare state rather than its individual components, that it is with the universal welfare state rather than its particular manifestation in any single country, and that this is an analysis of the welfare state only, and not of some larger system or purpose in relation to which the welfare state could be seen as an instrument. The welfare state is an institution common, albeit with variations, to the industrial democracies. Research results show striking similarities across nations both in its impact on socio-economic conditions and in the response of the citizenry to its influence. From one country to another, the same questions are asked about its effectiveness and the same concerns raised about its inefficiencies. It is this institution as such that is analysed here. I shall try to find out if the welfare state works, but not if it helps society to work.

The approach of the study is that of rational choice. I see public policies, ideally and theoretically, as a choice on the part of citizens. I assume citizens to be rational, which is to say only that they want their choices to be effective. In its simplest possible formulation, the criterion of successful choice is that what we get is what we want. Public policies are the result of a large number of choices made over a long span of time. This may give rise to two kinds of irrationalities: first, that the aggregate outcome of all choices may turn out to be unintended, and second, that developments during the period from choices are made until their results materialize may lead the citizenry to reject the intended consequences of its own choices.

The 1970s provide a natural laboratory for the study of the welfare state. That decade saw a combination of ever more ambitious social policies and a change of economic circumstances and political orientations because of slow growth. As the welfare state matured, it was set to the test of performing in an economically and politically hostile environment. By looking back now on what happened then, we can see not only if the welfare state vessel floats but if it can sail through economic tempest and political gale.

The academic literature on the welfare state is a wasteland of facts and fiction in which what we know is not always carefully distinguished from what we believe, what we guess, what we hope, and what we suggest. Much of what is presented as established wisdom is no more than statements of opinion derived from ideological premises or mere deductions following from theoretical assumptions which may or may not be reasonable. This needs not be so. The policies of the welfare state, and their expansion, have long enough been a practical reality in our societies for them now to be discussed on the basis of experience and not mere speculation. During the last ten or fifteen years, in particular, the development of the welfare state has been carefully observed and the observations recorded in a large body of high-quality social policy research in many countries and disciplines, notably economics, political science, and sociology. We now know a great deal about how the welfare state works; we need only look it up, sort out the most credible information, piece it together, and interpret it within a relevant framework. While politicians are free to speculate about this as much as and in any direction they may find opportune, the task of a scientific inquiry should be to establish how much can be said by considering only what is known. The aim here is to present an empirically based interpretation of the welfare state.

In the first two chapters, I raise a framework of analysis which results in a set of empirically formulated questions. In the six subsequent chapters, I attempt to answer these questions, taking care not to say more than I think is warranted by the requirement of a solid basis of factual observation. I here draw as much as possible on available material in the literature, but add original material where I have found that to be necessary and possible. In the final chapter, the loose ends are pulled together.

One question I ask in this study: Does the welfare state work? One question I do not ask: Is the welfare state a good thing? I attempt to sort out the experience of the welfare state such as it has been tried, and that alone. Nothing will here be said about how the welfare state should look in the future. This is a study in our recent social history.

Acknowledgements

I decided to write this book when I, in 1983, joined the Institute for Social Research at the University of Stockholm as a visiting, later acting, professor of welfare studies. But the work had started earlier while I was Head of Research in the Department of Income Policy of the Norwegian Ministry of Consumer Affairs and Government Administration (an exceptionally broad-minded civil service unit) and there synthesized a number of smaller studies into a pamphlet called *Er velferdsstaten realistisk?* (Is the welfare state realistic?). Most of the issues pursued in the book were formulated in the pamphlet, but some of the answers of the two publications are different. The process from pamphlet to book has been a rewarding experience of seeing that careful research matters and that it is possible, pretty much, to let facts speak.

I want to express my gratitude to my colleagues at the Institute for Social Research, in particular to Robert Erikson, Peter Hedström, Walter Korpi, Jan Selén and Eskil Wadensjö for continuous discussion and co-operation, and for their comments on endless working papers and early drafts, to Miljan Vuksanović for help with programming and data processing, and to Eva Carlsson, Ulla Carlstedt, Anne-Maj Folmer-Hansen, Eleonor Rapier, and in particular Gudrun Österman for their competent work on the manuscript in its various stages. I could not have completed this book without the kind of stimulating multi-disciplinary atmosphere of this fine Institute.

I have been fortunate to spend time while working on the book at The Jerusalem Institute for Israel Studies (in March–April 1985), at the Max-Planck-Institut für Bildungsforschung in Berlin (where the final editing of the manuscript was completed in May and June of 1986), and on numerous occasions at the Institute for Applied Social Research in Oslo (whenever I felt a need to escape the heavy influence of the Swedish welfare state).

More friends and colleagues than can be listed have given useful help and kind support, but I would like to mention Gösta Esping Andersen, Irv Garfinkel, John Goldthorpe, Björn Gustafsson, Ingemar Hansson, Ken Judge, Jon Eivind Kolberg, Michael O'Higgins, Casten von Otter, Natalie Rogoff Ramsøy, Peter Saunders,

Michael Shalev, Hans Tson Söderström, Peter Taylor-Gooby, Tim Tilton, Mariken Vaa, Kari Waerness, Rune Ågberg, and my brothers Anders and Knut (who both happen to be in more or less the same business). Hannu Uusitalo read the entire manuscript (except for the concluding chapter) in its next to final version.

The Norwegian and Swedish data used in Chapter 8 were made available by the respective Central Statistical Agencies. I want to thank in particular Yngve Bergstrøm, Håkan Björk, and Grethe Sparby for their painstaking assistance. Financial support for the preparation of these data was granted by the Norwegian Ministry of Consumer Affairs and Government administration and the Scientific Fund of Statistics Sweden.

An early version of Chapter 1 was presented at a seminar at the Department of Government at the University of Uppsala in March 1985 and later at the Jerusalem Institute for Israel Studies in April. A vast working paper which eventually developed into Chapters 4 and 5 was discussed at the Fourth Nordic Research Conference on Social Policy in Stockholm in October 1984. A first paper in the spirit of Chapter 7 was read to the Research Committee on Inequality, Poverty, and Social Policy of the International Sociological Association in Budapest in August 1981 and later presented to various seminars (The Policy Studies Institute and the Civil Service College, both in London; The Centre for the Analysis of Social Policy, University of Bath; The Department of Sociology, California State University at Northridge; the Department of Economics, New York University; and at the Clarke/Luxembourg Conference on Poverty and Inequality at the University of Clarke, Massachussetts, in September 1983). A fuller report on the income comparisons in Chapter 8 was written for the Export Group for Studies in Public Finance of the Swedish Ministry of Finance and was discussed in draft form by its 'reference group'. Early versions of Chapters 1, 2, 3, and 7 have been discussed in a regular social policy work shop under the Swedish Delegation for Social Research. A preliminary version of Chapter 9 was discussed at a seminar at the Department of Sociology at the University of Stockholm in April 1986, the day before I left the University, and again at the Zentralinstitut für sozialwissenschaftliche Forschung of the Freie Universität, Berlin in June. On all these occasions, I have received comments and suggestions which have been useful and important in the completion of the book, and for which I here record my gratitude.

Contents

1
The Strategy of Redistribution

The welfare state is an experiment in politics. It is an attempt to bring the distribution of welfare in the population under the control of deliberate political action. We can now speak of this attempt as an experiment since it is no longer merely an idea but has been tried in real life, and since it has been tried we can judge its results. This is what the present book is about. I want to establish from recent experience whether the welfare state works.

The Experiment

Men and women who have pondered over the nature of human coexistence have sometimes believed or hoped that our societies could be so wisely arranged that if we were only free individually to pursue our own good, we would together inadvertently create an environment which would encourage each of us to act so as to advance the common good. From this they have concluded that the authority of the state in economic matters should be limited to protecting the market against monopolizations and to balance market imperfections. This was the dominant theory of the state during the age of liberalism in the nineteenth century and the beginning of this century.

Other theoreticians and ideologists have believed that free markets, far from being to the benefit of all, result in chaos, inefficiency, and unfairness. There is no such thing, they have said, as a common good which exists in itself but at best only a common interest which

A note on notes: Footnotes are used extensively for reference, documentation, qualifications, and discussion of methodological issues. Appendices are used for concentrating the presentation and discussion of technical material. The careful reader will need to pay close attention to footnotes and appendices (but the general reader may want to skip them)—in particular Appendices C and F without which the arguments in Chapters 5 and 8 cannot be fully appreciated.

must be worked out explicitly through a process of agreement and which must be protected and advanced by a central authority. Instead of setting their trust in the invisible hand of the market, they have advocated the method of politics, whereby central planning rather than self-regulation is used for the co-ordination of economic activity and far-reaching authority to regulate markets and redistribute income is entrusted in the state.[1]

In the advanced industrial democracies, as well as in other systems, we have during this century more and more come to rely on the method of politics,[2] as can be witnessed by economic policies, social policies, labour market policies, environmental policies, regional policies, industrial policies, incomes policies, housing policies, consumer policies, family policies, and so on endlessly; and by public planning, the growth of central and local government budgets and bureaucracies, and ever more penetrating regulations; by the tendency of individuals, groups, organizations and businesses to take their case to government whenever they are in difficulty. In particular the crises of the 1920s and 1930s, the 'Keynesian revolution' in economic theory, and the experiences of the Second World War led to a new faith in government. During the last three or four decades, the balance between markets and politics has shifted strongly in favour of politics. The post-war period can be regarded as a Large-Scale Experiment of trying out in practice the theory of using politics to protect and promote the common interest. The welfare state is part of this endeavour. With a considerable over-simplification we can say that the experiment consists of economic policy for the management of the problem of production and social policy for the management of the problem of distribution.

Today, we are in the midst of a Grand Debate over how successful the experiment has been. Half a century ago, there was intense disagreement about the wisdom of launching it on a grand scale. Then, for a time, while the method of politics was being tried, the mood was apprehensive. Now that we start to see the results, there is again a sharply divided controversy over just what these results show. There are some who see this controversy as a sign of 'crisis' in

---

[1] I take the term *politics* to mean *public politics*, and use the terms *government* and *state* to refer to all agencies of public politics without distinguishing between different kinds of agencies, for instance central and local government.

[2] Of course, in a longer historical perspective, going back to mercantilism, there is nothing new in giving politics priority above markets.

the political system. This is a little odd. The markets vs. politics issue is at least two centuries old. The only thing that is new today is that we can now discuss these matters on the basis of experience. I choose to see the Grand Debate as an exercise in self-criticism. Critical evaluation is part of any serious experiment. The time has come to take stock of what has been achieved. We have wanted to gain control over the material circumstances of our lives. For this purpose we have entrusted vast authority in government and let the state develop into a machine of enormous power. Public politics are no invention of the twentieth century, but the democratic state with its contemporary extensive power is a new phenomenon. We have created this state to use it for our benefit; we are now asking if it has turned out as intended or if our creation has grown into a Franken-steinian monster that we no longer control and that may turn against us. This is a troublesome question. But it would have been more troublesome had it not been asked.

The present book aims to contribute to the Grand Debate over the experiment in politics. I have picked out for closer scrutiny only one part of the larger experiment, the welfare state, but will thereby inevitably comment also on the experiment as such. To attempt to answer the question 'Does the welfare state work?', is indirectly to say something about the larger question 'Is politics possible?'. And if it were not that I already have more than a reasonable share of broad questions on my plate I might have been tempted to add, 'Is democracy possible?'[3]

Definition

There are about as many definitions of 'welfare state' as there are members of the growing profession of writers about the welfare state, and not only are their definitions many in number, they are also different in kind. The welfare state is sometimes a political sector (for example, the 'social sector' as distinguished from the 'economic sector'), sometimes a kind of government (for example, a government which has been given a high degree of responsibility

---

[3] Others, more daring than I, have accepted this challenge. See e.g. Britain (1975); Buchanan & Wagner (1977); Rose & Peters (1978); Usher (1981).

for the welfare of the population), sometimes a kind of socio-economic system (for example, a system with a dominant public sector), and sometimes even a kind of society or civilization, in which case the terms welfare state and welfare society tend to become confused.[4] As a concept, welfare state is at the very least ambiguous and perhaps more to be reckoned as a slogan. Richard Titmuss, for one, recognized this when he set the term within quotation-marks in the title of his now classic *Essays on the 'Welfare State'*, first published in 1958, and thereby inaugurated what has become a solid tradition of using the term as a catch-word or heading under which selected policies are discussed. I shall follow suit and use the term welfare state in a restricted meaning to describe a specific set of policies in a limited set of nations.

Means

Governments can use several types of policies to influence the distribution of welfare. Policies which have distributional consequences can be classified according to whether they are introduced early or late in the distributive process. *Redistributive policies* are used towards the end of the distributive process to modify primary distributions or to repair damage or compensate dis-welfares which have arisen in earlier stages of the process. These policies aim, for example, to redistribute market income after the market has done its job. Income maintenance belongs to this category: for example, old age pensions, sickness insurance, and unemployment compensation. Health care is to a large extent a matter of treating illness or injury after it has occurred. Progressive taxation is intended to reduce income inequalities after they have arisen. Food subsidies are used to adjust a price structure which is considered to be problematic from a welfare point of view.

Regulatory policies are used in the earlier parts of the distributive process to regulate mechanisms which might otherwise result in inequalities, damage, or dis-welfares. These policies are introduced to influence the distribution of market income or other primary distributions or to prevent problems from arising in the first place.

[4] For an analysis of the concept of *welfare state*, see e.g. Kuhnle (1983:Ch. 3). For examples of different definitions, see e.g. Schottland (1967).

One of the goals of incomes policy has been to influence the distribution of pre-tax/transfer income, for instance through special measures to prevent the use of very low wages. An objective of employment policy is obviously the prevention of unemployment, and a wide range of health policies are preventive more than they are curative. Consumer protection is intended to keep damaging products away from the market, and family policies to avert later problems which might be caused by childhood deprivation. Environmental protection is very much a question of preventing problems which might be caused by polluted or dangerous environments.[5]

The welfare state concept used in this study is limited to redistributive policies and does not include regulatory policies. More precisely, this is a study of the effects of transfers and taxes, with special reference to progressive income taxes and household transfers in the form of cash income maintenance, consumer subsidies, and free or subsidized services. This I call *the strategy of redistribution*. The policies of this strategy are, for simplicity and convenience, sometimes referred to as *redistributive policies* and sometimes as *social policies*. The idea of the welfare state is to distribute again, by way of politics, what has already once been distributed in the market.

An alternative approach could have been to include all policies which have or might have distributional effects. That might have been relevant since many policies which are not considered here— labour market policies, environmental policies, and regional policies, to mention a few—can clearly have considerable distributional effects, perhaps stronger effects than the policies which are considered. The reason for choosing a more limited use of the

---

[5] The theoretical distinction between redistributive and regulatory policies is in practice not clear cut. Many policies can have both before-the-fact and after-the-fact effects. Family allowance aims both to prevent poverty and to redistribute purchasing power. Home care for the elderly compensates their inability to cope with all their daily requirements but may also save them from having to move to an old-age institution. Sometimes policies have before-the-fact and after-the-fact effects which pull in different directions. Progressive taxes may reduce inequality in post-tax income, but may also encourage increased inequality in pre-tax income if those wage earners who are hit most severely by high marginal tax rates bring the tax question into their wage negotiations and successfully demand extra wages to compensate their tax burden. The concepts of redistributive and regulatory policies have been used previously by other writers in a different meaning from how they are used here, cf. e.g. Lowi (1972).

concept is that this reflects a vision, as simple as it is bold, which has been one of the most important inspirations for the development of social policies to their present scope. The vision in question can be expressed thus: yes, we need policies to promote social goals; no, these policies should not change the nature of our societies. This exceedingly optimistic outlook rests on a theory which goes back to John Stuart Mill's distinction, in *Principles of Political Economy* (1848), between the laws of production, which he considered to be natural and technological, and the laws of distribution, which he considered to be 'social'. A practical application of this theory has been taken to be that economic goals should be influenced by one set of policies and social goals by another set, and that social policies should be introduced late in the process so as not to interfere with the mechanisms of production. Among modern theorists, Richard Titmuss in particular has argued for the separation of economic and social policies and the potential of the strategy of redistribution.[6] Although few today might be willing to subscribe uncritically to the separation of social laws from economic laws and although no state lives according to this learning, the theory remains immensely influential. It is politically attractive because it promises equality without radically affecting the system of production, ownership, and power; and it is pragmatically attractive because it promises equality without inefficiency. This is the theory which has found its practical manifestation in the modern welfare state. Social policy is not and has hardly ever been seen as an instrument to tame the forces of the market, but is primarily a way of modifying some of the effects of these forces.

This analysis, concentrating on the strategy of redistribution, is not a full analysis of the problem of distribution. I shall not attempt to explain the distribution of welfare, but only to find out how it is influenced by social policies. Nor is this a full analysis of the distributive effects of all policies or of the potential for creating equality by political means. I shall analyse only the effects of redistributive policies. It is a study of one among several possible political strategies; a strategy through which it is attempted to promote equality without regulating the basic processes which generate inequality. The object of this study is the power of the strategy of redistribution.

[6] See in particular Titmuss (1968:Part III).

The limitation of the welfare state concept to include only redistribution gives a more precise meaning to the concept of politics as considered here. The welfare state is an experiment in politics but not in any kind of politics; it is an experiment in *reform*. The essence of reformism, I think, is that, for fear of intolerable side-effects, limitations are imposed on the use of means, even to the extent of excluding a wide range of means which are recognized as effective in relation to given goals. This, of course, gives rise to a debate about the possibility of reform. Can we achieve what we want if we a priori deprive ourselves of the freedom to use the most effective means, or is reformism merely the refuge of the timid who cannot stomach action and a trap of political paralysis? Is the idea of politics without side-effects at all realistic, or is it a form of escapism for those who will not see that even careful reform gradually escalates to powerful interventions which do more harm than good?

Exactly where to set the dividing line between reform and more drastic or revolutionary approaches is a matter for much debate, but some political strategies are clearly more reformist than others. The strategy of redistribution, being limited to policies which are introduced after the fact with no intention of regulating underlying economic processes, is a case of pure reform. On a more general level, then, the object of the study is the power of political reform.

Goals

The immediate goal of redistributive policies is *equality* (or fairness or some degree of equality or fairness) in the distribution of available goods and unavoidable burdens (however the concepts of equality or fairness are interpreted in the political culture of the society in question). The welfare state is aimed to make the distribution of welfare more egalitarian or fair than it is assumed it would have been in the absence of social policies.

That equality is a goal in the welfare state we know from what politicians say, from what we can read in policy documents,[7] and from the existence of policies that cannot be understood independently of some redistributive intention. The clearest example of the

[7] As documented by e.g. Bjerve (1959); Le Grand (1982:Ch. 2); Hechscher (1984:227 ff.)

latter is the progressive income tax which has been a common feature in the tax systems of the industrial nations.

The sincerity of the goal of equality can be and often is questioned, but this is not necessarily to question the existence of the goal in itself. Equality is a controversial principle, clear enough, but those who support an ideology of equality have managed at least to get it established as one among several goals of public policy. Whether policies are enacted which in fact generate equality is a different question. It might be, for example, that those who are opposed to equality have seen themselves forced to accept the principle in the formulation of goals but have still been able to prevent effective means from being taken into use. Policy goals have a life of their own. We cannot argue as if the only goals that are real are those which are followed up by effective means. If we for a moment disregard completely the question of what means are implemented and look only at the intention which has been formulated through the political process, it is clear that equality, in some understanding of the term, is part of this intention. The existence and growth of the welfare state cannot be understood without taking into consideration, among other factors, some commitment to an egalitarian or fair distribution of welfare.

The goal of equality can be given a weak or a strong interpretation. In its weak interpretation, it implies a guaranteed *minimum standard* for all members of society, including economic security in case of inability to earn one's own income (through, for example, social security, sickness and unemployment compensation, or, as a last resort, social assistance) and the right to certain basic services, such as elementary education and necessary treatment and care during illness or disability, or for orphans and the permanently handicapped. In its strong formulation, the redistributive goal refers not only to the minimum standard but to the entire *structure of inequality*, such as the distribution of income, purchasing power, or consumption, the general standard of educational and other social services, and the degree to which members of, for example, different socio-economic or income groups have the same opportunities or access to services of the same quality. In the first case, the ambition is to eliminate destitution and individual misery, in the second case to eliminate, in addition, societal cleavages which might cause conflict and tension in society.[8]

---

[8] Terminology: The term *societal* is used in the meaning 'of society' or 'of society as a whole', as distinguished from the term *social* as used in e.g. 'social policy'.

To say that equality is the immediate goal of the welfare state is not to say that this is its only or ultimate goal or that the quest for equality explains the existence of the welfare state. The welfare state is a part of the total system of public policy and this total system obviously has general goals on a higher level than the immediate goals of each part of the system, such as, for example, to consolidate the power of the prevailing regime or the stability of the economic system, to protect capitalism, to develop socialism, to advance economic prosperity, or to create a harmonious society. However this may be, the immediate goal of the welfare state is still equality, even if the achievement of this goal can also be seen as a means in relation to more general goals. The present analysis is of the welfare state as such, rather than of its historical or societal role in relation to what may or may not be some more ultimate aim or purpose, and is consequently conducted in relation to its immediate goal of equality.

Welfare state nations

The welfare state is found in democratic nations only. Not all analysts of social policy distinguish between democratic and non-democratic systems, and for many purposes this is, of course, not necessary. But, although this distinction does not strictly follow from my welfare state definition, and although non-democratic systems can and do have active social policies,[9] it is for me a completely obvious one to make in the present analysis.

Democracy is, among other things, a method for establishing what the common interest is. In a perfect democracy, every citizen has equal access to participation in the political process and equal power to influence it. The outcome of this process corresponds, by definition, to the common interest. Real democracies, however, are never perfect and even when democracy works reasonably well, such as in contemporary Western democracies, the distribution of power and of access to and participation in the political process is

[9] For example, social insurance was not discontinued in Nazi-Germany, and the East European nations today have highly developed social policies. See e.g. Pryor (1968); Ferge (1979).

far from egalitarian. It can, therefore, not be assumed that public policies in real democracies necessarily correspond to the common interest; this is in each case an empirical question. On the other hand, it can be assumed that in non-democratic systems there is a conflict between the policies of the state and the common interest since there would be no need to maintain a dictatorship unless there was such a conflict.

Since dictatorships can only maintain themselves by suppressing the people, it makes no sense to describe a dictatorial state as committed to the welfare of its population. In democracies, the population has won basic and equal civil and political rights, in the form of legal security, freedom of expression and faith, eligibility, and universal suffrage. The welfare state can be seen as a further development of democracy in that the promise of a decent standard of living is granted to all not as a charity but as a right.[10] The significance of social policies depends not only on these policies themselves, but also on the society in which they are used. Social policies cannot expand the democratic nature of society unless there is already legal and political democracy, and they may have very different functions in societies where people are denied their basic rights from those in which these rights have been obtained. One of the more general functions of redistribution has been seen as to contribute to societal consensus. This is legitimate in a society where people have the right to vote for competing parties and are free to voice their discontent and to promote openly their interests or what they see as right, but potentially manipulative and oppressive in a society where such rights and freedoms are suppressed.[11]

The group of welfare state nations is further limited to nations where the state has been entrusted with considerable responsibility and authority in socio-economic affairs and where the strategy of redistribution has been implemented, that is, where considerable

---

[10] As has been argued by Marshall (1964, 1977).

[11] It is, of course, not unproblematic even in societies where such freedoms are secured. It can justifiably be argued that there is always an element in social policy of making things look better than they are, but it is hardly reasonable to regard the social policies of democratic systems exclusively or even mainly as manipulation from above. In their much discussed *Regulating the Poor* (1972), Piven & Cloward interpreted social policy in the United States in light of a theory of manipulation, but they have later, in *The New Class War* (1982), significantly modified this interpretation.

transfers are in effect and the level of taxation consequently high, and where more or less progressive rates of income taxation are applied. A state with the ambition of redistributing welfare is no welfare state unless it also has the economic resources and means to follow this ambition up with practical action.

These criteria, conveniently, limit the analysis to the industrial democracies of Western Europe, North America, and the Far East, in short, roughly the OECD[12] countries. About these nations, I assume that redistributive egalitarianism is part of their political culture—at least in the weak interpretation of the goal of equality—and that the strategy of redistribution has been implemented with some force. Some might perhaps question whether the egalitarian commitment is still alive, in for example Britain under 'Thatcherism' or in the United States under 'Reaganism', but my criteria are not so strong as to exclude these nations, in particular since this is chiefly a study of events during the 1970s. It may be that in some nations the first steps have been taken in the direction of 'dismantling' the welfare state, but this we cannot yet know, and if so it will probably be as long and gradual a process as has been the evolution of the welfare state.

Types

A quantitative distinction between welfare states is possible without much ado, for example on the basis of how much money governments spend for social purposes. For instance, according to OECD statistics, public spending on the welfare state around 1980 was in Denmark and Holland on a level corresponding to about 35 per cent of the gross domestic product, in Germany and Italy about 30 per cent, in Great Britain about 25 per cent, and in Australia, Japan, and the United States about 20 per cent.[13] These are all welfare state nations but their welfare states differ from each other in their relative size; some are *small*, others *large*.

A qualitative distinction has been suggested between so-called *marginal* and *institutional* welfare states.[14] The marginal welfare

---

[12] The Organization for Economic Co-operation and Development.
[13] Saunders & Klau (1985:Table 9).
[14] By e.g. Korpi (1980), following Titmuss (1974). See also e.g. Mishra (1977); Kuttner (1984).

state is described as having goals of limited ambition, corresponding to my weak interpretation of the redistributive goal, and using
mainly selective and income-tested anti-poverty policies. The
institutional type has more ambitious goals, corresponding to my
strong interpretation of the redistributive goal, and tends to use
universal programmes, by which is meant that all citizens with the
same needs are treated equally, irrespective of 'irrelevant' differences between them, as, for example, in income. These types are
seen as qualitatively different from each other because, in one,
social policies single out a recipient group in the population and
may have the effect of turning this and other groups against each
other, while in the other, they cover all groups and thereby contribute to the unity of the population. In the marginal type, the clients
are a minority, they may suffer stigmatization or resentment by the
majority, and are often offered services of a secondary quality. In
the institutional type, the clients are a majority, the separation of
those who get and those who pay is largely eliminated, and clients
with the same needs have the same right to the best available
services irrespective of income. One is believed to separate, the
other to integrate.

This distinction works quite well as far as goals are concerned.
While the goal of minimal security is a promise that no one shall fall
out of society, the goal of modifying the structure of inequality is a
promise to integrate everyone into the mainstream. This is not only
to promise more, it is to promise something different, what T. H.
Marshall has called 'citizenship', meaning 'full membership of a
community'.[15]

But as for means, the distinction is more difficult. Some welfare
states use income testing in almost all programmes, as, for example,
in the United States. This is not the case to the same degree in many
European nations, but truly universal programmes are, in fact, very
rare. Even large welfare states commonly have a large number of
income-tested benefits, such as social assistance, housing support,
and family support for child care. Progressive taxation, often the
pride of an ambitious welfare state, is a kind of income-tested
policy, and, as it seems from the intense debate over it, a policy
which tends to throw those who think they lose and those who think
they benefit into intense conflict with each other. Other policies

[15] Marshall (1964):70.

may be selective, although not necessarily by income. Many countries, including for instance Denmark and Sweden, have a union-based unemployment insurance, a system which tends to discriminate against non-unionized workers in unemployment compensation.[16] A search for selectivity in the Swedish welfare state, presumably the model institutional type, has revealed that, although selectivity by income is not widespread, the system is thoroughly selective by occupational experience so that clients with different careers in gainful employment have different rights to benefits.[17] A large welfare state obviously has benefits which cover a larger part of the population and probably tends to use more generous benefits, and it is likely that there is less stigma attached to being a recipient in the large welfare state than in the small one. But this may simply be because of the size of the welfare state and does not necessarily have anything to do with an additional quality of universality in the use of means. It is not obvious that large welfare states—all things considered—are less selective in their policies than are small welfare states. Nor is it obvious that universality gives rise to integration while selectivity causes conflict. The large and/or universal welfare state may be seen as wasteful and as giving benefits to people who do not need them, at the cost of unnecessarily high taxes, and the small welfare state as more effective because selective and targeted policies give more bang for the buck. And, indeed, in contemporary controversy over the welfare state there are ample signs of new conflicts arising as a consequence of the growth of social policies. The degree of institutionalism in welfare states needs to be demonstrated empirically but has hitherto for the most part been postulated as a property of particular welfare states. Such empirical inquiries as have been made suggest that the distinction in the use of means between marginal and institutional types may not be tenable.

For a basic categorization of welfare states, I shall stick to the quantitative distinction between large and small ones. In this way I avoid the ideologically loaded concepts of marginal and institutional welfare states and can leave the burden of proof for the relevance of this distinction to those who feel impelled to use it.

The distinction between types of welfare states is of considerable

[16] See e.g. Björklund & Holmlund (1983).
[17] Marklund & Svallfors (1985).

importance in the present analysis. Although the welfare state has become controversial and is debated intensely, the controversy is still relative and not absolute. The debate is not really *pro* or *con* the welfare state but rather about the rationality of the 'advanced' welfare state. Everyone (almost) accepts the need in modern, industrial democracies for at least a minimal welfare state. The question is how extensive it should be and whether the trend towards a large welfare state should continue, halt, or be reversed. Although this is a study of the welfare state as such, the perspective is generally that of the large welfare state.

Welfare

The goal of the welfare state is to redistribute welfare—but what is welfare? We strive for equality—but equality of what?

Even the most cursory survey of the literature will reveal a state of profound confusion over the concept of welfare. It is given different meanings by different authors. Attempts to clarify its meaning tend to lead the theorist into a wilderness of difficult and intricately interrelated terms from which it is hard to escape alive: preferences, utility, choice, rationality, rights, capabilities, resources, consumption, way of life, and so on for ever.[18] In spite of intense struggle over the meaning of welfare, no consensus has developed and no consensus is in sight. Each student of welfare, unless he is willing to accept ambiguity, must make his own choice as to the meaning of this fundamental concept.

There is a paradoxical disagreement between the dominant theoretical and empirical approaches in welfare research. While the most sophisticated theoretical treatises, notably in welfare economics, discuss welfare as a question of *subjective* satisfaction (utility), the most sophisticated empirical analyses deal with *objective* living conditions, mainly income. This disagreement may have a methodological explanation—it is easier to measure objective conditions than subjective utility—but it also reflects a basic controversy over the meaning of welfare. Should we evaluate social

---

[18] For an admirable demonstration of the complexity of these issues, see Sen (1982, 1985c).

policies by their ability to equalize subjective satisfactions or objective living conditions? Since subjective satisfaction does not follow from and is not closely correlated with objective conditions,[19] the choice of welfare concept can have considerable consequences for the study of social policy and for our conclusions about its effects.

The conceptualization of welfare is in part a philosophical problem—what is the meaning of the phenomenon of welfare?—and in part a political one—what should the policies of the welfare state redistribute? My position is in favour of the objective concept which I hold to be both philosophically superior to the subjective concept and politically 'safer'.[20]

Philosophical considerations

The subjective concept of welfare rests on the utilitarian understanding of human nature, according to which people are guided in their activities, at least ultimately, by the quest for pleasure or happiness.[21] In addition, the concept is argued as non-authoritarian: only the individual himself or herself is competent to judge how well he or she lives. The concept has its basis in utilitarianism and its quality in non-authoritarianism.

The principle of non-authoritarianism is an important one and should for obvious reasons be retained in any concept of welfare to be used for the purpose of policy analysis in relation to democratic politics. But the importance that is attached to the quest for pleasure as a determinant of human behaviour is less obvious. Man is, in the utilitarian *Weltanschauung*, seen as a one-dimensional and simple-minded being, as if we in life seek one reward and one reward only. This is, in effect, to accept an extremely radical assumption about human nature. To say that people are pleasure

[19] As demonstrated by Allardt (1975).

[20] Among welfare economists, there has long been virtual unanimity about the subjective welfare concept based on utility. Indeed, the matter has, for some mysterious reason, been considered almost obvious and beyond question. But there is not full agreement. For instance, Sen (1980) and Le Grand (1984) have argued for an objective approach as a basis for equity/equality evaluations along much the same lines as I do here.

[21] For those who might have a preference for penetrating the philosophical minefield of utilitarianism, I suggest Sen & Williams (1982). (That should cure them of one preference!)

seekers is for the theorist to say that he knows, or takes the liberty of assuming that he knows, what people want to get out of their activities and the choices they make. It is clear enough that people seek pleasure in life, but it is not clear that they seek pleasure only. It may be that they also seek survival, fulfilment of duty, dignity, freedom, unity with God, love, friendship, respect, fame, wealth, power, excitement, challenge, or whatever; and it may be that different people seek different things, that people seek different things from different activities, different things in different situations, and different things in the short and long perspectives. We could, perhaps, define all this as pleasure and take that to be a catch-all for whatever it is people seek, but that would be no more than a conjurer's trick with words. The man who seeks power may be willing to accept a great deal of suffering in the attempt to win it and have no illusion that power will ultimately bring him happiness. All we can say with confidence here is that no one knows what it is man seeks in and from his activities and choices. This is one of the great mysteries of life; to make any specific assumption is to take a considerable risk of being wrong; to assume that we always seek pleasure (or any other single reward) is to reduce the mystery of life to a triviality.

Considering how little we truly know about human nature, we should prefer theories which depend on conservative assumptions to theories which depend on radical assumptions.[22] Having accepted non-authoritarianism as a criterion of quality in the concept of welfare, this raises the question of the possibility of an alternative definition, more open with regard to human nature without violating the principle of non-authoritarianism.

It is difficult to imagine a concept of welfare that is totally independent of any assumption about human nature, but it is not necessary to go as far as the utilitarians do. Instead of assuming that people are pleasure seekers, assume simply that they are choosers. This does not exclude the possibility that people are in fact pleasure seekers, but nor does it exclude the possibility that they seek other things than pleasure. It is assumed that people seek *something* from what they do, but it is left open what that might be. This requires only that we believe there to be some rationality in human action, in

---

[22] In fact, we should *always* prefer theories based on the least possible radical assumptions because of their more general validity.

the sense that people do not act arbitrarily or purely by instinct. This, too, is an assumption about human nature, but to say that people are choosers is to say a great deal less than that they are choosers and that their choices are dictated by the quest for pleasure.

While the utilitarian approach results in a conceptualization of welfare in relation to the *outcome of choice*, the more careful assumption that people are choosers results in a concept where welfare is defined in terms of the *circumstances of choice*. In the first case, people are said to live well depending on what choices they make and what their consequences are; in the second case depending on what possibilities they have for making choices.

Welfare as the outcome of choice can be defined either subjectively—as satisfaction—or objectively—for example as consumption—but welfare as the circumstances of choice can only be defined objectively. We may not be aware of or understand our true possibilities for making choices, but the possibilities themselves are independent of our subjective perception of them.

To say that people live well if they can themselves choose how to live is every bit as non-authoritarian as to say that people live well if they take pleasure in how they live. Freedom of choice is an eminent non-authoritarian principle. The fact that objective welfare can (in principle) be observed, described, and measured by others than the individual himself or herself, does not mean that it is determined by others. My welfare is still determined by the situation in which I live, precisely as if it were defined in terms of pleasure, with the only difference that, under the objective concept, this situation can be described independently of my perception of it. Welfare defined objectively as the circumstances of choice is a concept which has the quality of being non-authoritarian while at the same time being dependent on less radical assumptions about human nature than is the subjective concept of welfare.

Political considerations

The first pragmatic advantage of the objective concept over the subjective one is that it corresponds to what public policy is, in fact, about. Politicians may on festive occasions speak about the happiness of the population, but everyday political concern is with more prosaic problems. The object of social policy is income distribution and social services, not human happiness.

The second advantage is that the objective concept corresponds to what public policy should be about. It is not realistic to believe that what government does can make much of a difference one way or the other for the happiness or unhappiness of individual citizens. Politics can—I should add 'perhaps', since this is the issue to be investigated in the present study—contribute to making individual lives comfortable or difficult, but to cast this in terms of happiness is fundamentally to misjudge people's ingenuity for coping in the most different of situations, the complexity of human nature, and man's extraordinary capacity for happiness as well as unhappiness irrespective of poverty or affluence. Nor is it desirable that the state should be entrusted with responsibility for the happiness of its subjects. Ralf Dahrendorf has pointed out that some authoritarian regimes have written a commitment of this kind into their constitutions but that democratic regimes have respected that the responsibility for happiness lies in a private domain into which government should not penetrate.[23] If the state wanted to make people happy, its most effective means might be propaganda (as authoritarian regimes realize well enough), but this would inevitably make the state repressive. In this way, paradoxically, a non-authoritarian concept of welfare could be used to justify authoritarian policies.

In addition, to see the ultimate purpose of politics as to influence subjective satisfactions is problematic because of the consequences one might find oneself forced to accept by being faithful to one's philosophical principle. Since people have different capacities for enjoyment (for example for deriving satisfaction from consumption), egalitarian goals in terms of subjective welfare would most likely have the strange implication of making inequalities in the distribution of objective living conditions, such as income, acceptable or necessary in order to obtain equality of satisfaction. Having accepted the concept of subjective welfare, it would be perfectly logical to defend income inequalities because, under this theory, income has no independent importance except for the satisfaction that can be derived from it.

---

[23] Dahrendorf (1977). The observation is an element in his critique of 'happiness research'.

Measurement

The circumstances of choice can be seen as a function of the resources the individual commands and the options of choice which his environment offers. The most convenient measure is income. If we are willing to assume that income is the essential individual resource for choice, that all individuals make their choices in (roughly) the same market, and that we are able to measure income with reasonable accuracy, then we could simply take income as a proxy for welfare, as is commonly done in welfare research. But if we believe that other individual resources matter in addition to income (for example property, education or knowledge, or other personal capacities, such as health), either because they influence our choices directly or because they affect our ability to make good use of income, or that markets are differentiated (for example through regional differentiations of housing and labour markets), or that our measurements of income have shortcomings (for example because we are not able to incorporate in a realistic manner income from the 'shadow economy', from barter, or from fringe benefits), we would need a broader measurement. Income would still be an important indicator, but we would in addition need indicators of other resources and of environmental structures which determine how individuals can transform resources into consumption or way of life. More will be said about broad measurements of welfare in Chapters 6 and 7 on activity and poverty.

Rationality

Assuming that government is not an individual actor, that politicians are only agents acting on behalf of citizens, and that the individual citizen is, in theory, the 'real' actor in democratic political life, the method of politics can be seen as a form of collective action on the part of the citizenry. It is one way in which we try to achieve things we want by acting together, instead of each individually relying on his or her own efforts only. The core issue in the Grand Debate is the success or failure of this kind of collective action. My key to the door into the analysis of this issue is the concept of *rationality*.

The meaning of rationality

I take rationality to be a universal criterion of successful action.[24]
Action is rational if actors have intentions with what they do and if
they are able to use available means so as to advance their intention.
It is irrational to the extent that the course of action chosen does
not correspond to the intention behind it—as in Paul's complaint, 'For the good I would I do not; but the evil which I would
not, that I do'[25]—or turns out to be counterintentional in its
effects—as when someone tries so hard to please that he
becomes a pest.

The criteria of rationality in public policy are *legitimacy*, *effectiveness*, and the absence of unanticipated negative *side-effects*. This is
consistent with what Jon Elster has called the 'broad' theory of
rationality whereby rational action is seen as a question of both
the instrumental choice of means and the ethical choice of
intention.[26]

Cost-effectiveness in the use of means is an obvious element in
any understanding of rational action. The concept of rationality can
be limited to the choice of means (what Elster calls the 'thin'
theory). In this case the problem is seen as a purely technical one of
making optimal decisions in relation to given intentions. Thus

---

[24] The theoretical basis for this approach is the methodological individualism of *la
sociologie de l'action* (Boudon, 1984). The basic assumptions in this theory are that
all societal phenomena are the result of action and that all action is ultimately
individual. If we in addition assume individuals to be rational we can, in collective as
well as in individual action, take the correspondence between intention, action and
outcome as a criterion of success. The main alternative and competing theory is that
of functionalism (cf. Elster, 1982) whereby societal phenomena are explained by the
position they fill or the function they perform in a larger system independently of
human intention or action. This approach could be used to analyse the success of the
welfare state if we could postulate some function that it is supposed to fulfil. On
theoretical grounds I do not accept that functions in this meaning exist in themselves
beyond intentions that are formulated by people. But it could be that the founding
fathers of the welfare state or today's politicians have had or have some ultimate
purpose with the welfare state beyond the redistribution of welfare. If so, the
advancement of this purpose could be taken to be the 'real' function of the welfare
state. But this would simply be to move beyond an analysis of the welfare state as
such to an analysis of its contribution to some process of socio-economic development or some ultimate goal, which is an approach I have above determined to lie
outside of the scope of the present study. On rational action and societal analysis, see
also Barth (1981).
[25] Romans 7:19.
[26] Elster (1983).

understood, the theory of rational action will encourage a political analysis centered on the behaviour of 'decision makers'. Public policy is often analysed in this technical way, for example according to the 'conventional' theory of public planning where the formulation of goals is taken to be 'exogenous'.[27] Theorists of the public-choice school have criticized the mainstream of public finance economics and public policy analysis for ignoring the political problem in public policy, by working on the basis of 'the benevolent despot model', as if politicians were autonomous actors independent of a political setting.[28] It can, however, be argued that the ethical choice of intention should be included as part of the problem of rationality since even ethical choices can be irrational if they are made through an irrational process, as, for example, when we hold people with twisted minds to be irrational because of what they want to do no matter how shrewd or clever they are in the way they go about it. In this understanding, rational action is associated not only with the outcome of choice but also with how choice is made. When applied to politics, this broad concept leads beyond a technical analysis of the politicians' use of means to an analysis of the political process through which goals as well as means are chosen. The broader approach is applied here. We shall see in particular in the analysis of economic efficiency that the political process approach makes a difference, compared to the decision making approach, for the interpretation of the observations which are made.

The meaning of legitimacy is as follows. Since public policy is a form of collective action, there is the problem of formulating collective intentions on the basis of individual preferences, and since we are concerned with democratic politics, there is the problem of doing this so that collective intentions reflect the preferences of the citizenry. It would hardly be meaningful to say that democratic politics are rational if they are effective in relation to goals which the population rejects or conducted with the use of means which most people find objectionable. In a discussion of rationality in democratic politics, the necessity of including the process whereby choices are made should be obvious enough.

[27] See e.g. Johansen (1977).
[28] See e.g. Brennan & Buchanan (1980, 1985); Frey (1983).

Barring unanimity as a realistic basis for collective action,[29] collective intentions can be said to correspond to the preferences of the citizenry if intentions are chosen in a way all citizens accept as a just method of balancing conflicting individual interests. The logic behind this position is that individual actors, if they are rational, acknowledge that some collective action is necessary or advantageous but that full agreement is not possible, and, therefore, conclude that they are better off accepting the outcome of a process in which they have confidence, even when the outcome turns out to be different from what they would ideally have preferred, than to risk the stalemate that would follow if everyone insisted on a veto. From this it follows that popular acceptance (as opposed to popular agreement) can be taken as an indicator of the correspon dence between political decisions and the preferences of the citizenry.

The concept of effectiveness is, at first sight, straightforward: means are effective to the degree that they advance their intended goal. But there are some difficulties. First, a goal can be realized independently of the means chosen to advance it. For instance, certain anti-poverty policies are introduced. They turn out to have no effect but, because of economic growth, poverty is still reduced. We have the intended result, which is fortunate, but since it is not produced in the intended way this result cannot be taken as a sign of rationality in the policy under consideration. Second, the means which are used to further some goal may turn out to be without the intended effect but instead to have some unanticipated effect which is held to be positive. A nuclear energy plant proves to be uneconomical from the point of view of the production of energy, but the spill-water heats up the adjacent bay making it ideal for the breeding of fish. The action has a positive result, which again is

[29] Since people must be expected to disagree on important matters, the effect of requiring unanimity would be to exclude by definition the possibility of rational collective action except for trivial purposes, either because unanimity would be so costly for some actors that they should not be expected to accept the effort (cf. Buchanan & Tullock, 1962) or because it is simply impossible (cf. Arrow's 'impossibility theorem' whereby the impossibility of unanimity is proved on the basis of assumptions that are usually described as reasonable). The application of the 'pareto principle' in welfare economics is an example of an approach to public policy based on the principle of unanimity. Brennan & Buchanan (1985) have suggested a compromise between the requirement of unanimity and the acceptance of disagreement, taking unanimity about rules but not outcomes as a normative basis for public policy. I here weaken this criterion by using the term acceptance rather than agreement.

fortunate, but since it is not the intended result this has nothing to do with rationality.

These two cases boil down to the following: luck does not count when the question is of rationality. Action is rational only if there are positive results in relation to the intended goal and only if these results are produced by the means applied. In order to judge the rationality of some action we must take care not to confuse the matter by considering effects which are coincidental to the means and goals under consideration, including effects that everyone would be glad to see.[30]

In the previous sections of this chapter, the problem under consideration has been limited in relation to both means and goals. Means are limited to those of the strategy of redistribution. Other means are thereby coincidental to this analysis even if they may affect the distribution of welfare. If, for example, employment policies succeed in reducing unemployment and this has the secondary effect of making the distribution of income less inegalitarian, all is good and well. But this would still not be a sign of success in the strategy of redistribution since employment policies are not a part of that strategy as defined here. Goals are limited to distributional ones. This means that any benefits which the application of redistributive policies may have, beyond the distribution of welfare, are coincidental and, therefore, in the present context irrelevant. This is not to say, to repeat, that I believe redistributive policies to be the only policies which may influence the distribution of welfare or that there may not be more ultimate intentions behind the welfare state than the immediate goal of equalizing the distribution of welfare. It is only to make clear how the problem of the study is defined and what the consequences are of applying the theory of rational action to its analysis.

An important consequence of these delimitations is that two-thirds of the macro-economic problem of inequality and redistribution is defined as out of bounds in this study. What is included is the problem of economic inefficiency which may result from redistribu-

---

[30] To illustrate, if x_2 are the means and y_2 the goals which define a certain policy, and if the arrows reflect causality, only arrow x_2y_2 is relevant to the rationality of the policy in question while all other effects, such as those described by arrows x_1y_2 and x_2y_3, are coincidental and irrelevant.

tional efforts. It would, of course, be meaningless to discuss the
rationality of redistribution without considering its costs.
(Although luck does not count, misfortune does.) What is not
included is the question of distributional effects of macro-economic
policies, which would in my schema be classified as regulatory
policies, as well as the question of possible gains in economic
efficiency resulting from welfare state policies, which would here be
considered as luck.

This latter point has some relevance for an issue which has
recently come to the forefront in the debate over the welfare state,
that of social policy and employment. It has been demonstrated that
the expansion of the welfare state has created a large number of new
jobs. This is hardly surprising—services do not produce themselves
but must be produced by people—but it is still part of the total story
of the welfare state.[31] Since employment is a good thing and a goal
of public policy, this has been taken as an argument in favour of the
welfare state, all the more so since a great many of the jobs in the
welfare state turn out to be taken by women. Without in any way
denying that the welfare state has created jobs and that this may be
fortunate, it is still, in my perspective, not relevant to take this as a
sign of success in the strategy of redistribution. For one thing, we do
not know what would have happened without the welfare state. If
there is a genuine demand in the population for the services that are
delivered through the welfare state, the same jobs might have been
created in the market, at least if income had been redistributed so
that those who need the services had the purchasing power to buy
them. But more significantly here, new jobs in the welfare state are
not a sign that the strategy of redistribution works, as the creation of
new jobs is not a goal of this strategy. It may be a goal of economic
policy or of employment policy, but not of social policy as defined
here. Redistributive policies are enacted primarily to redistribute
welfare, not to create jobs. It is fortunate if they create jobs, but
they are still not successful unless they do what they are intended to
do. To see the jobs created as a result of redistributive policies as an
argument for these policies is similar to seeing the jobs created in
the armaments industry as an argument for military build-ups. In
the same way that military build-ups must be justified by their

---

[31] The issue of the 'social welfare labour market' has been raised in particular by
Rein (1985a, 1985b).

purpose, which is presumably national security, the test of successful redistribution must be effectiveness in relation to the redistributive goal. If, in addition, there are positive secondary effects, all the
better, but there is no rationality without effectiveness in relation to
intended goals.[32]

As for negative side-effects, it is necessary to distinguish between
anticipated costs, which are considered a part of the policy in
question, and unanticipated consequences. There are always costs
in human action; to make choices is to prefer some things and to
give up other things. The existence of a cost is no sign of irrationality
in a choice. If we want something and are willing to give up what it
costs to have it, this cost cannot, on rational grounds, be considered
a problem in the choice we make. But if we make a choice, for
example of a policy, and later find that the balance between costs
and effects is less favourable than we had anticipated or that there
are indirect negative consequences which we are not willing to
regard as a part of the price to be paid for the policy in question, we
have a problem. In the first case, what we get is what we want; in the
latter case, we make a choice but do not get the intended and
anticipated result. This distinction between anticipated costs and
unanticipated side-effects becomes clear through the application of
the political process approach and will play a considerable role in
the discussion of efficiency in Chapter 6.

Political rationality is here defined so as to mean both legitimacy and
cost-effectiveness. No matter how effective policies are, they are not
rational if they are not also accepted by the population, nor are they
rational if they enjoy full acceptance without being effective. On the
other hand, perfect rationality is not possible (nor hardly desirable) in
the real world. Legitimacy depends on *sufficient* acceptance and cost-
effectiveness on a *reasonable* balance between costs and effects.

Sources of irrationality

There are two main processes through which public policy and its
effects are determined. The first is the political process of choosing
goals and means, and the second is that of individual reaction to the

---

[32] Strictly speaking, the jobs established to deliver social services are not even a
side-effect of social service policies, but simply a part of those policies. You cannot
take the instrument established to implement a policy as evidence that the policy has
positive effects. Side-effects of the welfare state in the form of new jobs would have
to be jobs stimulated outside of the welfare state.

policies that are enacted. First we decide collectively on a set of goals and means, such as the use of progressive taxation to redistribute income. The implementation of such collective decisions changes, in the next round, the environment within which individuals act, in this case the tax structure. We then react individually to what has been decided collectively, for example by changing our economic behaviour in response to new taxes. Individual reactions may, in turn, add up in a way that influences the effects of the policies that have been implemented. High-income groups may, for example, conceal part of their income from taxation and thereby pervert the intended redistribution.

Both these processes may give rise to irrationalities, the political process because of 'imperfections' and the second process if individual reactions contradict collective intentions. The main forms of imperfection in the political process are ignorance, which may result in sub-optimal choices of means, and abuse of power, which may result in political intentions that are not representative of the preferences of the citizenry. Individual responses are contrary to political intentions, firstly, if we individually disagree with or otherwise do not accept what has been decided collectively. This may be the case, of course, if there are imperfections in the political process. But it can also occur without such imperfections, for example, if we apply different preferences in our private and political activities or if we change our minds during the time between policies being decided and their effects experienced. Contradictions may, furthermore, arise because of behavioural responses which either undermine intended policy effects, as in the tax example above, or produce negative side-effects that were not collectively anticipated, as, for example, if redistribution is achieved at the cost of weakening the family.

The Test of Rationality

Now, finally, the welfare state can be said to work if the strategy of redistribution is successful. The success of the strategy of redistribution depends on the political choice of goals and means, on the individual reactions to these choices, and on the harmony between these two processes. Goals and means should enjoy popular support, means should be effective in relation to the goal of redistributing welfare, and the implementation of redistributive policies should not give rise to behavioural responses which undermine their intentions or result in unanticipated side-effects.

2
Issues

Following the growth of the welfare state we have seen a predictable growth in the literature on the welfare state. There is
a large specialized literature on individual social policies such
as health care, pension policies, unemployment compensation,
home-help services, and so on, and now, with the maturing of the
welfare state, a general literature on the welfare state as a whole.[1]
The problems discussed in the general literature have to do, on the
one hand, with the origin, background, and development of the
welfare state, and, on the other hand, with its consequences and
effects.

Origins

In 1981, a conference of social scientists was held in West Berlin to
celebrate the centenary of the welfare state, setting its birth to 15
February 1881 when Bismarck's proposal for social insurance for
workers was introduced in the German *Reichstag*.[2] This celebration
was, in several ways, justified. Bismarck's proposal was a decisive
step away from poor-relief and towards general transfers. It radically expanded the social responsibility and role of the state, and

---

[1] A sample of general literature (by country of origin): Okun (1975); Wilensky
(1975); Janowitz (1976); Campbell (1977); Rogers (1982); Gilbert (1983); Lampman
(1984): United States. Gough (1979); Marsh (1980); Mishra (1984); George &
Wilding (1984): Britain. Rosanvallon (1981): France. Donati (1984): Italy. Matzner
(1982): Austria. Greycar (1983); Jones (1983): Australia. Spiro & Yuchtman-Yaar
(1983); Eisenstadt & Ahimeir (1985): international conferences, Israel; Flora &
Heidenheimer (1981): international conference, West Germany. Offe (1984);
Schmid (1984): West Germany. Rold Andersen (1984); Goul Andersen, Hansen &
Borre (1984): Denmark. Olavsson (1984): Iceland. Ringen (1981a); Kolberg
(1983a); Kuhnle (1983): Norway. Lindbeck (1981b, 1983b); Korpi (1980, 1983);
Hechscher (1984): Sweden. OECD (1981). See also the papers published in *Govern-
ment and Opposition*, 1985 no.3.

[2] The conference papers are published in Köhler & Zacher (1983).

represented a new theory of social policy. While the goal of poor-relief had mainly been seen as the provision of minimum support for the most desolate of the needy, Bismarck's proposal was clearly understood to be not only about helping the poor but also (or perhaps rather) about helping society (*his* society, that is). Industrialization and the growth of the working class created tensions which the established order saw as threatening. Social insurance was one of Bismarck's instruments for dealing with *die Arbeiterfrage*.

Although 1881 does represent a leap forward, the birth of the welfare state cannot be pinned down to this or any other point in time. In several European countries, limited social insurance schemes had been adopted before 1880, and poor-relief goes much further back in history. Although usually the responsibility of private institutions (family, neighbourhood, church, guilds), traditional poor-relief was to some extent regulated by the state. In Norway, for example, the responsibility of the extended family, and of the neighbourhood for those who had no family to support them, was regulated by law from the twelfth and thirteenth centuries. Poor-relief is still an important component of social policy (now usually called 'social assistance' or, in the United States, 'welfare') and the administration by private institutions of state regulated provisions is not unusual in the modern welfare state.[3] In the areas of education and public health, state involvement started earlier than in social insurance. To take the case of Norway again, after independence in 1814, the first major acts on public education were passed in 1827 and 1848 and on public health in 1860. The first general social insurance act (accident insurance) was passed in 1894.

The growth of social policy over the last one hundred years or so has been continuous but not linear. The period has been sub-divided into experimentation (from the 1870s to the 1920s), consolidation (during the 1930s and 1940s), and expansion (from the 1950s). Whether the welfare state was born in the 1880s and 1890s or, as often suggested, during the economically and politically turbulent 1920s and 1930s or in

---

[3] See Kramer (1981). Kolberg (1984) has demonstrated for the case of Norway that voluntary humanitarian and social organizations during the 1960s and 1970s expanded their budgets and activities parallel to the growth of public social budgets.

1945, it did not reach maturity until after the middle of this century.[4]

Forces

The long-term development of the industrial democracies is often described under the label of modernization. This term indicates that we have to do with a single development which has several aspects (economic, social, political), that the relationship between these aspects is one of mutual interdependence (economic change influences social change and social change influences economic change), and that the overall direction of development is progressive. Low productivity economies have been turned into efficient industrial systems, subsistence economies into capitalist market systems and mass consumption, élitest polities into democracies and organizational pluralism, *laissez-faire* into political planning and regulation, and marginal poor-relief into universal welfare states. The growth of the welfare state is a part of the process of modernization, both resulting from it and contributing to bringing it about. To explain the origins of the welfare state is to identify the 'forces of modernization'.

What these forces are, and the relationships between them, are

[4] The sub-periods are according to Heclo (1981), and similarily Seip (1981). On the history of social policy and the welfare state, see, in addition, Rimlinger (1971); Wilensky (1975); Flora & Heidenheimer (1981); Mommsen (1981); Kuhnle (1983); Seip (1984). For an admirable illustration of continuity in social policy development, see 'the index of social insurance coverage' by Flora & Alber (1981). See also Alestalo, Flora & Uusitalo (1985). To illustrate the rapid expansion after about 1945, consider the timing of major social legislation in Norway:

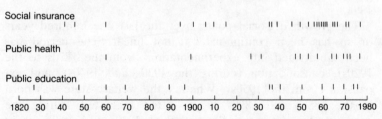

Note: Norway has had independent legislative power since 1814. From 1814 to 1905, Norway was in a union with Sweden but with her own elected Parliament (Storting). This figure covers the major legislation in these areas during independence.

highly complicated and controversial problems which are the subject of vast research efforts and not of single books, and certainly not of this book which is about the effects of social policies and not their background. What follows is merely a brief exposé of some forces which are important for understanding the roots of the modern welfare state.

The increasingly complex society. It has become so commonplace to speak of the complexity of modern societies that it often sounds banal, but it is, in fact, very true and important. One aspect of modernization is simply an increasing number of activities, in economic, political, and private life, which run parallel and which we perform or participate in. Each activity becomes more sophisticated. There is an increasing differentiation between activities, such as the division of labour and the division in time and place between work, family, recreation, and civic participation. The pace of life has increased, both in the performance of single activities and the shifting from one activity to another.

Social policy is part of what keeps modern society running at its elevated pace. Businesses need institutions which relieve them of outlays and responsibilities they would otherwise incur.[5] Restructuring of economic activity is necessary for progress, but it also produces new burdens. One of the functions of social policy is to provide a knowledgeable and healthy work force for a productive economy. Individuals and families need the security of social policies in an unstable environment. To be able to keep up with the increasing complexity of society, we must have new knowledge and more information. Social policies help us to enjoy the pleasures and bear the dangers of modern living.

Democratization. One way of interpreting the process of democratization is to see it as a transformation in the relationship between the 'individual' and the 'system'. In non-democratic societies, the individual is subordinated to the system and expected to accept such circumstances or sacrifices as are deemed necessary for the system, as interpreted by the ruling élite. In democratic societies, the indi-

---

[5] For example, when accident insurance for industrial workers was introduced in Norway in 1894, this was a result of pressure from both workers and businesses. During the 1870s, the courts had started to force industrial businesses to pay compensation for work accidents on objective grounds, i.e. irrespective of subjective neglect in each single case. This unpredictable risk became a problem, and instead many businesses preferred a predictable system of fixed insurance premiums.

vidual has gained priority over the system and it is recognized that
the system must be justified by its service to and usefulness for the
individual. This results in a need for policies to regulate how the
system 'treats' individuals, among them social policies.

The process of democratization is associated with the rise of new
classes (particularly the working class) as socio-economic conditions change, and with the struggle of these classes for a fair share
and a rightful position in society. The working class grows in size
and strength and gains power through its importance in production
and the dependency of other groups on its performance, and by
organizing in unions and political parties. Social policies are at the
same time a concession given by the ruling classes and a victory won
by the new classes. The class struggle has differed in form and
intensity from one country to another, but social policy has always
been an issue in this struggle.

New interests. As the welfare state grows, it gives rise to new
interests and political constellations. The clients of the welfare
state, obviously, have an interest in its preservation and expansion,
and so do the providers and others who depend on the welfare state
for jobs, income, and status. Together, these groups form a coalition of considerable size, gradually approaching perhaps half of the
electorate,[6] which in addition to the power of numbers has the
advantage of being able to argue its own interests with moral and
altruistic arguments and to portray those who do not accept these
arguments as cold-hearted and mean. Like other groups, they have
seen the advantage of organization. In Sweden, in the early 1980s,
the Union of Municipal Workers became the largest union in the
Federation of Trade Unions. In many countries, 'unions' of pensioners and other client groups have become a considerable force,
the system often working so that trade union officers 'retire' to
positions in pensioners' organizations, thus bringing their skills to
bear in favour of client groups and cementing the coalition between
clients and providers.

Economic growth. The economic basis for the welfare state lies in
growth. Poor nations have been transformed into wealthy ones and

---

[6] Producers and clients of the welfare state together made up 40 per cent, 37 per
cent, and 44 per cent of the electorate in Denmark, Norway, and Sweden respectively in 1980, up from 22, 17, and 23 per cent in 1960. Estimated by Kolberg (1983).
Producers: personnel in health, social services, and education. Clients: recipients of
public pensions for old age and disability, and survivors.

brought up to a level of national income which can sustain a large and costly system of social policies. During this process, additional income has constantly become available, thus allowing not only for a large social policy system but for a constantly growing one. In addition, growth has served as the great solver of conflicts. The magic of the post-war period is that there has been enough growth to provide for both increased private consumption and increased public budgets. This has been of the utmost importance for creating and maintaining a spirit of solidarity. Most groups have experienced improvements in their private economic situation and no group has had reason to feel that the expansion of the welfare state has occurred at their expense. Some groups have seen a deterioration of their relative standard of living but that has been easily accepted since their absolute standard has increased.[7]

In addition to making social policy expansion possible, economic growth is a pressures for such expansion. Those who are dependent on pensions or other transfers, or on the help and care of others, require an improvement of their standard of living. This boosts the social services and causes a shift from private to professional responsibility in care giving. Growth, as is well known, is a mixed blessing. It does create new resources, but also new losers. It is a process of constant change which is to the collective benefit, but also involves burdens which tend to be distributed inequitably. Social policies are, among other things, an effort to counterbalance

---

[7] Technically, social policy expansion is of course possible without economic growth, if it can be financed by increased taxation (or in the short run by public borrowing) or if new social policies can be financed by moving funds from other areas of public expenditure. But such expansions are politically difficult since they require someone to make do with a lower standard of living in absolute and not only relative terms. It can be done, but not without creating new conflict. The low rates of economic growth of the 1970s and 1980s have brought the welfare state under considerable strain and the strain would undoubtedly have been greater had there been economic stagnation or decline. The difficulties caused by low growth are sufficient to speculate that perhaps, politically if not technically, in a somewhat longer perspective social policy expansion without economic growth is not possible and that a lack of social policy expansion would after some time threaten the continued vitality of the welfare state no matter how advanced it had become before stagnation. The welfare state clearly thrives on expansion, new reforms and additional policies, and it may be that economic growth not only facilitates the welfare state but is a necessary condition for it. In the final analysis, one of the main functions of the welfare state is to reduce conflict and promote consensus. A social policy which creates new conflicts is not only difficult, but in a sense contrary to the very idea of the welfare state.

the price of growth. They help us to solve or live with problems which would otherwise make growth less acceptable, and they help those who would otherwise have experienced growth mainly as a burden to share its benefits.

Demographic change. At the turn of the century, average life expectancy for Norwegians was about 55 years, today it is about 75. In Sweden, over the same period, fertility rates are down from about four children per woman to about 1.6. These are typical trends for the industrial nations and have resulted, among other things, in a dramatic rise in the proportion of elderly in the population. In Norway in 1950, there were 12 persons of retirement age (67 and older) per 100 persons in occupational age 16–66 years). By 1980, this ratio had increased to 20 and it is expected to reach 25 by the year 2025.[8]

Families have become smaller, women have a much shorter period of caring for young children, and housework has become easier. Married women have increasingly come to seek jobs outside the home. The population has become more mobile. More often than previously, the grandparent and parent generations do not live in the same place or near each other. Neighbourhood contacts and friendships are interrupted because someone moves. Divorce has become more frequent.

Because of these and other demographic influences, new social needs arise and some old needs, which had previously been met within the family or among friends and neighbours, have to be satisfied with the help of professional, and usually public, agencies. Informal family care is still the dominant form of care, but there has also been increased responsibility for professional institutions.

Dramatic events. Through the great crises after the First World War, in particular the crash of 1929 and the mass unemployment of the 1930s, the *laissez-faire* theory of political economy lost its credibility and a new theory about the relationship between government and the economy emerged. This change of view had been going on for some time, but these events demonstrated irrevocably that the market on its own is vulnerable both with regard to stability and efficiency and to giving the mass of the population economic security. A new theory won acceptance according to which there is a need to inject in the market a vaccine of regulation against crisis or,

[8] Hatland (1984:162–3).

if this could not be achieved, at least to establish social policies which would protect the population against some of the human misery which had previously accompanied economic depression. The two goals were seen as compatible in that social policies were a part of those mechanisms which would make the economy less vulnerable.

In allied and neutral countries, at least, the Second World War was another push ahead for the welfare state. Both the years before the war and the war experience had demonstrated how dependent all groups are on each other in times of hardship and how important it is under such circumstances to be able to co-operate. During the war, new experiences of public administration were gained and an apparatus created which, with peace, could take on the job of planning the economy and running the welfare state. Promises of social reform had been used to boost war morale. The populations of these nations came out of the war with a strong feeling of unity as they prepared for the task of reconstruction under conditions of extreme austerity. In Norway, for example, the political parties agreed on a *Common Programme* during the last year of war, a coalition government ruled the first half year of peace on the basis of this programme until elections could be held, and even when the Labour Party could form a majority government on its own after the elections, consensus politics were the rule and the *Common Programme* still a basic policy document. In Britain, T. H. Marshall writes, '. . . solidarity grew without a break through the war and into the first years of peace. The Beveridge Report was a best-seller because it offered, while the war was still in progress, a blue-print of what the nation was fighting for. British war aims were expressed in terms of social justice. The Welfare State could enjoy a ready-made consensus.'[9]

The role of political struggle

There has been some considerable controversy over how to explain the growth of the welfare state. One group of theorists have suggested that the welfare state is best understood as 'a particular

[9] Marshall (1961:299).

manifestation of Western democratic societies'[10] while others have interpreted it primarily as the outcome of power struggle and of ideologically motivated decisions.[11] In the first case, the welfare state is seen as an adaption to objective circumstances and possibilities, such as demographic change, economic growth, and new modes of production, whereas in the second case it is seen as the outcome of a political struggle resulting from changes in the relative size and strength of classes or socio-economic groups, new political institutions (e.g. universal suffrage and unionization), and a radicalization of parliaments and governments. To put the controversy bluntly: is the welfare state a result of social democratic politics?

Rather too much, I believe, has been made out of this controversy. No one would presumably suggest that politics can do anything without consideration of economic realities. Only the most extreme functionalist would accept the notion of an objective need for society as an explanation of the existence of societal institutions, in this case the welfare state, without incorporating into the explanation some mechanism through which the need is interpreted and acted upon. I have not seen anyone suggest such functional explanations. Harold Wilensky, for example, who in *The Welfare State and Equality* has explained the growth of the welfare state mainly as a product of economic modernization and who has been regarded as the typical objectivist, has taken into consideration political variables such as the size of the working class and the nature of its organization in explaining differences between the welfare states of nations on more or less the same level of economic development. Since there would be not the slightest trace of a welfare state without political decisions, the mechanism in question could only be the system of political decision making. Both modes of explanation are, therefore, political. Objective and political factors do not make up alternative models for explaining the welfare state but are supplementary factors to be incorporated into a larger model. Assar Lindbeck, for example, has suggested that redistributive policies should be seen as the outcome of political decisions, that these decisions result from certain motives, that the possibility of going from motive to decision is explained by the prevailing dis-

---

[10] As formulated by Richard Titmuss. See e.g. Wilensky (1975); Kuhnle (1983); Flora (1985); Wilensky, Luebbert, Hahn & Jamieson (1985).

[11] See e.g. Furniss & Tilton (1977); Castles (1978, 1981); Korpi (1980).

tribution of power, and that this distribution is explained by structural factors at a higher level of generality.[12]

In this way the issue is reduced to the importance of the ideological orientation of governments as one among many factors of explanation. Those who have studied this question tend to disagree strongly with each other, but in a review of the literature, Hannu Uusitalo finds that their disagreement is to a large extent the result of methodological differences between studies and that the strength of the controversy is 'not warranted by reality'.[13] In another review, Michael Shalev concludes that the welfare state has grown with or without 'a strong and coherent social democratic labour movement' but that 'its emergence is hastened (and) its growth is speeded . . . under social democracy',[14] and thereby confirms the common sense experience that politics matter but also that politics are always conducted under the pressure of objective socio-economic circumstances.

Effects

Karl Popper has recommended 'piecemeal reform' as an alternative to authoritarian government. He has been heard! If the welfare state is anything, it is piecemeal reform. Its ambition is to reduce misery, but it makes no promise of happiness; its goal is to enrich the lives of ordinary women and men, but it has no grand vision of a paradise at the end of the road. Its method is the pragmatic avenue of one small step at a time. It rejects *laissez-faire*, but does not accept revolution. It remains what Marquis Childs called it as early as in 1936, 'the middle way'.[15]

Old and new criticisms

The welfare state, being a case of middle-of-the-road politics, is what everyone loves to hate. It is criticized from the Right for taking politics too far and from the Left for not doing enough; its goals are

---

[12] Lindbeck (1985).
[13] Uusitalo (1984:404).
[14] Shalev (1983:46).
[15] This, incidentally, was also the title of a political tract published in 1938 by Harold Macmillan, the British Conservative politician.

seen by some as trivial and by others as utopian; its means are believed to be without consequence as well as to interfere deeply in the mechanisms of societal life.

The normative problem of goals is not discussed in this book and I deliberately bypass the debate for and against equality.[16] I observe that the state acts on the basis of egalitarian goals and am here concerned with goals only in relation to the problem of legitimacy. For the rest, my concern is with intended effects and unintended side-effects in the use of means.

The dominant criticism of the welfare state used to be that its means were not effective. In spite of considerable efforts, inequalities persisted and poverty prevailed. The strategy of redistribution had proved to be merely a surface phenomenon which did not have much real impact. It was, to quote from the title of an early and influential Norwegian book of leftist criticism, a 'myth'.[17] The welfare state was useless.

This old criticism, although far from muted, has now been pushed into the background by a new and completely opposite criticism. It is now believed that redistributive means, far from being ineffective, are too effective, and that because of their effectiveness they give rise to side-effects which we want to avoid as much as or more than we want equality. To quote from an American study, 'most easy gains have been made';[18] henceforth, more equality can be achieved only at the cost of ever increasing inefficiencies. The welfare state has become impossible.

Is the welfare state possible?

Does the strategy of redistribution contain in its success the seeds of its own destruction?[19] It has always been recognized that the welfare state is rich in dilemmas and that its implementation is fraught with difficulties, but the new critics are now saying that in the mature welfare state dilemmas have turned into contradictions and diffi-

---

[16] I have discussed this issue elsewhere (Ringen, 1981a:Ch.2).
[17] Lingås (1970).
[18] Danziger, Haveman & Plotnick (1981:1019).
[19] Since the problem of side-effects is the main issue in the contemporary debate on the welfare state, and the most intriguing one, I here ignore logic and start by discussing side-effects before establishing whether there are intended effects from which side-effects might arise.

culties into crises. I shall look into four areas in which it has been suggested that contradictions have appeared in the wake of welfare state development.

Firstly, the problem of *legitimacy*. A recurring theme in the literature is that redistribution has gradually grown into something different from what was intended and that the population, once it sees the total result of all individual policies, turns its back on the welfare state. There is probably an unlimited demand for welfare benefits in the population but it does not follow from this that there is also unlimited support for the welfare state. The population may want benefits but hesitate to pay the bill, it may want each benefit on its own but not the sum total of all benefits, or benefits may be demanded by different groups which each support their own slice of the welfare state but do not agree to support the total welfare state.

The most common argument is simply that the welfare state has been taken further than the majority of the population is inclined to accept. Hence Bent Rold Andersen writes in a paper commenting on the Scandinavian welfare state, 'The core of the crisis is that the ordinary citizen not only openly and without compunction takes part in the underground economy and exploits the system of public services, but also hails others who do, and considers any attempts by the authorities to restrain this tendency as an infringement of his rights. That expenses have to be financed is accepted logically but denied emotionally.'[20]

The problem of legitimacy can be analysed on a grander scale than this by asking not merely if the welfare state is legitimate but if it lends legitimacy to the larger system of which it is a part, for example, to the state as such or to 'welfare capitalism'. Jürgen Habermas[21] and Claus Offe[22] have found in the modern (welfare) state a logic of contradiction rising out of its growing role in all aspects of societal life under advanced capitalism. Increasingly, the responsibility for economic stability and progress comes to be entrusted in the state. The state takes over production directly and supports private production indirectly, for example by accepting social responsibilities. In this capacity, the function of the state is to make further accumulation and investment possible. Since the state

---

[20] Rold Andersen (1984:135).
[21] Habermas (1975). See also Held (1982).
[22] Offe (1984).

operates in a capitalist economy, the *content* of state policies is primarily to fulfil this function, and doing this implies a distribution of income in favour of capital. However, in a democracy, the state cannot perform its functions without popular support and state policies would not work unless most people were willing to comply with them. The state must demonstrate, therefore, that its policies are to the benefit of the population. It must justify them in terms of welfare and at least give the appearance of distributing income in favour of labour. This makes ever more ambitious and costly social policies necessary, but these policies are primarily a matter of *form* and do not basically affect the content of the state. The state is trying to do two opposite things at the same time, or rather to conceal what it is really doing by means which are contrary to its true purpose. These contradictory efforts result in an '. . . increasingly visible conflict between the promise and experience, form and content of state policies (which) can lead . . . to a growing difficulty for state policies to win acceptance . . . '[23]

This is a broad analysis of political legitimacy in the Weberian tradition which goes beyond the scope of the present study and which is rather more functional in its approach than I feel comfortable with. While Habermas and Offe see the welfare state as a particular kind of state (the state under advanced capitalism), I have defined the welfare state in a more limited way as a set of policies (the strategy of redistribution). I am more in line with Rold Andersen, being concerned with the legitimacy of redistribution rather than of the total system of which the welfare state is a part. I observe that governments enact redistributive policies and I want to know if those who have taken the existence of such policies as proof of a 'social preference for equality'[24] are right.

Secondly, the problem of *governability*. The welfare state is an enormous machine. There is nothing new in a concern about how to run the machine of public policy effectively and to get its different parts into tandem. But it is now suggested not only that government, through the growth of the welfare state, has taken on more social tasks than it can manage effectively, but that it may have taken on a greater burden and responsibility than it can manage in any way whatsoever, the result being not only substandard manage-

[23] Ibid., p. 144.
[24] The term and logic are by Okun (1977:14).

ment but political paralysis, general government impotence, or policies which are not under political control.

Morris Janowitz, in one of the early general studies of the welfare state,[25] raised the question of whether its development was under what he called 'social control'. He discussed several problems of institutional and political nature which indicated that social policies could develop either in an arbitrary manner or in a way contrary to the interests of the population, such as weak political regimes and the lack of effective parliamentary control over politics, the inability of political élites to 'articulate the national interest', the inadequacy of popular participation in the political process, the strength of special interest groups, and the lack of institutions for working out national priorities. James O'Connor, in an analysis akin to that of Habermas and Offe, has suggested that increased claims on government, following the necessity of state support for advanced capitalism, will tend to surpass a level of taxation which the population will accept or the economy can support, the result being a 'fiscal crisis of the state'.[26] Richard Rose and Guy Peters have seen signs in Western democracies of government mismanagement so serious that they have coined the term 'political bankruptcy', which is the fate of governments that lose both effectiveness in decision making and popular consent.[27] A study of the structure of power in Norway has concluded that the power of interest groups to coerce government into accepting their claims is not paralleled by government power to mediate between groups and to balance their claims against each other.[28]

ability of the political process to reconcile ends and means, or—if you will—the power of governments to acquire the means which they need to fulfil their promises or to limit promises to what is within their means. This is relevant to the welfare state since, to a large degree, what populations claim of governments and what governments promise populations are social benefits. I shall approach the problem by looking into the nature of public budget deficits and discuss the role of social policies in generating what is now rampant deficit budgeting and whether these deficits can be seen as a sign of slipping governability.

[25] Janowitz (1976).
[26] O'Connor (1973).
[27] Rose & Peters (1978).
[28] Maktutredningen (1982).

Thirdly, the problem of economic *efficiency*. This is the most discussed of all contradictions assumed to be following the growth of the welfare state: what some may gain from redistribution today, all will have to pay for tomorrow in the form of less total income. It is part of the established wisdom of neo-classical economics that there is a dilemma between equality and efficiency. Inequalities have a function in the economic system and help it to perform efficiently. 'It is', write the Friedmans, 'important to recognize how much we benefit from the very unfairness we deplore'.[29] If politicians interfere in the market and make the distribution of income less inegalitarian than is 'natural', economic actors will be discouraged from efficiency, the economic system will perform poorly, and we will all have less income to share than we might have had if we had chosen wiser politicians. In addition, the political administration of money and the public production of services is costly. Households do not receive from government a value in the form of direct transfers and services corresponding to the income they give up in the form of taxes; something gets lost in the process.

As long as income redistribution was moderate (for example, mainly in the form of helping the poor), the dilemma was generally not considered serious and the cause was seen as good enough to be worth sacrificing some income for. But as ambitions have grown, so has the concern that we may be sacrificing too much income for a cause which is not worthy enough, and once Arthur Okun in 1975 had elevated the dilemma to 'the big tradeoff', strong voices were heard in countries with small and large welfare states alike, explaining all but the most careful of redistribution to be a folly. In Sweden, Assar Lindbeck has warned that in high-tax welfare states the inefficiencies following from redistribution have 'tended to become quite important (and that) the sum of all the effects of all policy measures may. . . be substantial in the long run',[30] and, even for the small American welfare state, scholars believe, as we have seen, that the easy gains have now been made. If these warnings are right, we have started a process of buying equality at the price of poverty.

Fourthly, the problem of *activity*. One element in contemporary criticism of the welfare state is that it influences not only what we

---

[29] Friedman & Friedman (1979:137).
[30] Lindbeck (1981b:61).

have but also constrains what we do. Although we (or some of us) may benefit from social policies in our capacity as clients, we do not benefit as people. Though material resources may be redistributed, activity is not stimulated and could be discouraged. The very policies which create security undermine individuality. Instead of stimulating self-reliance and initiative, the welfare state causes people to adopt a spirit of dependency and a life style of passivity, and reduces them from being participants to becoming dependents. The outer comforts of life are won but the inner meaning is lost. Hence Irving Kristol, in a discussion of egalitarianism, asks, 'What kind of civilization do we want to live in?' He contrasts 'the egalitarian society', which he finds overregulated, boring, and to be experienced as boring by those who live in it, and a society of the present American type. 'I am not saying there cannot be a decent society with a large state, a bureaucratic state, an intrusive state, a state that imposes a high degree of equality. But that is not the kind of society I want . . . because, I think, our society is in many respects more interesting, more varied, more lively, and more creative than any such egalitarian society.'[31]

The underlying question here is that of redistribution and productivity. Does the welfare state simply reshuffle what we have or does it leave us with either less or more of what we want; is there a welfare loss implicit in redistribution or do we in the process make some welfare gain in addition to equality? This question is closely related to the problem of economic efficiency but since income is not the only thing we value, I shall not be content with discussing it in economic terms only. I shall also look into the sphere of private lives and ask what individuals and families do in the welfare state and if social policies either discourage or stimulate private activity.

Is the welfare state useful?

Has the strategy of redistribution had the intended equalizing effect? The question can be divided into two sub-questions depending on whether the redistributional goal is given a weak or a strong interpretation: Has poverty been eliminated? Has the full span of inequality been modified?

It was long considered common sense that poverty would go

[31] In Campbell (1977:62–3).

down as the standard of living rose, and statistical evidence was found in support of this assumption. Seehbom Rowntree, the pioneer of empirical poverty research, in his first study of poverty in York in 1899, found 9.9 per cent of the population to live below the poverty line. By 1936, the percentage was down to 3.9 and by 1950 to 1.7.[32] A society without poverty appeared to be around the corner. However, sociologists soon came to question these results on the ground that they were based on an inadequate understanding of the problem of poverty. The meaning of poverty, they claimed, must be seen in relation to the society in which it occurs. The higher the standard of living in a society and the more complex its structure, the more resources each individual and family needs in order to avoid poverty. Peter Townsend has given the new approach a no-nonsense justification: 'Poverty can be defined objectively and applied consistently only in terms of the concept of relative deprivation.'[33] This theory led to a 'rediscovery' of poverty in the industrial nations and to new statistics which show the proportion of the population living in poverty to be considerably higher than Rowntree's most recent results indicate, and the size of the poverty population relative to the entire population not to have changed much during the period of post-war welfare state expansion.

There are many unanswered questions about recent trends in income distribution. Evidence from some countries, including so different ones as the United States and Norway, seems to show that income inequality has remained roughly stable since about 1950,[34] but there are signs that inequality has been reduced in other countries, for example in Sweden during the 1970s.[35] The trend in inequality, however, does not really answer the question of how effective or ineffective redistributive policies may have been. Even if inequality remains stable, redistributive policies might have had their intended effect if the trend without these policies would have been towards more inequality.[36] Economists have tried, therefore, to isolate the effect of redistributive policies on the distribution of

[32] Rowntree (1901, 1941); Rowntree & Lavers (1951).
[33] Townsend (1979:31).
[34] Williamson & Lindert (1980); Pechman & Mazur (1984); Ringen (1982).
[35] Åberg, Selén & Tham (1984).
[36] Danziger & Plotnick (1980) have suggested that in the United States between the mid-1960s and mid-1970s, the distribution of market income became more inegalitarian but that this was counterbalanced by the effects of transfers so that the distribution of gross income remained roughly unchanged.

income and for this purpose developed a method whereby the distribution after transfers and taxes is compared to the pre-tax/transfer distribution and the difference between the two distributions is taken to express the redistributive impact of transfers and taxes. With certain variations, this method has now been applied in a large number of countries and has universally shown that post-tax/transfer distributions are less inegalitarian than pre-tax/transfer distributions.

While the issue of side-effects of redistributive policies is open and controversial, the question of intended effects is, to a greater extent, regarded as closed. The sociological theory of poverty has won broad recognition and poverty is again held to be a problem of significant magnitude in the industrial nations. The method of comparing the distributions of pre- and post-tax/transfer income is considered to be the best available way to study redistribution, and from the conclusions of such studies the welfare state tends to be regarded as effective in relation to the redistributive goal. Since empirical research has come up with more categorical answers to the questions of intended effects than of side-effects, my treatment of these two main issues will be somewhat different. In the case of side-effects I shall try to establish facts; in the case of intended effects I shall question facts established.

Ultimate issues

Some critics of the welfare state, or of the experiment of politics in general, have feared, following Hayek's warning in *The Road to Serfdom*, that its ultimate price could be the loss of freedom. Some proponents of the welfare state, such as Ernst Wigforss, the early Swedish theoretician of democratic socialism, have hoped that it would be at least 'a whistle-stop on the track towards socialism'.[37] Today, most commentators are more cautious, for good reason I think.

Norway and Sweden have, for better or worse, highly advanced welfare states. I know these societies intimately from experience and observation. Political democracy and human rights are here firmly established, actively used, and vigorously defended, and infringements of civil freedoms loudly protested and effectively

[37] According to Korpi (1982):55.

rejected. The welfare state has undermined none of this. I think also that no one who knows the scope of private ownership of capital, the concentration of wealth, or the concessions made to business profitability in these economies can find much socialism there.

I am in no doubt that a good welfare state would enrich the society that implemented it and make it a better place for people to live. I also recognize that the experiment could fail and that, if so, it might be costly. But the possible outcomes need to be set in their proper perspective. The welfare state is a set of practical policies which may affect the circumstances people live and work under but which are still very much a part of the established order in the societies in which they are used.

3
Legitimacy

One way the population can react to the welfare state is to reject it.
Many observers now see this to be happening. Some doubt that the
welfare state was ever wanted by the mass of the population and
believe it to be a result of disproportionate power for a minority of
egalitarians.[1] But most commentators give the democratic system
enough credit to assume that the development of the welfare state
can be taken as a sign that it has been wanted so that the question is
whether it is becoming unwanted.

The Meaning of Legitimacy

In one of the many books on the popular topic of 'crisis', Ramesh
Mishra has identified a set of factors which he believes '. . . gave
legitimacy to the post-war welfare state: a buoyant economy, the
Keynes–Beveridge rationale for state intervention, theories of
industrial society and post-capitalism, the promise of a science of
society, and the pursuit of socialism through welfare'. But by the
end of the 1970s, 'most of these supports had been seriously weakened (and so had) the broad consensus concerning the mixed economy and the welfare state so characteristic of western societies
since the second world war. . . The welfare state is faced with a
crisis of legitimacy'.[2] When the OECD in 1980 convened a
conference of politicians, Civil Servants, and academics to discuss
'social policies in the 1980s', the participants heard that '. . .
general attitudes have changed considerably and the ruling
thought nowadays is more probably that the continued
growth of the Welfare State is neither likely nor even desirable'[3]
and that there is '. . . a growing sense, in many advanced

[1] See e.g. Nisbet (1977).
[2] Mishra (1984:18, 25).
[3] Cazes (1981:151).

countries, that the growth of social policy . . . is reaching a limit'.[4]

There are several reasons to expect that popular attitudes to the welfare state could be changing. In the United States, a general trend of declining confidence in government has been observed from about the mid–1960s.[5] The industrial nations are said to be in a process of transformation towards 'post-industrialism', a part of which is the evolution of 'new values' such as 'post-materialist' and 'individualistic' values which are assumed to square poorly with the more 'materialist' and 'collectivistic' values underlying the welfare state.[6] It has been suggested that a stronger middle class orientation of popular opinion following changes in the socio-economic composition of the population might result in weaker support for egalitarian policies.[7] We have now experienced what the welfare state does, and it is possible that people are disappointed with its effectiveness or disillusioned with inefficiencies which they see as arising from redistribution.

But Mishra and some of his co-plaintiffs take a few short cuts in pronouncing their verdict. For one thing, they are worried about the loss of something that has never existed. There never was a consensus over the welfare state. Social policy reforms have always had to be fought through against opposition, at times against fierce opposition. This was as true in the now idealized 1950s and 1960s as it had been previously, and it is as true for those nations which have developed large welfare states as it is for nations with less encompassing social policy systems.[8] What is new is not that there is disagreement about social policy or that the welfare state is being criticized, but that there appears to be more credibility in the

---

[4] Glazer (1981:240).

[5] See Lipset & Schneider (1983).

[6] On 'new values', see e.g. Inglehart (1977); Yankelovich (1983).

[7] See Martinussen (1981).

[8] According to Korpi (1983:199), out of six Social Democratic government resignations in Sweden, four have been related to controversies involving the development of the welfare state. The struggle over the supplementary pension scheme in the late 1950s was perhaps the most divisive political conflict in the post-war period, including the more recent conflict over 'wage earners funds', resulting in extraordinary elections to the *Riksdag* and adoption in 1959 by a majority of one vote. In contrast, Norway adopted a similar scheme seven years later with very little conflict and by a unanimous vote in the *Storting*, something which has in part been interpreted as a result of the struggle having been taken in Sweden and the disastrous subsequent election results there for the parties which had opposed the reform (Kuhnle, 1983). On the issue of conflict and consensus, see also Taylor-Gooby, (1985c).

criticism because of the economic troubles of the welfare state nations. Furthermore, they conclude that the welfare state has lost its legitimacy because *theorists* have started to change their minds about it. But legitimacy is not a question of a 'buoyant economy' or of Keynesian principles, but of the attitudes of the *population*. Even if those who thought that social reform was a road to socialism have lost their faith, it does not follow that the public has turned away from the pragmatic policies which make up the welfare state. The problem of legitimacy is a question of how people react to the experience of redistribution: do they accept social policies and play along with them or do they oppose these policies and try to beat the system? The legitimacy of the welfare state does not depend on theoretical fashions but on the opinions and behaviour of the population. It must be investigated on the grass-roots level and not on the level of élites. Legitimacy does not come from above and it cannot be lost from above.

Expressions of Protest

In a brilliant triad of concepts—exist, voice, and loyalty—Albert Hirschman has sketched a theory of reaction on the part of individuals who experience disorder in systems they belong to or depend on. They can either speak up in protest and try to change the system from within or they can leave the system behind them and try to escape its influence. Systems in this understanding can be, for instance, family, neighbourhood, town, country, work place, organization, political party, or—as in the present case—a set of public policies such as transfers and taxes. Non-action is also possible; we often experience dissatisfaction with our environment without doing anything about it, be it because of suppression, indifference, or impotence, or for want of alternatives to turn to. But if we are compelled to act, we can choose between speaking up or leaving, between turning against the system or turning away from it.[9]

If we have previously not experienced disorder in the system in question, we have probably built up some loyalty to it. Such loyalty will tend to make us hesitate in reacting once we experience dis-

---

[9] Exit and voice are not necessarily mutually exclusive forms of reaction. For instance, not all politicians who leave their party do so in silence.

order; we may postpone taking action or we may react only moderately. Even careful reactions against a system which has previously enjoyed loyalty can, therefore, be a sign that disorder is strongly experienced.

Applied to the welfare state, these simple concepts lead us to see that two different avenues of protest are open for people who disagree with its principles or are dissatisfied with its performance. They can express their protest through their opinions or through their behaviour (or both). Furthermore, if we assume, as we should, that the welfare state would not have expanded without popular support, we must also assume that the population has invested a great deal of loyalty in it. We shall later see this confirmed. Consequently, we should not under any circumstances expect to see strong or sudden expressions of protest. We should instead look for small signs of changes in popular opinion or behaviour and we should interpret even moderate shifts in the balance between support and rejection which can be observed on the surface as a sign of possibly more radical shifts in 'true' underlying attitudes.

Popular acceptance of the welfare state depends on loyalty in opinions as well as behaviour. People may act according to the rules of the welfare state without agreeing with them. This could be the case if the government used an elaborate system of controls to enforce its will. It is also possible that people could agree with the welfare state but still not comply with its rules. This could be the case if pro-welfare state opinions were not strong enough to influence practical behaviour or if people found themselves caught in a dilemma where each would have wanted to comply with the rules but found this difficult out of fear that no one else would. Redistribution is a little like prohibition: there are good reasons to support it in principle but also, at least for a part of the population, to avoid its practical effects. We can reject the welfare state by voting against it with our feet, even if we vote for it at the ballot box. A policy is not accepted unless popular opinion is for it, but the true test of support lies in the willingness to accept the practical consequences of the policies we value in principle, in particular, the burden of discomfort which is a necessary part of any policy. If people see the burden as small relative to the benefit, it will be easy to bear, but if the burden comes to be seen as outweighing the benefit, people will naturally resent and try to escape it.

There is some difference in the meaning of exit and voice as a reaction to disorder. Exit is a more drastic reaction (although this is not necessarily true in dictatorial systems). People who protest care; people who turn away have given up protesting or couldn't care less. Exit is the ultimate form of rejection.

Voice

The voice of the people can and should be observed directly in popular opinion. This is now done on a broad scale in social research with the use of advanced survey techniques.

It can be argued that opinion data do not necessarily reveal 'true' public opinion: the survey situation is artificial, questions may be leading or not precisely formulated, respondents are free to express opinions without having to stand by what they say. It can also be argued that individual opinions are merely the raw material for collective preferences and that the latter are developed in a process where opinions are tested against counterarguments and where those who express opinions must be prepared to accept challenge and to motivate and defend their views. Under this argument we should look not for any opinion but for 'mature' opinion, as expressed in voting behaviour, for example, or in the policy positions formulated by parties or organizations.

I do not agree with these criticisms of opinion surveys and the use of survey evidence. Modern survey technique is sufficiently sophisticated to monitor opinions with reasonable accuracy. At least for social policy opinion there is now enough material available for us not to have to rely on individual results but to be able to draw conclusions from patterns of opinion which emerge from a large number of independent surveys. Voting is determined by so many factors that it is not possible to read social policy preferences out of the choice between a limited number of parties. To accept the positions of parties and organizations as true statements of the will of the people is to believe that they are governed by perfect internal democracy and to disregard the possibility both that those who are in power in organizations can impose their will on members instead of the other way around, and that those who do not belong to or participate in organizations may have opinions of their own. This, clearly, would be an impossible starting-point in a study where one of the questions is precisely how well processes which are in principle democratic in fact work.

The interpretation of opinion data is not without problems, but it nevertheless makes good sense to say that if we want to know what people think about the institutions of their society or the policies of their government, the best way to find out is still to ask the people.

Exit

From the viewpoint of individual citizens, the welfare state is a set of rules which specify their rights to benefits and their duties to bear a part of the tax burden. We must assume that people understand that if they do not, on the whole, comply with the rules of public policy they are, each in their own small way, undermining the possibility of its being effective. Consequently, compliance can be taken as a sign of support and free-riding in the form of misuse of benefits or evasion of taxes as a sign of indifference or protest.[10]

The misuse of benefits and the evasion of taxes are, however, not altogether parallel occurrences as far as acts of protest against the welfare state are concerned. In any welfare state there are necessarily a good deal of people who are on the margin of receiving some benefit. It may be illegal for them to try to manipulate themselves over on the 'right side' of the border, but this is still understandable and hardly something that needs to be interpreted as a rejection of the policies in question or of the welfare state in general. There probably is a good deal of misuse, in particular when benefits are income tested,[11] but it appears that in terms of magnitude this is still not a very serious problem. Evidence from several countries indicates that there tends to be more underconsumption than overcon-

---

[10] Misuse: the consumption of social benefits by individuals or families who, according to prevailing laws or rules, are not eligible for these benefits. Tax evasion: less tax actually being paid than should have been, according to prevailing laws/rules on the taxable income of the individual or family in question.

[11] According to Donnison (1982:70), on the British Supplementary Benefit: 'As for fraud, there was certainly plenty of it—arising mainly from the concealment of earnings. It is a serious problem, although it scarcely justified the overheated attention later focused upon it . . . '.

sumption of social benefits.[12] It is also questionable whether misuse should be seen as a serious moral problem or a form of anti-welfare-state behaviour. True, those who misuse benefits do not respect the rules of existing social policies, but if this is done to get around a restrictive system of income testing, it is both heartless and illogical to see it as a vote against the welfare state. If anything, it is a vote for more generous policies and a peculiar way of turning to the welfare state instead of away from it. Rather than being seen as a reflection of a real problem, the often expressed concern about 'fraud' is probably best understood as a psychological reaction resulting from a combination of ignorance and a deeply rooted feeling that the welfare state should, but does not properly, distinguish between the 'worthy' and the 'unworthy' poor. It is a problem for the welfare state if people try to exploit benefits beyond their rights, but this is still not really a sign of protest or rejection. It is only a case of that widespread occurrence in all human activity: the attempt to get something for nothing.

Tax evasion is a different matter. Taxes are not something we want for their own sake but merely the consequence of our wanting something else; they are the burden we have to accept in order to enjoy the benefits we want. If we do not accept the tax burden, we are in effect saying that we do not want the public benefits they finance enough to be willing to pay for them. We may want the benefits but do not accept the consequences. It is in our willingness to accept the tax burden that we show our support for and confidence in public policies. If people are turning their backs on the welfare state, it is not primarily by cheating on benefits but by resisting taxation. Hence, for symptoms of exit behaviour we should look for traces of *tax revolt*.

A tax revolt should be understood as more than a protest against

[12] A UN Expert Group Meeting on 'Use and Abuse of Social Services and Benefits', held in 1980, concluded: 'All the experts, some of whom presented statistical evidence, agreed that only a small proportion of those receiving benefits were involved in fraud or abuse (typically 1 per cent to 3 per cent). The vast majority of users of these programmes are legally entitled to them and are intended by social policy to receive them. Far more important than the problem of over-use, in terms of magnitude and social consequences, is the problem of non-use. Several experts reported that in their country substantial numbers of persons legally entitled to social services or social assistance are not receiving their entitlements. In many countries, particular problems of non-use and inaccessibility were observed for various social services and benefits (in some cases up to 50 per cent).' (European Center . . . 1980). For a summary of equivalent findings for Norway, see Hoven (1981).

taxes, which is a perfectly normal and understandable thing that may be as much an attempt to enforce prudence in the public use of funds as an expression of disloyalty against government, and anyway would come under the category of 'voice'. Instead, a tax revolt should meaningfully be seen as an active attempt to avoid paying 'necessary' taxes. To any set of public policies there is, in principle, a corresponding necessary level of taxation. The political interpretation of the necessary tax burden is expressed in a set of rules and rates of taxation. An attempt on the part of individual tax payers to avoid the tax burden implicit in prevailing rules and rates is a sure sign that they do not support the prevailing system of public policy. They either do not agree sufficiently with the adopted policies to be willing to contribute to paying what they cost, or they do not believe that the adopted tax burden is necessary or accept its distribution. For whatever reason, by trying to avoid a 'necessary' burden they show that they do not have confidence in the prevailing system of public policy.

There is, of course, nothing new in attempts to avoid taxes. Some level of tax resistance must be expected under any system of public policy. But if popular support of and confidence in government is constant, tax resistance also should be constant. This should be true even if the level of taxation rises, since new taxes would then be accepted as necessary to finance new policies which have the same popular support as previous policies. Hence, a tax revolt should be recognized not simply in tax resistance, but in an *increasing* tendency in the population to try to avoid the tax burden that has politically been interpreted as necessary.

The way for tax payers to avoid the intended tax burden is to contract their taxable income so that prevailing tax rates are applied to a smaller than intended proportion of total income. This they can do politically, for example by coercing government into handing out 'bribes' in the form of special tax reliefs to selected groups in return for their support of the system. But since this is an attempt to change the system from within rather than to escape its effects, it again comes under the category of voice and can be disregarded as a sign of exit behaviour.[13]

[13] Also, tax reliefs can be a perfectly sensible policy instrument, then called tax expenditure, either as an alternative to transfers (e.g. tax credits for families with children) or to encourage certain desired behaviours on the part of households (e.g. the tax deduction of mortgage interest to encourage a high standard of housing). On tax expenditures, see Owens (1983); OECD (1984); Surrey & McDaniel (1985).

That leaves for consideration regular tax evasion, whereby taxable income is concealed from taxation.

Social Policy Opinion

From public opinion research we now have enough information to draw a fairly reliable, albeit rough, picture of public opinion on social policy in Western industrial nations. We do not have all the information we might want, and the data we have are somewhat ramshackle in that they are taken from surveys which are not always strictly comparable. But what we have is sufficient for the purpose of the present analysis. Social policies are different in each country and so is public opinion, but there are remarkable similarities between the welfare state nations in the structure of social policy opinion. The picture to emerge below will emphasize these similarities but it should be understood that this is not to say that there are no differences.

The pattern of opinion

Appendix A contains tables of survey data on social policy opinion in several countries. What follows here is, in the form of four statements, a summary presentation of this material.

1. Ideological orientations cannot be taken as expressions of social policy opinions. When interpreting public opinion on social policy, it is necessary to distinguish between the level of ideology and the level of specific policies and to observe that opinion trends in these two levels are not necessarily 'consistent'. It is well known from opinion research that there is not always a very close correlation between general value orientations and specific policy opinions. In the area of social policy it has been demonstrated that value orientations are not necessarily followed by the 'expected' policy opinions. In early surveys of American public opinion, Free and Cantril found that their respondents tended to reply differently to ideological and specific questions and concluded that Americans were 'ideological conservatives' and 'operational liberals'.[14] This has been upheld in later surveys of social policy opinion and appears, in the light of the recent conservative climate in many

---

[14] Free & Cantril (1968).

industrial nations, to be the situation not only in the United States.

—In a summary of recent survey data for the United States, Ladd has demonstrated that the majority of the population agrees that government is too powerful but also that it should do more in a number of specific social areas, and that the federal government is, in general, spending too much but, when asked about itemized social policies, that it should spend more (see Table A1 in Appendix A).

—The same pattern of response is reported from the Danish 1979 election survey. A majority of the respondents agree that 'politicians spend the tax payers' money too freely' but also that in most specific social policy areas (except unemployment compensation) public spending is only adequate or too low (see Table A2).

—A conservative ideological trend has been found in Norwegian election surveys but this trend is not reflected in the pattern of response to a more specificly formulated question on social security (see Table A3). Finnish data for the period 1975 to 1985 show 'inconsistent' trends in the responses to general and specific questions (see Table A4).

The distinction between the level of ideology and the level of specific policies is significant for interpreting trends in popular opinion on social policy issues in two ways. Firstly, changing ideologies should not in themselves be taken as signs of changing opinions with regard to social policies. Political observers and commentators sometimes assume that public opinion is 'consistent' so that one can make inferences from ideological trends to specific issues, but that is simply not the case. Many people clearly have no problem, for example, in regarding themselves as conservative without adopting all specific opinions which conservative ideologists associate with conservatism. Secondly, it has a bearing on the much discussed question of 'new values'. We may or may not be experiencing a shift towards 'post-industrialism' or 'post-materialism' in the value structure of the populations of the industrial democracies. This is a controversial question which we need not take up here.[15] What should be said, though, is that even if there is such a shift it is in no way clear what implications, if any, this might have for social policy opinion. 'New values' are on the level of

[15] See e.g. the criticism by Wilensky (1981) of Inglehart's *The Silent Revolution*.

ideology while social policy opinion is issue oriented. 'New individualism', for example, if that is an element of 'post-materialist
values', could perhaps be expected to result in changing opinions on
social policy questions, but the one does not necessarily follow from
the other. General value orientations are not issue opinions. If we
want to say something about opinions on matters of social policy we
need to investigate opinions directly on the level of specific issues
and cannot rely on observations of ideological trends or take it for
granted that certain opinions follow directly from certain value
orientations.

2. The level of popular support for social policies is generally
high. In most countries, the majority of the population supports
such social policies as are in operation, and there is typically more
support for expanding social policies than for cutting back.

—The most comprehensive and reliable information on social policy opinion in several industrial nations is that compiled by Coughlin and based on a re-analysis of comparable data from eight
countries with very different forms of social policies (Australia,
Canada, Denmark, France, Sweden, United Kingdom, United
States, and West Germany; see Table A5).[16] This study has found
that the pattern of social policy opinion is very similar across
these countries. Over the last twenty to thirty years, a high level
of public support has persistently been observed in each country
for the social policies which have, at any time, been in operation.
There is some difference between the countries in that public
opinion tends to be somewhat more pro-social-policy in nations
with a larger social policy sector. Within countries, there is some
difference of opinion between population groups[17] but on the
whole more agreement than disagreement. Popular support is
uniformly strong for heavy social programmes, such as old age
pensions, health care, and education, in most cases strongly in
favour of family and child allowance (except in Britain), less
strong for unemployment compensation and social assistance,

[16] For an independent corresponding summary of survey material for Sweden, see
Korpi (1983:199–204).

[17] The self-employed tend to be more sceptical to social policies in their opinions
than other groups, and the same goes for conservative voters as compared to centrist,
liberal, or leftist voters, men compared to women, and perhaps for lower status
groups as compared to higher status groups (demonstrated for Norway by Kolberg &
Pettersen, 1981).

and in one case—'welfare' in the US—there is very little popular support.

—In the United States, an overview of opinion research going as far back as the 1930s[18] shows a high level of support for social policies (with the exception of 'welfare'). In an analysis of 1980 election data,[19] it is demonstrated that there was no erosion of public support for government policies in the main social fields of health and education behind the Reagan election, in spite of the clear anti-welfare-state ideology of his campaign.

—In Britain, opinion data from the early 1950s to the early 1970s show that '. . . by and large, there is a high degree of satisfaction with the services provided . . .' and that 'With remarkable consistency over the years there is a very large majority which favours raising pensions, and a very large minority which is highly critical of family allowance . . .'[20] Similar results are reported in a 1980–1 survey (see Table A6).

—In Norway, election surveys from the mid 1960s to 1980 have demonstrated that there is (with the exception of some brief irregularity in the early 1970s) a stable and considerable majority for maintaining social security at its present level or for expanding it, and that a minority (less than 10 per cent of the electorate) is in favour of reducing social security (see Table A3). Finnish data for 1975, 1980 and 1985 give roughly the same picture, although somewhat more mixed (see Table A4).

—In Denmark, the home of the 'welfare backlash', public opinion has not permanently turned against social reforms. In the late 1960s, there was a solid majority for maintaining or expanding social reforms. By the early or mid 1970s, public opinion had turned so that there was now a small majority expressing a preference for cutting back on social reforms. This opinion, however, which was fairly unique among the industrial nations and must be described as an exception from the general rule of a pro-social-policy majority, did not persist. By the end of the 1970s, the old majority was back, although not as solid as before (see Table A7).

This statement deals with public opinion on the level of specific

[18] Martin (1982).
[19] Miller (1981).
[20] Klein (1974:410).

social policies. It is demonstrated here, firstly, that in welfare state nations there is, for the most part, a fairly good correspondence between opinion and policy. Social programmes generally have broad popular support; this is true, in particular, for heavy programmes and in particular in nations which have a large social policy sector. Secondly, it is demonstrated that popular support for social policies has not been eroded during the 1970s and early 1980s. In both large and small welfare states, popular support for most social programmes has remained at a high level. The alleged 'welfare backlash' is not reflected in long-term public opinion, and has occurred, if at all, only temporarily. There were some signs of a backlash in several countries during the early 1970s, but these are now in hindsight and in the light of new data interpreted as situation-specific rather than as a permanent turn of opinion.[21] There remains in the populations of the industrial democracies a pro-social-policy majority.

3. Public opinion on taxes parallels that on benefits. There is a reasonable understanding that supporting public spending for social benefits also implies accepting a correspondingly high level of taxation. Research on social policy opinion has concentrated on benefits. This has led some observers to question the validity of the opinion material and to suggest that it exaggerates public support for social policies since respondents in opinion surveys are not forced to take into consideration the cost in the form of taxation of the programmes they support. Naturally, everyone would prefer more benefits and less taxes and one should expect some 'inconsis-

---

[21] 'Proposition 13' in California, whereby property tax limitations were imposed on local government, was one such sign. According the Lipset & Raab (1978) this should be interpreted as a reaction against the tax effects of an unprecedented and unanticipated real-estate inflation rather than as a frontal attack on 'government'. 'The message of Proposition 13', they have found on the basis of a broad survey of opinion material, is not so much that the taxpayers simply want to keep their money as that they want to get 'their money's worth'. (See also Lipset & Schneider, 1983:343–6.) The remarkable success in Denmark of the tax revolt party (ironically called *The Progress Party*) in the 1973 election was another such sign. We now know that this wave of protest did not persist. The 1973 election is now interpreted as a temporary reaction against extraordinarily rapid increases in taxes and public spending in the preceding years (Andersen, 1982). The turn of opinion in Norway between 1965 and 1973 (see Table A3) was at the time interpreted as a sign of 'backlash'. Again, we now know that this was temporary, and Martinussen (1981) has since interpreted the 1973 figures as expressing some 'exhaustion' in the public after the introduction of the integrated public pension system in 1967–8, the most far-reaching single social policy reform ever in Norway.

tency' in public opinion on this point. For this reason and because taxes are used for other purposes in addition to social policy, a preference for cutting taxes does not necessarily imply a preference for reducing social spending. There is a good deal of evidence of a tax-weary opinion in the industrial nations but when opinions on taxes and social benefits are confronted in surveys, the apparent contradiction between pro-benefit and con-tax opinions breaks down.

—Coughlin has analysed data for France, Britain, West Germany, and Denmark based on surveys where the respondents were asked to choose between 'reducing taxes even if social security and health programmes are cut' and 'improving social security and health programmes even if this means higher taxes'. This analysis was conducted in 1975, which was probably near the height of the 'welfare backlash' in, for example, Denmark. The surveys demonstrate that in all four countries there was a larger proportion in favour of improving programmes and increasing taxes than of reducing taxes and cutting services (see Table A8). This pattern of response is confirmed in independent and more recent surveys in Britain.[22]

—A British survey in 1982 found that 83 per cent of a national sample replied that taxes should be reduced when asked simply 'Do you think taxes ought to be reduced or increased?', but that only 36 per cent continued to support tax reductions when they were confronted with the possibility of a corresponding fall in the standard of social services. In a survey three years earlier, 34 per cent had replied that taxes should be cut even if it meant some reduction in government services such as health, education, and welfare, another 34 per cent had replied that such services should be expanded even if it meant some increases in taxes, and 25 per cent thought things should be left as they were. This reflects a somewhat lower level of popular support for social policies once the tax question is taken into consideration compared to the results of surveys which ask only about benefits, but still a majority for maintaining or expanding both benefits and the tax level.[23]

—Some British studies have been interpreted to indicate that when given a choice, a majority of the population will opt for low taxes

[22] Taylor-Gooby (1985d:Tables 1 & 2).
[23] George & Wilding (1984:224–5).

and private welfare provisions rather than high taxes and public social policies,[24] but these studies have later been criticized on methodological grounds.[25] A recent survey in Britain has demonstrated that reported popular support for specific social programmes drops somewhat, but not much, if the tax issue is brought explicitly into the survey questioning (see Table A6).

—In a Norwegian poll in 1984, concentrating on financial problems in the social security system, 76 per cent of the respondents were willing to accept higher payroll taxes in order to maintain benefits, as compared to 23 per cent who were opposed to increased contributions.[26]

4. Within the framework of a pro-social-policy majority there is a trend towards falling support for and rising uncertainty about social policies. In spite of overall continued popular support for most social policies, there are uncertainties in public opinion about some social programmes and currently a somewhat more critical attitude than previously to the welfare state in general.

—Some social programmes are less popular than others. 'Welfare' in the United States, family allowance and unemployment compensation in Britain, unemployment compensation in Denmark and Finland, and social assistance in Sweden are examples of programmes which are more controversial than others or downright unpopular. The explanation usually given in the literature is that these programmes are often thought of as providing benefits for people who do not need or deserve them, or as being open to fraud.

—Except for temporary ups and downs, the time series reported in Appendix A show almost universally some reduced popular support for social policies. In the United States, the percentage of survey respondents replying that government was spending too much on 'welfare' increased from about 7 per cent in 1961 to about 58 per cent in 1980.[27] In Sweden, the percentage agreeing with a standard anti-social-policy statement went up from 42 to 67 per cent between 1968 and 1979 and the percentage disagreeing down from 51 to 27 (see Table A9). In Norway, between 1977 and

---

[24] See e.g. Harris & Seldon (1978).
[25] By Taylor-Gooby (1982, 1983), and others quoted by him.
[26] *Aftenposten*, 18 April 1984.
[27] Martin (1982:Fig. 3).

1980, there was no increase in the minority wanting social
security to be cut back but the proportion wanting it to be
expanded dropped from 36 to 23 per cent and the proportion
giving 'other answers' increased from 2 to 12 per cent (see Table
A3). This change has been interpreted as indicating a shift not so
much to more opposition against these programmes as to a
somewhat increasing 'scepticism to the administration of social
security'.[28] In Finland, the proportion answering that the increase
of social security was 'too slow' dropped from 31 to 21 per cent
between 1975 and 1985, those answering 'too fast' increased from
15 to 21 per cent, and the trend on specific policies is that fewer
respondents want spending to increase and more want it to
remain unchanged (see Table A4). In Denmark, the proportion
wanting social reforms to be cut back increased from 23 per cent
in the late 1960s to 31–2 per cent in the late 1970s (see Table A7).
—In Sweden, Zetterberg has found that 'doubt is mounting'. During the 1970s, the level of satisfaction with social services
remained high but at the same time more people came to be
uncertain about whether the quality of these services continued
to improve (see Table A10).

A change of heart?

Public opinion is generally supportive of the welfare state but it is
not uncritical. While a majority wants the welfare state to be
maintained or expanded, there is always a minority that wants it to
be cut back, and for some (usually comparatively minor and marginal) programmes there is only weak popular support. There is
rather more than less popular support behind large welfare states
than behind small ones. But the essential question here is not about
the level of popular support but about a possible change in popular
attitudes. The data show that public opinion has not been stable and
that the trend which is revealed in the available material for both
large and small welfare states is one of some falling support for
social policies.

It is not altogether obvious how this trend should be interpreted.
If the expectation were a massive 'welfare backlash', it is perhaps
not much to speak about. Popular support has fallen but not enough

[28] Martinussen (1981:444), based on the content of the 'other answers'.

for it to be correct to say that the population has changed its mind about the welfare state. One might even say that as the welfare state has expanded, it is only to be expected that there is gradually less support for further expansion (which is how many survey questions are formulated) and in this way dismiss the observed trend altogether.

But if, instead, we believe that public opinion usually changes only gradually and slowly and that enough loyalty has been invested in the welfare state to make popular opinion hesitate in turning against it, which is unquestionably a more reasonable starting-point than the expectation of a 'backlash', we should interpret the observed change of opinion as significant. Some changes are in fact dramatic, such as the complete turn around with regard to 'welfare' in the United States (a small welfare state) and the more ideologically formulated reorientation in Sweden (a large welfare state). It should be observed that the data show not only that fewer people want the welfare state to continue expanding but also, generally, that more want it to be cut back. The public is not only more frequently saying, 'We have enough,' but also, 'We have too much'. Hence, it appears that the best interpretation is that the welfare state *has* lost support. That being said, it is still necessary carefully to set this loss of support in perspective. The welfare state remains popular, only slightly less popular than in its best years. In view of the continued high level of public support it is simply nonsense to speak of a *crisis* of legitimacy,[29] but trends in public opinions reveal a *problem* of legitimacy. It is probably right that there is '. . . a growing sense, in many advanced countries, that the growth of social policy . . . is reaching a limit' but clearly wrong that '. . . general attitudes have changed considerably and (that) the ruling thought nowadays is more probably that the continued growth of the Welfare State is neither likely nor even desirable'.

Tax Revolt

With modern systems of national statistics and accounting, there is no problem knowing how much tax a population has paid or how

---

[29] For a more precise definition, discussion, and rejection of the 'crisis of legitimacy', see Lane (1979).

much income is taxed, but to find out how much income is *not* taxed and how much tax is *not* paid is an entirely different matter and so difficult a problem that no satisfactory solution has yet been found. Since successful tax evasion is not discovered, we cannot know exactly how large the tax base is, and since many forms of consumption are not recorded in national income statistics (for example, most of the consumption which is produced within households), we do not know how large total national income is (never mind the problem of *defining* total income). Figures from income statistics and national accounts are only more or less good approximations of these quantities.[30] Hence, we cannot know precisely how the tax base is developing relative to total income or how taxable or taxed income is developing relative to the tax base. To measure tax not paid is an exercise in measuring the unmeasurable.

During the last few years, economists have none the less, and with much energy and ingenuity, tried to do this under headings such as 'black economy', 'shadow economy', 'hidden economy', and so on. This has resulted in a large body of exciting and intriguing research but in very few hard and uncontested facts.

The income that is generated in the shadow economy is income that is withheld from taxation. If the shadow sector grows as a result of a response to rising taxes whereby more economic activity is moved into the shadow sector, this can be seen as an effort to escape the tax burden. Since the rise in the level of taxation has been caused by increasing public expenditures for social policies (as will be demonstrated in the next chapter), a tax revolt should necessarily be understood as a lack of willingness to accept the consequences of the welfare state.

Several ways have been tried for finding indicators of the size and development of the shadow sector.[31] An original and illuminating

---

[30] Using such approximations, Pechman (1983b:Table 3.2) has estimated that in the United States between 1947 and 1978, the difference between total income and taxable income increased but that the difference between taxable income and reported income decreased.

[31] See e.g. Feige (1979, 1980); Blades (1982); Denison (1982); Tanzi (1982); Carson (1984); Hansson (1984a); Gartner & Wenig (1985); Mogensen (1985); and the papers of the following international conferences/seminars: *International Conference on the Unobserved Economy* (Netherlands Institute for Advanced Study, Wassenaar, June 3–6, 1982), *Economia informale, conflitti sociali e avvenire delle società industriali* (Consiglio Italiano per le Scienze Sociali, Frascati, November 25–28, 1982), *The General Conference of the International Association for Research in Income and Wealth*, Session 6: The Unrecorded Economy (Luxembourg, August 21–27, 1983), *The Unofficial Economy: Consequences and Policies in the West and the East* (University of Trento, December 3–4, 1984).

method is the following. Instead of attempting to measure the unmeasurable, why not concentrate on factors which might reasonably be assumed to influence the size of the shadow economy, and for which reliable data are available, and estimate the 'expected' size of the shadow sector? The assumptions are that all economies have a shadow sector and that the size of this sector depends on the interaction of several economic and political factors. Estimates for seventeen Western industrial nations at different points in time during the 1960s and 1970s, based on a model which takes into consideration tax levels and other indicators of 'public sector burden', income levels, labour force participation, unemployment, hours worked, and economic growth, show firstly that the size of the shadow sector should be expected to be very different in different countries, secondly that it can be different in countries with roughly the same level of taxation even when the level of taxation is assumed to be one of the factors influencing its size, and thirdly that the development over time in the size of the shadow sector in different countries should not be expected to run parallel.[32]

This does not say anything directly about how large the shadow sector is, but it says some other things of importance. It is often taken for granted that the size of the shadow sector is more or less determined by the tax burden and, therefore, that in nations with a high level of taxation there tends to be a large shadow sector and that its size grows as the level of taxation increases. It is hardly a radical assumption to say that taxes are probably only one of several factors which might encourage people to move their economic activity into the shadow sector, yet this is enough to outrule simplistic notions that higher tax rates necessarily result in a contraction of the tax base relative to total income. Unfortunately, it is also enough to prevent changes in the size of the shadow sector from being accepted as indicators of reactions in the population to public policies. The size of the shadow sector can change for other reasons and it can remain unchanged even if there is a pressure from rising taxes to increase shadow economic activity.

Studies of tax compliance in the United States by the Internal Revenue Service, using a variety of data sources and methods, show non-reported income from both legal and illegal activities to be increasing. Between 1973 and 1981, the legal sector 'tax gap' is

[32] Frey *et al.* in Gartner & Wenig (1985).

estimated to have increased from 29 to 82 billion dollars, and the 'tax gap' due to illegal activities (drugs, gambling, and prostitution) from 2 to 9 billion dollars. Of the legal sector tax gap in 1981, 6 billion dollars is estimated to be corporate and the rest—about 75 billion dollars—to be household. Non-reported household income rose from 9 to 11 per cent of total household income.[33] Similar studies on the same scale are not available for other nations.

A method which has been applied in several countries is to estimate the difference between total taxable income according to prevailing rules and *de facto* taxed income, by comparing total income figures from national accounts with total income figures from tax statistics. In Sweden, for example, the use of this method shows non-reported income to be the equivalent of between 5 and 8 per cent of GNP around 1970 and falling to between 4 and 7 per cent around 1980.[34] Estimates for other countries fall within the range of between 1 and 3 per cent for Britain and about 20 per cent for Belgium and France. In some countries, a falling trend has been observed, in other countries a trend towards increasing non-reporting. Independent estimates for the same countries give different results on both the magnitude of and trend in unreported income.

A final major approach is to try to measure the volume of economic activity which is not captured by conventional measures, such as GNP. In Norway, estimates based on survey data have shown income from work in the shadow sector to be the equivalent of 2.3 per cent of recorded GNP in 1979 and about 2 per cent in 1983.[35] In several countries, so-called 'monetary methods' have been used, whereby the total volume of economic transactions is estimated from the volume and velocity of currency and other means of payment and this volume is compared to recorded GNP. These methods tend to show the shadow sector to be large and growing but the range of estimate results is even larger than for non-monetary methods.

There is a great deal of uncertainty in all methods used for measuring the shadow sector of the economy.[36] No concise and

---

[33] IRS (1983:Table I–1, III–2).

[34] Hansson (1984a:Fig. 1).

[35] Isachsen, Klovland & Strøm, (1982); Isachsen & Strøm, (1985).

[36] So much so that according to Denison (1984:34), with special reference to the monetary methods, their ' . . . case rests in part on anecdotes, often fictional, most of which were already stale in 1931 when Al Capone was convicted of income tax evasion . . . '

consistent definition of 'shadow sector' is applied. Comparing income reported for taxation to national account measures of income is problematic because these two measures are not entirely independent of each other and because total income may be under-estimated in the national accounts. In interview surveys, it must be expected that respondents are reluctant to report their more or less illegal activities. Monetary methods are suspect because it is vir-tually impossible to measure total income realistically on the basis of means of payment and because these methods typically assume a starting-point with no shadow economy whereafter the shadow sector is assumed to have grown to its present size.

Research on the shadow economy has undoubtedly given some insight into the structure of economic activity in advanced industrial societies but it has so far proved impossible to arrive at reliable quantitative estimates. We know that the industrial nations have shadow sectors in their economies and that they may be of some considerable size, but we do not know how alike or different from each other the industrial nations are in this respect; we do not know how large the shadow sectors of these economies are; and we do not know if they are typically growing, declining, or remaining of stable size.

The conclusion here must be that as long as we want to stick to what is empirically established, nothing can be said with certainty. The development of the shadow sector is no more than a tentative indicator of tax revolt, since it can be influenced by other factors than reactions to rising taxes or other elements of public policy, and attempts to measure the size and development of the shadow sector are plagued with uncertainty and give results which point in all directions.

Wretched as it is, this lack of conclusion is still significant, but significant only because we are forced to emphasize what we do *not* know. Studies using different methodologies and conducted in different countries have produced no authoritative evidence con-sistent with the tax revolt hypothesis. This means, on the one hand, that statements about the growth of the shadow sector remain speculative: nothing is known. But on the other hand, the evidence is not sufficient to dismiss the hypothesis. We simply do not know if more income is concealed from taxation because of the expansion of the welfare state than what would otherwise have been the case. The question of tax revolt must be left open.

Legitimacy Lost?

A trend of falling support for the welfare state in popular opinion can be observed in the material that is investigated; a weak trend, it is true, but the direction of change is unquestionable. Clear signs that the population is increasingly sabotaging the welfare state by its economic behaviour have not been found, but we cannot rule out the possibility that this may be happening as well or that changing opinions may eventually be followed by changing behaviour as loyalty wears increasingly thin. Although it would be to put it much too strongly to say that the population has rejected the welfare state, it is necessary to conclude that the tendency in public opinion is towards less support and more criticism. Legitimacy is not lost, but weakened.

That much being established, it is tempting to raise additional questions: Does the shift of balance between support and criticism reflect a reconsideration of the *principle* of the welfare state (goals), or disillusion with its *praxis* (the use of means)? Is what we see the embryo of a new ideology which may ultimately reject the welfare state or is it a more pragmatic criticism of its present performance?

No more than a guess can be ventured in response to these questions. Public opinion does not readily distinguish between goals and means, and the two possible reactions are not mutually exclusive. But there are some signs which make possible at least a moderately educated guess. One such sign is that clear evidence of a tax revolt—the ultimate form of criticism—has not been found. People complain about the tax burden, but they have always done so. There have been occasional dramatic uproars against taxes but they are explained by special circumstances. Survey data suggest that, by and large, the population is willing to pay what government asks. Tax evasion may be more prevalent, as suggested by US tax compliance data, but the opposite may be the case in Norway, for instance, or Sweden; we do not really know. Much is uncertain about all of this, but, impressionistically, it does not look as if the population is turning away from the welfare state. Against it to some degree, yes. But away from it? Probably not.

Another sign is the discrepancy between public opinion on the levels of ideology and of specific policies. Instead of dismissing this as an 'inconsistency', it can be interpreted as a rational expression of opinion which reflects an ambiguity in the public with regard to government policies. According to Ladd, 'the US population has not become more conservative in its attitude toward government (but) more demanding of governmental services . . . Over and over again, when people are asked whether they want to cut back on spending for public services, they have come down overwhelmingly in favour of sustaining or increasing current levels (but) almost every major survey on the topic documents the exceptional emphasis voters place on governmental waste and inefficiency . . . The essential message is a sober call for improved performance.'[37] In their massive study of public opinion in the United States, Lipset and Schneider have found that the majority of Americans have confidence in the institutions and norms of their society but that they are increasingly disillusioned with the use leaders in government (and the private sector) have made of the confidence entrusted in them. Americans believe that 'there is nothing wrong with this country that good leadership couldn't cure'.[38]

A further sign is that heavy and costly programmes tend to have strong support whereas the policies that have least support tend to be minor ones which are perceived—rightly or wrongly—as being not very useful or effective. If people were against the principle of the welfare state, we would expect them to turn against the policies which matter most and are most expensive. It appears, instead, that they turn against policies they think are ineffective. A final sign is what Martinussen has found in Norwegian public opinion and what Zetterberg has recorded in Sweden, namely that the change of opinion is coming in the form of increasing scepticism to the administration of social security and that doubt is mounting about the quality of services.

My guess is that the shift of balance in public opinion should not primarily be interpreted as opposition to *what* is being done, but rather as a criticism of *how* it is being done. The populations of the industrial democracies want their governments to be active in the field of social policy but they are, to some extent, increasingly uncertain about the ability of their governments to do what they think ought to be done. What we see is not a reconsideration of goals but some change of heart stemming from the experience of how means are used. The public has not changed its mind about the welfare state as such and a large majority continue to see it as a good idea, but some increasing uncertainty is developing about the competence of government to turn the idea into practical reality.

[37] Ladd (1979:49, 51, 52).
[38] Lipset & Schneider (1983:390). For a similar conclusion, see Lane (1979).

4

Governability

Politicians complain that they have little influence over politics because most decisions are dictated by some kind of necessity which is imposed upon them from the outside or as a consequence of previous decisions. Former US president Gerald Ford, for example, is said to have experienced that the 'size and growth of the Federal budget has taken on a life of its own'.[1] Theoreticians of politics, in particular followers of the public choice school, have suggested that, increasingly, the outcome of the political process is more or less arbitrary in relation to the preferences and decisions of those who take part in the process. 'The public sector may indeed be 'out of control' in the sense that its development is no longer related to the desires of the ultimate 'purchasers' of government services.'[2] Hence, warnings about a loss of control in politics are voiced by participants and observers alike.

The Control over Politics

In one sense, politics are necessarily under perfect control. Political decisions do not make themselves but are always the result of choices that politicians make, if only the choice between action and non-action. But to have control over each individual decision is not necessarily to have control over the aggregate of all decisions. This could still be arbitrary if individual decisions are not consistent with each other.

The central assumption behind the hypothesis of loss of control is that the political and administrative process has a systematic bias in favour of perpetually increasing public spending. This bias is a result of a tacit 'conspiracy' between politicians and voters against the common interest and of the complexities of the modern state, in

---

[1] According to Rose & Peters (1978:117).
[2] Buchanan & Tullock (1977:150).

particular its major component, the welfare state. Politicians prefer the easy pleasure of spending to the difficult duty of taxing. The majority of voters, having lower than average incomes, believe they will benefit from the redistribution implicit in taxing and public spending. Special interest groups try to win benefits for themselves at the expense of others. The welfare state confronts politicians with problems they cannot manage and voters with temptations they cannot resist. The rapid growth of the public sector over the last two or three decades is seen as a result of a weakening of political control, but, at the same time, as one of the factors which have caused politics to escape control. The scope of politics has expanded at such speed and to such proportions that politicians have not been able to keep pace with the developments they have themselves released. Public policy has become ungovernable.

The politicians' problem

The modern state combines the reality of vast size and the ideology of unconstrained politics. Our politicians are the guardians of streams of money, the directors of service production, and the members of decision-making bodies of supreme authority. They discharge their duties with a minimum of guidelines and at their own discretion, bound only by the expectations of their constituencies.

Up to half of the national income, or more, passes through the hands of politicians, one way in the form of taxes and the other way in the form of transfers and purchases. In addition, the politicians have the responsibility and authority to regulate private activities by laws or other forms of rules and to influence them through societal planning. This vastness of government is thought to result in uncontrollability because the system of democratic and parliamentary decision making, and in particular the budgetary process, is not up to the complexity of the task. Former decisions are considered binding and entitlements are built into the structure of taxing and spending so that the range of choice to affect change tends to be limited. Politicians avoid the larger problems and take refuge in protracted debate and struggle over minor issues which happen to be on the immediate agenda. Special interests always have advocates but the common interest is left undefended. The co-ordination of decisions—central and local, long-term and short-term, yesterday's and today's, political and bureaucratic, spending and taxing—is neglected.

A basic principle of democracy is that decisions shall be made by those who are affected by them. Historically speaking, this means that today's decisions should be made by today's politicians, unconstrained by restrictions handed down by previous politicians. The idea of democracy, therefore, is in a sense the idea of politics without constraints. This, together with theories of the pre-eminence of politics, such as 'Keynesianism', has given rise to the conviction that today's politicians alone are competent to judge what decisions are the right ones and that it is the privilege and duty of today's population and politicians to make today's decisions as they themselves see fit. Of course, politicians can never act without any formal constraints—laws are binding until they are changed and constitutions can be changed only slowly, if at all—but historians have seen in the political development of Western democracies a trend towards the demise of the *Rechtsstaat* and the substitution of 'rule by discretion' for 'rule by law'.[3] One often mentioned sign of this is the increasing tendency to pass laws which delegate authority to decide, instead of laws which prescribe certain decisions in certain situations.

Public choice theorists argue that the way political decisions are made is not fundamentally different from the way people make other kinds of decisions. Political decisions should, therefore, be understood in light of the preferences and motivations of the decision makers and the incentives they are offered in the political process.[4] Even if it were in the common interest to restrict public spending, it tends to be in the private interest of most politicians and the majority of voters to expand spending. With the concentration of power in the modern state, there are not enough checks and balances to discourage this bias. Constraining rules on political action have been removed or weakened. Politicians are only people and as prone as the next man to make mistakes and to become

---

[3] See e.g. Sejersted (1984) for an interpretation of Norwegian political history during the 19th and 20th centuries in this spirit. Here, parallel to democratization is seen a removal of constraints from the political process. The historical role of conservative parties is interpreted as protecting the integrity of political life against the perils of unconstrained politics, in opposition to the more conventional interpretation in which conservative parties are seen as breaks on progress.

[4] On 'public choice', see e.g. Brennan & Buchanan (1980, 1985).

blinded, vain, or corrupted by the power with which they are entrusted. The expansion of politics has given them the opportunity and excuse, it has been said, for 'acting out their natural proclivities to spend without taxing'.[5]

It is not easy to argue against the principle that today's politicians should be responsible for today's decisions, but there may still be a dilemma between this principle and the necessity of control over political decisions. It may be in the public interest for politicians to have incentives which encourage fiscal prudence, for instance a constitutional requirement to balance the budget, and it may be in the public interest for politicians to be armed with objective constraints which they can use to defend themselves against the fusillade of claims from the public to increase spending or reduce taxing.

The public's problem

The welfare state is a mixed blessing. It is a combination of burdens that it is tempting for people to try to avoid or pass on to someone else, and benefits, of which it is tempting to try to secure as much as possible for oneself. To illustrate, take the case of Norway, a large welfare state but still smaller than some.

Gross taxes (including direct and indirect taxes to central and local government) were in 1980 on the level of 51 per cent of the gross national product, having risen from 32 per cent in 1960.[6] This puts Norway in the top tax league among the OECD countries (the equivalent figures for Britain and the US were 41 and 33 per cent). Net taxes (net of subsidies and transfers to private households) were of course lower: 29 per cent of GNP, as compared to 23 and 20 per cent in Britain and the US, and up from 20 per cent in 1960.

The level of income taxation (including payroll taxes) on an annual taxable income (i.e. after deductions) in 1980 of 80,000 kroner (about average earnings for an industrial worker) was for a single person 33 per cent. His marginal rate of taxation would be 48 per cent. A couple without children with this income would pay 27 per cent and have a marginal rate of 43 per cent, and a couple with

---

[5] Buchanan (1984:7).
[6] All data from Central Bureau of Statistics *Aktuelle skattetall*, *Skatter og overføringer til private*.

two children would pay 17 per cent (including child allowance calculated as a negative tax) and have a marginal rate of 43 per cent. With a taxable income of 150,000 kroner, the single person would pay 47 per cent (70 per cent marginal), the couple without children 40 per cent (70 per cent), and the couple with two children 35 per cent (70 per cent).

Wage earners pay an income tax consisting of, firstly, a payroll tax of approximately 10 per cent (flat rate except for very low and very high wages; employers' contribution: in most cases 16.8 per cent of total wage costs, except in some areas where the rate is lower as an element of regional policy), secondly, a local tax of 21 per cent or in some areas slightly less (flat rate above a level of about 25 per cent of average wages), and thirdly, a central government tax which is strongly progressive above a level slightly lower than average wages. A good deal of deductions are accepted, including a standard basic deduction, travel expenses to and from work, all interest on mortgages and other loans, certain standard deductions for families with supported children, and a myriad of complex deduction possibilities.[7] Pensioners are allowed larger basic deductions than wage earners. The wealth tax is such that 'normal household wealth' for the most part is exempt, and above that level it is progressive up to a rate of 2.6 per cent.

There are a large number of indirect consumer taxes. Firstly, a value added tax of 20 per cent on virtually all goods and services, including food and with only very few exceptions (one being books, journals, and newspapers). In addition, there are special indirect taxes on alcoholic beverages, tobacco, soft drinks, chocolate and candy, sugar (as of 1983, mainly for reasons of nutrition policy), perfume and cosmetic articles, radios, TV sets and recording equipment (and a viewer/listener's fee for public broadcasting), cars, pleasure boats, gasoline, oil, electricity, and a nice little tax on charter travel abroad. Most of these indirect taxes are, by international comparison, high.

On the benefit side, in 1981–2, out of 1,000 inhabitants there were[8]
132 old age pensioners

---

[7] In 1982 total deductions reduced taxable income to 74 per cent of gross recorded income (Central Bureau of Statistics, SU 1984:41).

[8] All data from Central Bureau of Statistics (*Yearbook of Statistics*, *Social Survey 1983*), except data on housing subsidies and housing allowances which are from The State Housing Bank.

  48 disability pensioners
  16 recipients of survivors' benefits
   4 recipients of benefits to unmarried supporters
   4 recipients of benefits to divorced or separated supporters
  94 cases of allowance during sickness or childbirth
   5 cases of rehabilitation allowance
  13 recipients of unemployment compensation
  17 cases receiving social assistance
167 patients in hospitals and nursing homes
  96 patients in home care or home nursing
145 consultations with doctors
156 patients in public dental care (including school dental care)
208 pupils and students
261 participants in adult education, broadly defined, and
  20 children in kindergartens and day care institutions.
Out of 1,000 households (including singles)
320 received child allowance
  86 received home-help services
400 to 450 lived in houses or apartments which were financed, in
     part or completely, by subsidized loans from the State Hous-
     ing Bank, and
  90 received housing allowance.

This does not include special group policies, such as assistance and care to groups of handicapped, orphans, children under protection, alcoholics, drug addicts, or victims of violence (within or outside of the family). Nor does it include various forms of consumer subsidies, such as on food (milk, cheese, flour/bread, meat), public transportation, electricity and fuel (in some regions), cultural and recreational activities, newspapers, magazines, books, and broadcasting. And it does not include production subsidies where redistribution is one among several motivational factors: for example, support for agriculture, fisheries, or the arts, regional policies for industry and commerce, labour market policies, or incomes policies. Finally, the list does not include defence, law and order, and general government administration, items which together take up about a third of all public expenditure.

In the modern welfare state, then, as we can see, no one escapes the tax burden, but also everyone benefits. Rose and Peters have calculated that on average each inhabitant in five European countries receives at least one major social benefit each year from government, and in for example Sweden almost two benefits.[9] In addition, it should be remembered that the direct beneficiaries of the welfare state are not only the clients but also the providers and others who depend on it for their jobs, and that there are indirect beneficiaries, for example families or private businesses which are relieved of some of the social responsibilities they might otherwise have had to accept.[10] Rose and Peters, again, have estimated that on average for advanced industrial nations about 30 to 40 per cent of all employees depend directly or indirectly on government for their jobs (the figure for Sweden is 58 per cent). In Scandinavia the producers and clients of the welfare state together make up between 40 and 50 per cent of the electorate.[11]

Hence, people have vested interests in the welfare state, interests which encourage the expansion of benefits (and of bureaucracies to produce, administer, and distribute benefits) and discourage the growth of the tax burden. Although most people are, as we have seen in the previous chapter, far from being without scruples in demanding benefits and resisting taxes, there is a constant signal from constituencies to politicians in favour of more benefits and in opposition to more taxes.

These signals can turn into uncontrollability in government through the mechanism of competitive politics. Political parties depend for their life and success on their ability to attract voters. It

[9] Rose & Peters (1978:73). The countries in question: Britain, France, Germany, Italy, Sweden.

[10] The question of who has a stake in the welfare state, which is of course important for explaining its expansion, is quite complex. One possibility is to assume altruism and consequently a pro-welfare state coalition beyond those who see themselves as benefiting personally. But several theories suggest that it is not necessary to give up the assumption of self-interest in order to put together a large, probable coalition for the welfare state. First, there are the consumers of services and the indirect beneficiaries (family, businesses) who would otherwise have had to provide services, who believe costs (and other burdens) to be shared by others than themselves. Second, there are those who get jobs as providers and who believe that their jobs would otherwise not be available or that private sector jobs would be less rewarding. Third, there are those who do not benefit today but who see the welfare state as an insurance for themselves in case of future need, the cost, again, being assumed shared more broadly than in private insurance. Finally, assuming income is redistributed, those who benefit from equality: the poor, the majority with less than average income (according to the 'median voter theory'), and those who have a preference for equality irrespective of their own relative income position. For further discussion, see e.g. Rogers (1974) and other papers in Hochman & Peterson (1974).

[11] See footnote 6 in Chapter 2.

is as tempting for party spokesmen to promise benefits without taxes as it is for voters to believe it is possible. And even if politicians understand the impossibility of giving benefits without imposing burdens, they may find themselves trapped in a choice between giving in to the competition of other parties or outbidding them. Parties that are totally irresponsible are usually not seen as credible, but even the most responsible party can be driven, in an election campaign, to promise more than it knows it can deliver.

The meaning of control

A large and/or rapidly growing public sector is in itself sometimes seen as a sign that politics are out of control.[12] This, however, is not meaningful. A concept of control whereby a large public sector is by definition out of control and only decisions that restrict the (growth of the) public sector are taken as signs of control makes no more sense than if I were to say that politics are under control only if the decisions taken are the ones I happen to approve of.

The problem of control can also be seen as a question of the correspondence between the preferences of the public (or of voters) and the policies of government, so that politics are under control to the extent that they reflect the preferences of the public, as exemplified in the quotation from Buchanan and Tullock in the introduction to this chapter. But this is equally inadequate since it is just another way of formulating the problem I have earlier discussed under the heading of legitimacy. This use of the concept of the control is misleading since it implies that there is an intrinsic tendency in government to take politics further that the public wants and that the public is necessarily interested in holding back government. The problem is over-simplified by being seen as one of conspiracy by politicians against voters, rather than of imperfections which may produce outcomes that no one has wanted.

Instead, I suggest a concept of control which is derived from the need for consistency in political decision making. Control is not a question of what decisions are made but of consistency between the decisions that are made, whatever their content may be. In this way I separate the concept of control both from that of legitimacy and from the issue of the size and growth of the public sector and the

---

[12] See e.g. a polemic by Beck (1981:4–7).

scope of politics. These are all important problems, but they are separate problems. Legitimacy has been dealt with in the previous chapter and the size of the public sector will be discussed in the next one; here I shall discuss control and that alone.

The problem of control has nothing to do *per se* with either limiting the domain of politics or securing its legitimacy, but is instead a question of reconciling goals and means or ambitions and resources. While legitimacy has to do with the relationship between popular preferences and political decisions—do politicians make the decisions the public wants and does the public accept the decisions politicians make?—control has to do with the relationship between the different decisions politicians make—are their decisions consistent with each other? Problems of legitimacy can make it difficult for politicians to maintain control, and politics out of control can give rise to problems of legitimacy, but the two problems are still conceptually separate. While legitimacy must be studied in popular opinion on the grass-roots level, control must be studied on the level of political decision making. It is in the behaviour of politicians that we can see if politics are under control.

Some political decisions are popular and easy to make, others are unpopular and difficult to make. Since easy decisions usually imply or depend on difficult ones, one of the main functions of the political process is to be a clearing house between easy and difficult decisions, so that no more easy decisions are made than can be followed up with the necessary difficult ones. Accordingly, politics can be said to be under control to the extent that easy and difficult decisions are reconciled or, in other words, to the extent that the innate bias of the political process is not allowed to result in easy decisions which are not covered by the necessary difficult ones.

The typical easy decision, of course, is a decision to spend, and the typical difficult one a decision to tax. A number of forces pull in the direction of overspending/undertaxing. Spending is 'good'; it is good because someone benefits directly and because it is often believed to stimulate the economy so that we all benefit indirectly. Taxing is, by the same standards, 'bad'. The public expects and demands benefits from government and dislikes taxation, and is always tempted to convince itself that it is possible to have more benefits without more taxes or less taxes without less benefits. Political parties are forced to outbid each other and are tempted to promise the kinds of tax/benefit miracles that the public is tempted to believe in. It is by spending that politicians can help people and win friends; by taxing they impose burdens and make enemies. In the absence of objective constraints in the process of decision making, politicians have no protection against, or anywhere to turn for help to resist, the pressures for overspending and undertaxing. Without firm control over politics we should expect to see spending in excess of taxation.

The public budget reflects the aggregate outcome of the many decisions on taxing and spending which politicians make and hence reflects the ability of government to be consistent in its decision making. The way government clears outlays and revenues is indicative of how able it is to follow up easy spending decisions with the necessary difficult ones on taxing, or to limit spending to what it is able to cover by taxing. Consequently, the balance between spending and taxing can be taken as an indicator of political control. Overspending in relation to taxing (or undertaxing in relation to spending) is a sign of politics out of control.

Overspending (or undertaxing) is independent of the level of spending. There is, in the present context, no such thing as too much spending in itself. Spending can be excessive only in relation to taxing. Hence, overspending must always be revealed in a budget deficit. But not any budget deficit is a sign that politics are out of control. Two conditions must be met. First, the deficit must be a result of political choice in the sense that it might have been avoided. We cannot put the blame on inadequacies in the political process if a deficit is unavoidable. Secondly, it must be unintended. If politicians decide on a budget deficit as an instrument of economic policy, we might discuss the wisdom of their decision but we could not say that the deficit was the result of a lack of control over politics. Only avoidable and unintended deficits are signs of lack of control. On the other hand, any deficit of this kind can be taken as proof that politics are not under control since there is no other possible explanation for such deficits than the inability of politicians within the system they operate to avoid what they themselves necessarily see as inconsistencies in their decision making.

The dilemma of control

The whole point of the expansion of politics in the modern state is to win control. We have wanted to use politics to control our environment and our destiny. The deeper meaning of the hypothesis of ungovernability is that this ambition is ultimately self defeating. Like Faust, who longs so strongly for perfection that he accepts the Devil's offer of unlimited power although he knows that he is thereby condemning himself to destruction, we want so strongly to win control through politics that we accept such expansions of the public sector that the state becomes ungovernable. The very concentration of power which is intended to win us control over our society has the perverse effect that we lose control over politics. A not uncommon experience in life is that he who tries too hard will not succeed.

It is easy to see that this hypothesis, if tenable, represents a dilemma for the welfare state. It is the welfare state that causes the public sector to grow. If the public sector can grow only at the cost of reduced control over politics, we face a trade-off between more redistribution and less political control, and must accept a political price on the welfare state in addition to its possible economic price.

The Nature of the Deficit

In most of the Western industrial nations, there developed during the 1970s huge deficits of tax revenues in relation to public spending. There is broad, although not perfect, agreement that these deficits represent some sort of problem.[13] But what kind of a problem is this? Are the deficits 'only' an unfortunate but unavoidable outcome of a difficult economic situation, or are they the result of an inability in the political system to make and implement necessary decisions? Are they a sign that governments are not able to govern?

Thanks to recent OECD studies, we now have good statistics on

[13] One source of disagreement is a controversy over the adequacy of the official method of measuring government debt and budget deficits. Eisner & Pieper (1984), for example, claim that the method is misleading for several reasons (e.g., financial asset accumulation is ignored, current and capital accounts are not separated, the effects of inflation are not properly incorporated) and that this has the effect of the government debt and the public budget deficit being exaggerated. On the basis of a re-estimation of the US federal budget, these authors claim that the real debt burden of the federal government has declined over the post-war period, including the 1970s. This controversy is of little importance here, since, as will be explained, what matters for the present analysis is the political perception of the deficit more than its reality and since the political perception follows the official method of measurement.

public revenue and expenditure in OECD countries at the beginning of the 1980s and their development during the 1960s and 1970s. Appendix B contains a detailed summary of the most important of this material. Although it is tedious, the reader is advised to study this material carefully in order to get a firm grasp of just how fast the public sector has grown, how large it has become, the very significant role of social expenditures in total public expenditure and expenditure growth, and the size of the present budget deficits in most of these countries.[14]

Origin

The essential facts about public expenditure and revenue trends in the industrial democracies from about 1960 to the early 1980s are the following:

1. Public expenditures and revenues[15] grew more rapidly than the national income and thereby dramatically increased the size of the public sector in these economies.

2. Social expenditure[16] is the largest component of public expenditure and grew considerably faster than total public expenditure. The growth of public expenditure relative to the national income is explained almost totally by the growth of social expenditure.

3. Public revenues more or less kept track with public expenditures up until the early or mid–1970s. During 1973–5, however, and

[14] The statistical information used here goes up to about 1982–3. The essential period for which information on public expenditure and revenue trends are needed for the present analysis is the 1970s. This was when the recession set in and the OECD countries went from being high-growth to low-growth or moderate-growth economies, and this was the period when the situation of rough budget balance for most of the OECD countries gave way to large and persistent deficits.

[15] Includes expenditure and revenue of central and local government; excludes government businesses which produce for sale in the market. Public expenditure/revenue in per cent of GDP is the most used but not the only possible measure of public sector size. Lybeck (1984) compares 13 different measures of public sector size and demonstrates, with data for Sweden for the period 1970 to 1981, that the expenditure/revenue measures are the ones which show the largest public sector and the most rapid public sector growth. Beck (1981) shows that after adjusting for price changes (the price of government products tends to rise faster than the general price level), government expenditure relative to the national income rises less rapidly than when measured, as here, without adjusting for price changes.

[16] Includes public expenditure for 'merit goods' (education, health, housing, other) and 'income maintenance' (pensions, sick-pay, family allocations, unemployment compensation, other).

again in 1979–80, expenditures continued to rise while the growth of revenues fell behind as a result of periods with close to zero economic growth. This created sudden and considerable gaps between expenditures and revenues and left most OECD countries with very sizeable government deficits.

4. The government budget deficit was not caused by extraordinary changes in expenditure or revenue policies but primarily by economic recession (the two periods of close to zero economic growth). The explanation behind the sudden deficit is not that governments adopted new spending programmes or cut tax rates but that the revenue base of government did not continue to grow fast enough for revenues to keep track with the 'normal' development of expenditure.

5. Both expenditure and revenue trends adjusted somewhat to lower growth rates. Expenditure, including social expenditures, continued to grow more rapidly than the national income, but, with the exception of the two periods of recession, slightly less so during the latter part of the 1970s and early 1980s than previously. Because effective tax rates continued to rise, revenues continued to grow relative to the national income at about the same pace during the 1970s and into the 1980s as they did earlier. But these adjustments were not sufficient to overcome the jump in the deficits during the two periods of recessions and to regain the rough public budget balance which most OECD countries had up to the early or mid-1970s.

6. The adjustments of public expenditure trends to lower growth rates were, for the most part, 'automatic' and were not, or only to a minor degree, the result of new budget policies (i.e. the result of 'built-in stabilizers' as opposed to 'discretionary' policy changes). They were caused above all by such factors as changes in the demographic composition of the population (e.g. decline of the school age population from the mid 1970s) and the fact that most of the increase in the scope of major social programmes had been completed during the 1960s (e.g. eligibility and coverage of social security, expansion of basic education). These effects would have materialized even if economic growth had continued at its previous rate, and it can be said to be pure luck that they did come in time to rescue public finances from even worse problems. Most OECD countries have tried to adopt

anti-deficit policies, but, at least up to the early 1980s, without much impact.[17]

7. The public budget deficits were caused mainly by 'automatic' pressure on expenditure and revenue, such as the effects of slower economic growth, inflation, and unemployment. But, in addition, certain policies contributed to increasing the deficits, for example the tendency to index some social benefits so that they grow in proportion to inflation or the wage level and to index some taxes so that they do not increase with inflation. In most OECD countries, the public budget deficit now has a 'structural' component. This means that the deficits are larger than can be explained by recession alone and that part of the growth of the deficit must be explained by policy changes. Although governments tried to adopt anti-deficit policies, these were either ineffective or more than outbalanced by the opposite effect of other policy changes. The size of the structural component of the deficit is uncertain. It appears to be moderate if seen in relation to pre-recession growth rates and capacity utilization, i.e. in relation to the main factors which have caused the deficit, but to be considerable if seen in relation to realistic expectations about economic growth over the next five or ten years.

All in all, the OECD countries typically entered the 1970s with a rough balance between public expenditure and revenue and left the decennium with expenditures far exceeding revenues. This change is explained mainly by economic recessions but also to some extent by a political response which has contributed to widening rather than narrowing the budget gap. It needs to be added that the picture drawn here does not fit as a description of all industrial democracies. It is a general description for the OECD area as a whole and fits fairly well for most of the countries in this area, although there are clearly differences between them in their public budget situation. For some countries the description does not apply at all: for example, Norway, which has until 1986 persistently had a public budget surplus.

Intention

The kind of budget deficit that became typical in the OECD area during the 1970s is now widely regarded as a problem that had best

---

[17] According to *OECD Economic Outlook 1985* (Table 3) deficits are in most member countries expected to fall somewhat in the latter part of the 1980s. This, however, is not expected in all countries, e.g. not in the United States (see Congressional Budget Office, 1985).

been avoided. While we know from experience that we can live very well with at least some deficit budgeting over a long period of time, it is argued that these deficits are not good old-fashioned practical deficits but that they are in several respects *different*. Some of the problems most frequently associated with these 'modern' deficits are the following.

First, they are exceptionally large. Until the early or mid–1970s, OECD countries (with some exceptions) would typically have deficits off and on, so that on average deficits might be, for example, less than or around 1 per cent of GNP. In the middle of the 1970s, the public budget deficits jumped to about 3 or 4 per cent of GNP. They went down again slightly towards the end of the 1970s (though not down to the pre–1975 level), but then rose again during the first years of the 1980s to an average level of between 4 and 5 per cent of the national income. Deficits on this scale, and the public borrowing that accompany them, may have adverse economic effects, at least in the long run, in terms of inflation, for example, or 'crowding out' of productive economic activity.

Secondly, they are not short term, but chronic (or, in the more technical language, structural). The present large deficits cannot be explained by outside circumstances alone, that is by slow economic growth, but have also to some extent been caused by internal decisions on expenditure and revenue policies. This means, again, that the deficits would not be overcome by a return to pre-recession growth rates and that, in light of what are now realistic growth prospects, an 'automatic' restoration of a rough budget balance in the foreseeable future is unlikely. Instead, because of the vicious circle of large-scale deficit budgeting, they threaten to grow and become permanent. This would make borrowing a normal source of 'revenue' for government and introduce an element of some sort of implicit taxation through borrowing which would make fiscal policy even more difficult to understand and control than it already is.

Thirdly, when deficit budgeting becomes chronic, the problem turns from being a practical matter to becoming one of principle with ethical elements. What a public sector deficit means is that we here and now have a higher sum of private income and public expenditure than the total available income, and consequently, that part of the cost for our present consumption will have to be paid later. With short-term cyclical deficits this is not so much of a problem, because for all intents and purposes we will ourselves have to pay off our own deficit in a few years time. We are, of course, entitled to borrow today and forsake tomorrow, in particular if we can hope that this will make us better off tomorrow than we would otherwise have been. What *we* overconsume today, *we* pay tomorrow. But with long-term chronic deficits the situation is different. We are postponing payment for part of our present consumption much more than a few years, or in other words passing the bill on to someone else in the future. What *we* overconsume today, *they* will pay tomorrow. This becomes an ethical problem because we are shifting the burden of payment on to someone who has no say in today's decision making. Of course, we make a large number of decisions today which affect future generations; that is unavoidable. But it is not unavoidable to hold a higher level of consumption than we are willing or able to pay for. In order to justify a long-term deficit today, we must at the very least feel confident that this policy is to the benefit of those we are passing the bill on to, that is, that we are now making investments which will pay off so that the next generation not only will be able to cover the bill we are leaving for them, but will also have a better standard of living than they would have had if we today had chosen other and less costly policies. If there is reason to fear that this will not be the result, then our present policies might be described as exploiting the future standard of living of our children.

It is not likely that present budget deficits are justifiable on these grounds. Since the major expenditure component, and the growing one, is the welfare state, the deficits must be said to be used primarily to finance present consumption by way of direct and indirect transfers and other social policies which are not covered by public revenues rather than to finance investments which might benefit future generations.[18] Social policies, for sure, are not merely consumption; they are a combination of consumption and investment. But a chronic deficit which is caused by social expenditures that are not covered by taxation can hardly be justified as being an investment in the interest of future generations.

Fourthly, through chronic deficits the political system loses its

---

[18] In fact, the investment component of public expenditure has gone down and the consumption component up. On average for the major 15 OECD countries, investment fell from 16 to 12 per cent as a proportion of total public spending during the 1970s, and general government savings, which represented over 3 per cent of GDP in 1970, have diminished almost to zero (OECD:CPE-WP1 (82)3, p. 10).

freedom of action. Very considerable resources are tied up in servicing the debt burden. Today, OECD countries on average use 4 to 5 per cent of their national income for interest payments. This amounts to 10 or 15 or even 20 per cent of total public expenditure. The interest bill alone is on average larger than the deficit, which means that many of these governments are now borrowing primarily to cover the cost of their accumulated debt. Had they had no debt and no borrowing, they would have had more money to spend at their discretion than they now have, including the money they borrow. In addition, governments may become dependent on lenders and may have to bend their policies to direct or indirect requirements set by the lenders.[19]

Finally, the deficits have not been acquired positively in relation to specific policy goals, but negatively in the sense that the political systems of these countries have not been able to avoid a situation of growing deficits. They are not intentional elements of economic policy but accidents we have found ourselves unable to escape and forced to accept.

The merits of most of these arguments are a matter of controversy. Economists disagree about the economic effects of large-scale deficits, and politicians disagree about their ethics. It can be argued that the inter-generation transfer implicit in long-term government borrowing is only one of paper claims and not of real resources so that there is no burden on the future unless public borrowing has a negative impact on economic growth (unless governments borrow abroad, as they generally do). Although the deficits are of unprecedented size, the public debt is perhaps not alarmingly large in relation to, for example, national or private wealth. We do not as yet have much practical experience with what it means economically and politically to live with deficits such as we have now acquired, so that much of what is said about the deficits is necessarily speculative. However, the merits of these various warnings against large-scale deficits are in themselves not of much importance for the present discussion. What matters here is not the 'true' nature of deficit budgeting but how the deficits are perceived by the politicians of these nations and in their political cultures. We are concerned not with the wisdom of the decisions that

---

[19] For a vivid illustration, see the *Sunday Times*' reports on the secret negotiations between the British government and the International Monetary Fund in 1976 (14, 21, and 28 May 1978; and the booklet *The Day the £ Nearly Died*, Sunday Times, June 1978).

politicians make but with their ability to make the decisions they themselves believe should be made. Politically, the deficits are a problem if they are perceived to be a problem.

While experts debate the deficits, there can be no doubt that politicians, and certainly politicians in power, have on the whole interpreted them as problematic. It is enough to look at the recent issues of the *OECD Economic Outlook* to see that according to the collective wisdom of the governments of the OECD nations, the deficit is now one of the most serious economic problems they confront, if not the most serious one. Governments may, of course, be wrong in their analysis but their anxiety is not without basis, and anyway what matters here is not really if they are right or wrong, but how they in fact analyse the situation. Some commentators warn against exaggerated fears over the deficits, but no one appears willing to praise them as a sign of wise economics and decisiveness in politics. It has been suggested that the deficits may have contributed to stimulating the economies of the OECD nations in the early 1980s,[20] but if so this is a slightly paradoxical and coincidental benefit from a situation the governments have wanted to avoid.[21] By authoritative political interpretation, the deficits are a problem. They were acquired not by choice but were forced upon us by economic circumstances that were mostly beyond our control. In conclusion, therefore, the 'modern' deficits in the OECD area must be classified as *unintended*.

Avoidability

Could the deficits have been avoided if politicians had been more forceful and austere in their decision making? Technically, of course, they could, if only expenditures had been cut and effective tax rates raised sufficiently, but realistically the answer is 'no'. The deficits were caused mainly by economic recessions in the form of two sudden drops in economic growth, and these drops were caused mainly by factors over which Western governments had no control, the 'oil shocks'. It was politically and economically impossible to cut spending and raise taxes overnight sufficiently to prevent the deficits from jumping to

[20] See e.g. Tobin (1983).
[21] See e.g. Tobin (1985).

new heights. It would, hence, not be correct to blame the unprecedented budget deficits we now see in the OECD area on politics, for
example, on the politician's 'natural proclivities to spend without
taxing'.

That being said, one can ask the following additional question:
Although some increasing deficit was unavoidable, could some of
the actual increase of the deficit have been avoided? Here the
answer is 'yes'. A trend towards growing deficits was apparent even
before the dramatic recessions of the 1970s, and warnings that fiscal
policy was threatening to grow out of control were heard, and not
only from commentators on the Right.[22] Since the deficits were
interpreted as problematic, we should have expected adjustment
policies, so that actual deficits were kept at least slightly lower than
what they would have been as a direct result of economic recession
and 'built-in stabilizers'. Instead we have seen that deficits have a
structural component, which means that they have grown more and
not less than can be explained by economic recession and 'automatic' adjustments alone. Politics, far from keeping actual deficits
lower than 'expected' deficits, contributed to making them higher.
Consequently, although the deficits cannot be explained as a result
of 'irresponsible' spending and taxing policies, their size must to
some extent be explained by the absence of adjustment policies
which we should have expected to see, given the politicians' interpretation of the nature of the deficits and assuming that they were
able to follow up their own analysis with the kinds of policies this
analysis suggests.

To this should be added one qualification. The recession of the
early 1970s was first interpreted as probably being short term, and
the deficits consequently as being cyclical ones which, although
large, would be corrected once recession was over. Specific anti-
deficit policies should therefore probably not be expected until after
some time when it was understood that the recession was more
serious and lasting than at first believed. During the period from the
early 1970s to the early 1980s, deficits rose considerably. Structural
factors are estimated to explain about a quarter of this change.[23] But
there are signs that the deficits may temporarily have been brought
slightly down during the years between the two recessions and that

[22] For a Marxist analysis leading to this conclusion, see O'Connor (1973).
[23] OECD: *Occasional Studies*, June 1983:19.

anti-deficit policies contributed to this. If so, this was interrupted by the second recession, and it is, therefore, perhaps still too early to pass final judgement on the ability of governments to adjust their fiscal policies to their own analysis of the deficits. Governments say that they are enacting anti-deficit policies; it remains to be seen how effective they are in a longer perspective.

From what we know today, the deficits as such must be classified as unavoidable. They are not a result of overspending or undertaxing in relation to alternative policies which were realistically open for the politicians to choose. But the deficits grew more than was unavoidable. Through their own analyses, politicians in effect said that fiscal policies should have subtracted from the deficits, but in fact they adopted policies which had the opposite result. The deficits were unavoidable, but fiscal policies that made the deficits larger than can be explained by recession cannot be classified as unavoidable.

Control Lost?

From 1960 to the early 1980s, public spending in OECD countries on average increased from the equivalent of about 25 per cent of GDP to almost 50 per cent. Politicians and students of politics have warned that this extraordinary growth of government is associated with a loss of control over politics. The growth of public spending relative to the national income is a result almost totally of the growth of expenditure within the welfare state. If politics, therefore, have grown out of control, this must be seen as a side-effect of the expansion of the welfare state and as a political price on the strategy of redistribution. This is all the more so since it is usually the entitlements which have been built into the welfare state that are thought of as uncontrollable.

Control over politics is a question of consistency in decision making. This can most conveniently be studied in the relationship between public spending and taxing. There is a bias in the political process in favour of spending and against taxing. To have politics under control is a question of being able to master this bias so that spending is covered by taxing. A lack of control will reveal itself in the form of a budget deficit which is politically unintended and could have been avoided.

During the first three decades of the post war period, the industrial nations enjoyed rapid and stable economic growth. Under these conditions it proved possible to expand public spending and taxing without serious difficulty. Increased spending could be 'financed from growth', and political control was not much of a problem. Then, during the 1970s, the basis for increasing tax revenues was eroded because of economic recession. The growth of revenue fell off automatically so that when spending continued to grow more or less at its previous pace the result was necessarily a budget deficit. Suddenly, political control was a difficult problem; the political process was set to the test of reconciling spending and taxing under less favourable conditions than politicians and voters had grown accustomed to. The true governability of the modern state would be revealed.

The welfare state nations typically responded to economic recession by developing unprecedented budget deficits. Through an analysis of the origins and structure of these deficits we have found that they must be classified as *unintended* and in part *avoidable*. The deficits were not created by fiscal policies, but nor were they effectively counteracted. They grew more than was the unavoidable result of economic recession and were stimulated rather than held back by fiscal policies. Consequently, although a lack of political control is not the main factor behind the deficits, it is a contributing factor. The deficits soon came to be seen as deeply problematic, but effective adjustment policies consistent with this analysis were generally not implemented. When new spending could no longer be financed through growth, there proved to be insufficient power in the political process to master the bias in favour of overspending.

The overall conclusion here is much the same as in the previous chapter on legitimacy. There the crisis of legitimacy was dismissed but a problem of legitimacy identified. Here we have seen that a lack of political control is not the main factor behind large scale deficits, but we must at the same time concede that, as revealed by the political response to the economic recessions of the 1970s, there is a problem of political control over the welfare state.

5

Efficiency

The leaky bucket—this is the famous 'Okunism' for the economic dilemma of redistribution: 'The money must be carried from the rich to the poor in a leaky bucket. Some of it will simply disappear in transit, so the poor will not receive all the money that is taken from the rich'.[1] Economists have always—or at least since Adam Smith more than two hundred years ago warned against the way British anti-poverty legislation was being implemented (but not against anti-poverty legislation as such) because he believed it prevented geographical mobility in the labour force—been concerned that the good intention of encouraging social progress through political intervention could backfire by at the same time discouraging economic progress. As soon as steady post-war economic growth started to slip in the 1970s, this turned from being a concern to becoming a major anxiety. The argument that redistribution could not be afforded—however desirable it might be—quickly became, as Julien Le Grand has put it, 'one of the major weapons in the non-egalitarian's armoury'.[2] With his simple and striking analogy, Arthur Okun explained for everyone to see how redistribution could be costly. Although his own discussion of the relationship between equality and efficiency is a model of academic broad-mindedness and without a trace of the vulgarism that has later become not unusual,[3] he thereby contributed to sharpening this weapon.

But the leaky bucket image, although admirably elegant, is not altogether accurate. How government handles money in transit is an important problem—a problem of good housekeeping—but it is not the only problem of economic efficiency in social policy, perhaps not the most important problem, and certainly not the problem Okun was most concerned with in his lectures on 'the big trade-

---

[1] Okun (1975:91).
[2] Le Grand (1982:148).
[3] The peak of vulgarism must be by George Gilder in *Wealth and Poverty* (p. 144): 'In order to succeed, the poor need most of all the spur of their poverty.'

off'. The members of a society together own a pool of income. From this pool government swoops out a good part in its big bucket, holds it for a while and then pours it back in again, hoping that it takes income out from the rich and pours it back in to the poor. This is done at a double risk. Some of the income may spill out of the bucket and go lost so that government has less income to pour back in than it took out; income is wasted. But in addition, private economic actors might find government's bucket—leaky or not—objectionable and react by withdrawing from economic activity, so that some of the streams that bring income into the pool in the first place dry up; income is not generated. These are two different ways that redistribution may cause our common pool to contain less income than it might have had. We can speak of internal and external inefficiencies.

Internal Efficiency

The social policy system of a welfare state consists not only of abstractions, such as 'programmes' and 'redistributions', but is also a huge physical apparatus of personnel, buildings, equipment, bank accounts, and so on. We want to know what comes out of this apparatus in the form of intended redistribution and unintended side-effects, but we can also ask what goes on inside it. Is it well run?

In any huge apparatus in the real world there are bound to be inefficiencies compared to the theoretical case of the best of all worlds. Our question should, therefore, not primarily be whether inefficiencies can be identified—that is obvious—but rather if there is more inefficiency than might realistically be expected and if this is a problem the welfare state is likely to grow into or grow out of.

A typology

As usual, a whole range of problems can be discussed. Off the cuff, I suggest four criteria of internal efficiency in social policy:

—The absence of waste in the use of funds and other resources.
—The ability to reach all individuals or groups that are intended to be supported under the existing regime, and to limit service and assistance accordingly.

—The ability to deliver services and assistance in accordance with the structure of needs.

—The ability to serve and treat the clients of the welfare state with expedience, courtesy, respect, and dignity.

Distinguishing between cash transfers and services, a typology of internal social policy inefficiencies can be set up as in the chart below. Since the subject here is economic efficiency I shall concentrate on the problem of productivity. But some brief remarks on the other issues in the chart are in order first.

Minor issues

Money lost in the process is not a very serious problem. In the Norwegian and Swedish social security systems, for example, only 1 to 2 per cent of total expenditure is for administration. The administrative cost of taxation is in Sweden estimated to be about 1 per cent of collected taxes.[4] Income-tested transfer programmes are likely to be relatively more cumbersome and expensive to adminis-

A Typology of Internal Social Policy Inefficiencies

	Cash transfers	Social services
Waste	Money lost in process	Low productivity
Target inefficiency	Underuse Overuse Fraud	Underuse Overuse Fraud
Needs not met	Cash when services are needed	Services when cash is needed Wrong kinds of services
Clients mistreated	Stigmatization 'Bureaucracy'	Stigmatization 'Bureaucracy'

[4] ESO (1983a, 1983b). This does not include 'compliance costs' for tax payers. Such costs have in the United States been estimated at 1.4 per cent of household income, including nearly 22 hours spent by the average household on the preparation of tax returns (an absolutely incredibly high figure for someone used to Scandinavian tax returns). See *NBER Digest*, April 1985.

ter than large universal programmes. But to redistribute cash income is technically not difficult.

Fraud may be a problem in small welfare states which rely heavily on income-tested benefits, but not to the same degree in welfare states which have more universal programmes. As far as we know, as mentioned in Chapter 3, underuse of social benefits is a more widespread problem than overuse.[5] This may be a problem welfare states grow into, since more rights established also means potentially more rights not claimed. Stigmatization of recipients of social benefits is a problem which is caused almost exclusively by income testing and which is, therefore, more typical of small than of large welfare states.[6]

The question of whether the welfare state delivers the right kind of support in relation to the structure of needs is highly complex. One school of social policy theory holds that cash transfers should, in most cases, be sufficient, since this would enable the individual to purchase the services he might need or want, but this is probably a serious over-simplification which ignores the importance of other resources than money for efficient consumption. The handicapped and the elderly, for example, are often prevented from (literally) entering consumer markets or from coping with the practical difficulties they meet there. For many of the needs of heavy social clients, cash transfers are close to being irrelevant.

A related problem lies in the distinction between caring and curing in the health services. Increasingly, health care clients are not patients in the conventional understanding but elderly who 'suffer' mainly from old age and who require care more than cure. Health service institutions and their personnel, however, tend to be geared to curing, the result being an over-supply of curing and under-supply of caring and possibly that many clients are 'treated' at a higher cost than necessary.[7] The institutionalization of clients who could have remained in their homes, and would have preferred to do so had there been a better system of home-help services, the hospitalization of clients whose needs are the services of a nursing home, and the lack of flexible combinations between institutionalization and non-institutionalization are examples of problems

---

[5] Overuse can occur independently of fraud: for example, if clear criteria for the allocation of benefits are not available, so that more recipients than intended can make claims.

[6] On stigmatization, see Rainwater (1982).

[7] See e.g. McKeown (1965); Wærness (1982).

which are, undoubtedly, a fact of life in small and large welfare states alike and which reflect both poor management of resources and needs not being met. So, of course, does the failure to provide institutional facilities for clients who need them.

'Bureaucracy' is, as everyone knows, a subject of heated debate and strong feelings. It is not clear what precisely the problem is but many people apparently feel that the provision of public services is too slow and clumsy, that the client is constantly sent from one office to another, that it is difficult or impossible to obtain proper information, that responsibility within the social services is not clearly defined, that there are too many forms to fill in and too many rules to comply with, that public 'bureaucrats' are unconcerned and rude, and so on. There is a mass of anecdotal criticism of 'bureaucracy' but there are also many thankful and satisfied clients.[8] It would not be surprising if 'the human factor' tended to be neglected in the vast apparatus of the modern welfare state, and no doubt it often is, but systematic, as opposed to anecdotal, evidence suggests that on the whole people are remarkably satisfied with how they are treated in their encounters with public agencies, be this because the service is good or because clients are too timid to complain.[9]

Productivity

The concept of productivity describes in economic terms the relationship between the resource inputs which are employed and the output which is produced. The more output in relation to input, or the better the quality, the higher the productivity. In this, nothing is

---

[8] An eloquent expression of such satisfaction is Richard Titmuss' 'Postscript' in his *Social Policy*, based on his own experience in old age as a National Health Service cancer patient.

[9] In Sweden, which probably has the most developed public bureaucracy of any democracy, the evidence is that the population is remarkably satisfied with public services. Surveys indicate that in general only 2 to 5 per cent of the adult population report that they have ever been treated 'wrongly or injustly' by any of a long list of public agencies (Johansson, 1981). Between 80 and 90 per cent of those who have been in contact with such agencies report that they are satisfied with the treatment they received (NSI, 1981). The tax authorities, understandably, are among the least popular agencies, but no more than 16 per cent report that they have been treated 'wrongly or injustly' and 77 per cent report satisfaction. There is not more dissatisfaction reported with public agencies, e.g. the postal service, than with private institutions, e.g. banks.

said about the usefulness of the output. For example, many people hold all war toys to be useless and harmful, but this does not mean that there cannot be more or less productivity in the production of war toys, depending on how economically raw materials are used, how durable the toys are, and so on. It is in this understanding of the concept that productivity in the social service is discussed here. We want to know if what is done is done well. Whether it is useful will be discussed later in relation to redistributive effectiveness.

In order to make a judgement about productivity in the welfare state, a standard of comparison is needed. The obvious choice is private sector production. This is an alternative form of production which is available for empirical comparison. Lower productivity in public than in private production would be proof that public production is behind not only a theoretical standard but also what has been demonstrated to be practically possible. (However, such proof would not necessarily be an argument for 'privatization', a question which is not discussed here.)

The public sector as a whole is usually assumed to improve its productivity more slowly than the private sector because relatively more of public production is service production.[10] But this is not the problem we are concerned with here since even if this were true, it would not necessarily reflect lower productivity in the public sector than might realistically have been expected. Our question is instead whether productivity is lower in public than in private production when we look at the same kind of production. If all we know is that more resources are used in public than in private production because different things are produced, we know nothing about productivity. It is only if more resources are used to produce the same thing that we can speak of lower productivity.

Common sense economics suggests several reasons why public agencies might be less productive than private companies. Since they are not privately owned and are often monopoly suppliers, there is no owner with a private interest in keeping costs low and no competition to give managers and workers incentives to keep efforts high. Decisions are made via negotiations and budgetary processes and with no market against which the allocation of resources can be tested. These are decision-making procedures which may encourage over-investment, over-hiring, and wages

---

[10] See e.g. Beck (1981).

which exceed the productive contribution of workers, and which may make the agencies slow in adapting to new demands. Of course, what sounds like common sense is not always necessarily correct—budgetary processes can, for example, be a powerful tool for controlling costs if politicians have the will and ability to restrict funds[11]—but there are nonetheless reasons at least to suspect that the way decisions are made in public agencies does not always encourage careful economizing.

There is now fairly solid empirical evidence from a number of countries that productivity, as measured by unit cost (only the quantity of output is measured), is often lower in public service production than in comparable production in the private sector. A survey of fifty recent studies from five industrial nations, covering nineteen areas of production (generally outside of the welfare state but including hospital services and housing), finds that only eight studies do not show this to be the case.[12] An exceptionally well-studied area is that of renovation. Several studies have compared purely public systems (public responsibility and production), mixed systems (public responsibility and private production under contract), and purely private systems (private responsibility and production). These studies have found the mixed system to be the most productive.[13] A study of fire fighting in Denmark, which is partly municipal and partly contracted out to a private company, has found that the private company provides comparable services at a lower cost.[14] A Swedish study of productivity in central government administration outside of the welfare state (covering about 30 per cent of total central government administration) finds an average annual decline in productivity, between 1970 and 1980, of 2 per cent.[15] Changes in both quantity and quality of output are incorporated, though quality changes necessarily on a tentative basis. During the same period, productivity in private sector service production increased.

More directly in the social policy field, a series of Swedish studies

---

[11] It has been suggested, for example, that the relatively low cost of health care in Britain compared to many other European countries and the US is best explained by restrictive budgeting in the National Health Service which has simply forced it to make do as best it could with relatively low funds. See Abel-Smith (1983).

[12] Borcherding, Pommerehne & Schneider (1982).

[13] Otter (1983).

[14] Kristensen (1982).

[15] Statskontoret (1985).

have confirmed that productivity tends to be low here too. These studies are part of a careful examination of productivity in the public sector conducted by the Ministry of Finance's 'Expert Group for Studies in Public Economics'. One study covers (mainly municipal) social services for children, elderly, handicapped, and other selected client groups. While the cost of these services grew from 3 to 4.7 per cent of GNP between 1970 and 1980, productivity is estimated to have declined by an average annual rate of between 1.6 and 4 per cent.[16] Here, only the volume of output is estimated. Changes in quality are discussed but not quantified, and are generally assumed not to have been such that they could significantly alter the estimated results. Studies of public health care, in the same series, find that between 1970 and 1979 the input of resources grew by 40 per cent but the volume of production by only 2 per cent.[17] Between 1960 and 1980, costs increased 1.8 times faster than GNP and productivity declined by an average annual rate of 3 per cent.[18] Again, changes in quality are not incorporated but it is pointed out that if quality improvements should account for the total growth of cost relative to the volume of output, the quality of services would in 1980 have to be understood as being twice as good as in 1970. It is indicated that a realistic incorporation of quality improvements might bring the decline in productivity down to an annual rate of between 1.5 and 2 per cent. Finally, a study of public and private dental care finds both that private dentists provide more services per patient and that the total cost per patient is lower.[19]

A Norwegian study of primary medical care in Oslo has come to similar conclusions as the Swedish study on dental care.[20] A British study of nursing homes finds that '. . . private residential homes in England and Wales are less costly and might represent better value for money than their non-profit counterparts in the public and voluntary sectors'.[21]

There is obviously a great deal of uncertainty in the available material. Productivity in the social services has started to be studied empirically but this cannot as yet be described as a thoroughly

---

[16] ESO (1985a).
[17] Ståhl (1983:150–1).
[18] ESO (1985b).
[19] Jönsson (1984).
[20] Buxrud, Forsén & Otterstad (1985).
[21] Judge & Knapp (1985:139).

examined area. Many of the studies which compare public and private production do not cover social services. Not all studies have come to the same conclusion. There are methodological problems which are usually not handled very well; in particular, it is difficult to find public and private productions which are truly parallel and it is difficult to take into consideration the quality of output.[22] Public agencies may produce some services that private companies are not able or willing to provide or have a different composition of clients than private companies do of customers. But many studies try to control for or incorporate such factors, or at least discuss the sensitivity of their estimated results, and it appears that, although the exact numerical results can often be debated, the general conclusion is robust enough. Productivity in the public production of social services has tended to fall during the period of welfare state expansion of the 1960s and 1970s. The Swedish material demonstrates this rather alarmingly.[23] When comparing public and private production of the same kinds of services, there is a fairly strong tendency in empirical studies to find that public production comes out as being less productive. The British, Norwegian, and Swedish comparisons show this to be the case. More remains to be said about productivity in the social services but we do have enough evidence to conclude that a problem of low productivity has been identified.

For our discussion of the welfare state this means that the population gets less output for the resources that are invested in the production of social services than has been demonstrated to be economically possible. We are, in other words, paying a price not only for the services that are produced but also for the way their production is organized. In the total analysis we may find that the price is worth paying, for example if the present form of production results in a better distribution, but that is a different matter. On the

---

[22] Millward, in a paper published in 1982, on methodological grounds does not accept the conclusion that the relative inefficiency of public provision is well sustained, but more material has since then become available, including the social service studies referred to here.

[23] To illustrate the magnitude of the problem, the Expert Group for Studies in Public Finance has incorporated public sector productivity development into national accounts growth estimates (which are otherwise based on the assumption of constant productivity in the public sector). Assuming an annual average productivity decline of 1.5% in the 70% of all public service production investigated, the result is to reduce average annual growth rates during the 1970s from 2% to 1.5% and GDP in 1980 relative to 1970 from 1.21 to 1.17. See ESO (1986).

limited question of productivity, the conclusion must be that the bucket is indeed leaky. How much it leaks is hard to say, but it does leak.

Explanations

The meaning of inefficiency in relation to productivity is that, of the resources that are put into a production, more than economically necessary are 'consumed' inside the apparatus and less than economically possible come out again in the form of a product someone else—clients or customers—can consume. We have enough evidence to say that a good deal of public service production, including social services, is in this sense inefficient. It is, however, more difficult to explain why this is so. The available studies give some clues but no firm answers.

One explanation can be excluded, namely that public production is necessarily inefficient because it is public. The Swedish studies, for example, find that, although productivity has fallen in most of the agencies or activities investigated, there are very considerable differences between public agencies in this respect and in some cases productivity has been found to rise. Also, they find that although productivity has fallen in the years from 1960 to 1980, it has tended to fall less towards the end of the period, and in some cases to have turned from falling to rising.

This suggests another explanation, one of internal organizational problems, which are frequent but not necessary in public production and which were acute in the early phase of rapid public sector growth, but are gradually being managed. This explanation is supported by the Swedish dental care study and the Norwegian medical care study, which both indicate that small-scale private businesses in these areas tend to be characterized by hard work and an economical use of personnel and equipment. The British nursing homes study finds that the distinctions between public and private and between profit and non-profit do not contribute significantly to explaining differences in cost and efficiency and point instead to the predominantly small-scale organization of private residential homes and, in particular, to the very considerable workload which many owners/managers accept and their strong feeling of responsibility for their clients and identification with the success of their enterprise.[24]

A third explanation which has been suggested is that the 'over-consumption' of resources in public production is not a result of inefficiency at all, but of a power struggle in which those who work in public agencies are able to bring about an implicit redistribution in their own favour by securing for themselves wages and working conditions which drive up the price of their products.[25] Although possibly part of the story, this public choice explanation does not add much to the previous explanation of internal organizational inefficiency, including uneconomical use of personnel, except a more provocative formulation. If those who work in public agencies enjoy their inefficiency, as they may well do if it takes the form of 'leisure at work', there is of course an implicit redistribution in their favour, but this does not prove the conspiratorial theory or exclude the possibility of simple inefficiency.

External Efficiency

In neo-classical economic theory, perfect markets by definition co-ordinate economic activity so that resources are used optimally, by which is understood that they are used in a way that corresponds to the preferences of the economic actors. Since real markets are never perfect, there are always inefficiencies in real economies. Inefficiencies result in a difference between the actual outcome of the economic game and the optimal outcome. This difference is commonly described as a welfare loss. It occurs because there are imperfections in real markets which prevent economic actors from making the choices they would ideally have preferred. They may, for example, not have a sufficiently wide range of choice or there may be incentives which encourage them to act differently from how they would otherwise have acted.

In everyday parlance, we usually think of inefficiency as having to

[24] This conclusion is supported by other studies in Britain (Knapp, 1984) and by studies in the US (Gilbert, 1984).

[25] By e.g. Borcherding, Pommerehne & Schneider (1982). These authors 'prove' that public sector inefficiency is impossible by arguing that economic theory predicts wasteful institutions not to survive. Since the public sector has in fact thrived, what we see as inefficiency 'must' therefore be 'a misinterpretation' of some perverse form of efficiency (p. 143).

do with something going lost; we have less income than we might have had because we are inefficient in the way we do things that determine our income. But this is not the general meaning of the concept of inefficiency, as used in economic theory. Here, firstly, *any* use of resources that results in a different outcome from the optimal one is inefficient. There may be inefficiencies which, paradoxically, cause us to have 'too much' income, as in the case when part time work is not available so everyone is forced to work full time (assuming no one can afford to go without work). And, secondly, *only* uses of resources that result in non-optimal outcomes are inefficient. There is no inefficiency involved if we choose to give up some income because we would rather have more leisure.

The concept of efficiency is, in the following, used in its most common economic meaning, that is, in relation to aggregate income and without regard to its distribution.[26] By 'income' I here understand monetary income. 'Potential income' is the theoretically maximum possible income, defined for example as the sum of actual income and the value of leisure. 'Optimal income' is the same as the preferred income: for example the income that would have been generated in a perfect market. I shall ignore the not so interesting possibility of too much income and say that there is inefficiency in the economic system if we are collectively forced, because of market imperfections, to give up income that we would have preferred

[26] The concept of efficiency is sensitive. It has to do with the use of resources and is a normative concept. One use of resources is more efficient than another because it promotes some goal. If our goal is economic growth, then whatever resource allocation promotes growth is efficient; if our goal is equality, whatever promotes equality is efficient. In economic literature the concept is often used in relation to the 'pareto principle', which can be taken to mean, according to Culyer (1980), that any reallocation of resources is efficient if someone approves of it and no one objects, but is usually interpreted as meaning that a reallocation of resources is efficient if it causes (more) growth and does not leave anyone worse off than they would otherwise have been. This criterion does not work if we believe that some goals of economic life should be pursued even if there is not complete agreement about them, for example if they are formulated through a political process where, in the end, the majority has its will. If it is decided that more equality is desirable, then 'pareto optimality' is irrelevant because there is no way of going from inequality to equality without anyone objecting or someone becoming worse off, if only in relative terms. According to Okun (1975:2), the economist's concept of efficiency 'implies that more is better, insofar as the "more" consists of items that people want to buy'. In the literature on social policy and economic efficiency, the concept is often used without careful definition but in relation to growth, so that efficiency is what promotes growth, and inefficiency what prevents such growth as might reasonably have been possible.

to have (consideration given to the sacrifices which would have been necessary in order to earn this income), or, in other words, if actual income falls short of optimal income. I underline the distinction between potential income and optimal income. The difference between actual and potential income is a cost; we have less income than we could have had. But only the difference between actual and optimal income is a welfare loss: we have less income than we would ideally have chosen to have. This corresponds to the distinction between anticipated costs and unanticipated side-effects which was made in Chapter 1. Observe also the role of market imperfections. Only welfare loss which is caused by market imperfections is a sign of economic inefficiency. If we have less than optimal income for some other reason than market imperfections, we are the victims of inefficiencies in some other system than the economic one, for example imperfections in the system of political decision making. We shall return to the distinctions between cost and welfare loss and between economic and non-economic inefficiencies later on and see that they are of the utmost importance for understanding the issue of redistribution and economic inefficiency.

Mechanisms

There are, theoretically, three main sources of market imperfection. The first lies in the behaviour of businesses. Instead of competing freely, a single or a few businesses may be so dominant in an area that they do not have to compete, or several businesses may agree not to compete.[27] The second source has to do with the behaviour of workers. Instead of acting independently on the labour market and competing for jobs, workers may merge their power through collective action and thereby more or less eliminate

---

[27] The elimination of monopolization is the one area of legitimate political intervention in economic life according to classical theory. Adam Smith recognized that it is always tempting for businesses to try to obtain monopoly and that there is, therefore, a need for political regulations to protect the market. Very radical regulations have been advocated on the basis of classical theory, for example by Simons (1948), who in a paper entitled *A Positive Program for Laissez Faire*, published in 1934, interpreted the contemporary economic crisis as a result of monopolization and made a number of suggestions to restore competition, including restrictions on the accumulation of property and shares, on the establishment of corporations, and on the use of advertisement, regulation of private banking, nationalization of businesses in branches where competition would not work, and stronger redistribution of income and wealth through taxes.

the relationship between what the individual worker puts into production and what he gets out of it.[28] Finally, imperfections can be created by politics. Instead of leaving the co-ordination of economic activity to the sensitive, invisible hand of the market, government may decide to intervene with the heavy, visible hand of politics. It is the third of these possible mechanisms we are concerned with here.

Political interventions in markets are believed to give rise to inefficiencies, in proportion to their magnitude, or as a result of their form. In the first case, macro-economic performance is influenced by the size or growth of the public sector which is believed to crowd out private economic activity, for instance by 'confiscating' capital or labour. To this can be added the concern that (large scale) budget deficits may have a similar effect of their own, for instance by crowding private lenders out of capital markets, driving up interest rates, stimulating inflation, and the like. As to the form of political intervention, micro-economic behaviour is affected because the redistribution of income, compared to the distribution which would have resulted in a free market, distorts the structure of economic incentives compared to the optimal case.

The problem of macro-economic performance is related to the welfare state because it is the growth of the welfare state that explains the growth of the public sector, at least as measured by public spending. But it is, above all, through the relationship between income redistribution and micro-economic behaviour that economic efficiency is related to social policy. Income inequality is one of the factors which, in neo-classical theory, is assumed to make markets work. It has the function of helping individuals to be efficient economic actors. In a perfect market, each worker is rewarded with an income which corresponds to his (marginal) productivity. There will usually be considerable differences in productivity between workers depending on what kinds of job they have and their personal abilities, and consequently, in a market economy, considerable inequalities of income. These inequalities

---

[28] A recent development of this part of classical economic theory is *The Rise and Decline of Nations* by Mancur Olson, in which he argues that collective action on the part of labour (and other economic actors) tends to cause 'institutional sclerosis' in the economic system and that this is a general cause of economic decline in systems which were previously dynamic, as witnessed, for example, by the present fate of several of the industrial democracies. For a critique, see e.g. Korpi (1985).

inform workers about where it is most profitable for them to work by showing them which jobs are better paid, and encourage them to be economically active and industrious by demonstrating that it is possible for them to obtain higher wages.[29] In this economy it is in the private interest of workers to make an extra effort in the job they have or to try to shift to another job. Since income inequalities correspond to underlying differences in productivity, workers will, by pursuing their private interests, contribute to a more efficient use of their labour power and in that way to increased aggregate income.

When politicians intervene in this system with redistributive policies, they more or less set these mechanisms out of play. Assuming policies are effective so that inequality is reduced, workers will no longer have the same information about where it is best for the economy that they invest their labour power, or the same incentive to move into more productive jobs or to make an effort in their work. And even if the policies are not effective in changing the distribution of income, they may make it more arbitrary in relation to the underlying pattern of productivity, in which case workers would still have an incentive to work hard in their private interest, but no longer thereby contribute as well to the common good. Or, at least, so the theory will have it.

Macro-economic performance

Although the relationship between economic efficiency and the size of the public sector is not irrelevant in our context, it is not possible here to discuss the problem in depth. This would lead into a full fledged macro-economic analysis of the modern economy and that is beyond the scope of the present book (and the competence of its author). Nevertheless, a few comments are appropriate.

It seems reasonable to believe that, as political intervention in the economy becomes more far-reaching and the public sector grows, this will sooner or later come to a point of doing more harm than good for economic performance. Economic actors may use up their energy coping with the politics of economic life, regulations may become more stifling than creative of order, the administration of a

---

[29] The same line of reasoning applies to the distribution of profits and the behaviour of investors.

circulatory system of transfers may grow to be a heavy burden, taxes become unbearable, and so on. The experiences of centralized economies in Eastern Europe, and the present efforts there in the interest of efficiency to release economic life from full political control, suggest that there is a limit to how much politics the economy can take. This is not to say that all political regulation of economic life must be paid for with a loss of efficiency—there is abundant experience to the contrary—but only that, at some point, new problems created will probably start to outbalance old ones solved.

Many economists now see signs that the limit has been reached or passed, at least in those nations which have the largest public sector.[30] It is true that such warnings have been heard all through this century, and before, but although the post-war combination of public sector expansion and economic growth has proved previous Cassandras wrong, our contemporary ones may be right. It has, however, been difficult to establish empirically what effect, if any, public sector size may have on economic performance, given the large number of other potentially relevant factors. Attempts have been made to get some grasp of the problem through systematic comparisons between nations which differ from one another both in public sector size and growth and in economic performance. The logic of the comparative method is simple enough: if there is a general relationship between these political and economic factors, one should expect to find some trace of this in a difference in economic performance between nations, depending on the size or growth of their public sectors. Although finding the expected correlations could hardly be taken as proof that a large or rapidly growing public sector has caused low economic performance, an absence of any correlation might reasonably be interpreted as an indication that these factors are independent of each other.

Statistical comparisons between OECD nations for the period from about 1960 to 1980 have generally not found macro-economy performance to be correlated with the size or growth of the public sector and have, hence, been taken as evidence that even with the contemporary size of the public sector in the most 'advanced' welfare state nations and its rapid growth during the 1960s and

---

[30] See e.g. Geiger & Geiger (1979); Lindbeck (1981b).

1970s, the limit has not yet been reached.[31] But these studies have not proved sufficiently conclusive to form a basis for a consensus on this matter. They do show that there is no direct correlation between the factors studied and, thereby, refute models which assume a universal effect on economic performance of public sector size or growth, irrespective of other circumstances in each individual nation. Such models are frequently implicit in political debate on economic policy. But they do not refute more complex models where public sector size or growth is assumed to affect economic performance in interaction with other factors. For this, it has until now not been possible in comparative studies to incorporate enough relevant variables or to specify sufficiently complex interactions between variables.

What we know, therefore, is that a large and/or rapidly growing public sector does not necessarily have a negative (or for that matter positive) effect on macro-economic performance, but we do not know that it may not have some effect under certain circumstances or that individual nations could not have had better economic performance had their public sector been smaller or grown less rapidly. The question of public sector size/growth and economic performance remains open. Instead of trusting the black box approach of simply correlating economic performance output indicators and government action input indicators, we must look into the black box and observe directly what processes government action releases in the economic system. We must turn out attention from the size of government to its structure, from *how much* government does *to what* it does.

Micro-economic behaviour

Our question here is whether the use of tax and transfer policies for redistributive purposes creates economic distortions which have the

---

[31] See Smith (1975); Gould (1983); Katz, Mahler & Franz (1983); Cameron (1984, 1985); Korpi (1985); Saunders (1985). Friedland & Sanders (1985) find that increasing cash transfers to households over a period are positively correlated with high rates of economic growth in a later period while increasing transfers in kind and tax levels are negatively correlated with economic growth. For a methodological discussion and interpretation, see Saunders (1986).

ultimate effect of us ending up with less income than we would have
had in the optimal case. The distortions in question are what
economists usually call 'disincentives', a concept which has been
defined as wedges between the societal and the private return to
economic effort.[32] The underlying assumption is that if the private
return is different from the societal return, the economic actor will
be encouraged to sub-optimal choices, for example to make less of
an effort than he would have made if the private return were
identical to the societal return—he may, for example, choose more
leisure and less work—or to turn his efforts to non-productive
activities, such as investing in art instead of in production. To the
extent that redistribution does create disincentives, what we gain
in equality today must be paid for by less than optimal income
tomorrow.

As usual, there are different hunches among experts about the
facts of economic life. Some believe that people tend go about their
business as usual, irrespective of the burden of government. Hence,
the late Erik Brofoss, while Minister of Finance in Norway,
learned—with some delight, one would think—that ' . . . it is
quite astonishing how much people can bear of taxes once they
get used to them'.[33] That was forty years ago, but Lester Thurow
has recently said much the same when describing the efficiency
argument against further movements toward equality as a 'smoke
screen that cannot be backed up with hard economic data'.[34]
Others believe that the discouragements arising from social policies
are so strong and that individuals are so sensitive to them that
economic progress itself is at stake. For example, Arthur Burns,
the American economist and ambassador, thinks that Europe
is slipping behind the United States in economic vitality and,
in his own diplomatic way, puts the blame on the welfare
state: 'Europe is strangulating itself through its overblown welfare
programs.'[35]

The reason experts disagree so much about this is that the problem is too complex to be resolved by theoretical reasoning alone.
We are faced not with one simple question but with three difficult
ones. First, what effects do redistributional policies have on the

[32] Lindbeck (1981b:28).
[33] *Morgenbladet*, 25 Nov. 1947.
[34] Thurow (1981:140).
[35] *Challenge*, Jan.-Feb., 1985, p. 23.

economic structure, including the structure of incentives? Second, how do individuals react and adapt their behaviour to changes in the economic structure? And third, how do these individual behavioural responses add up to an aggregate impact on total income?

It is clear enough that social policies have some impact on the economic structure. Taxes and transfers are a part of the environment that people take into consideration when they make decisions about work, consumption, saving, investment, and so on. This we all know from personal experience. It is also clear that some of these effects have the form of disincentives. If I do a piece of work that I sell for 100 kroner but can keep only 30 kroner because my marginal tax rate is 70 per cent, there is clearly a wedge between my private return and the societal return on this work effort. But it is not clear what the total effect of transfers and taxes are on the economic environment. In particular, discussions of disincentives focus only on the supply of factors of production, such as labour and capital, and disregard the demand side. Since social policies may have economic effects which are relevant for demand as well as supply—cash transfers influence consumer demand, health care and education services create a direct demand for labour to produce the services—we should, in a discussion of the economics of social policy, ideally take into consideration all structural effects and not only those that are relevant for supply. And on the supply side we should consider not only behaviour but also resources, which may be influenced positively by the human capital investments which are a part of many social policies.

It must be assumed that individuals adapt their behaviour to changes in their economic environment; rational people do, and even not-so-rational people when faced with so strong a motivational force as pecuniary loss or gain. But we cannot know in advance how they will react. There is first the question of the strength of the behavioural response. Even if purely economic considerations might suggest strong responses, it must be remembered that people in real life make their choices in a social context. Their range of choice is limited, they have obligations to family or otherwise, they have made investments in their present form of economic activity, and they may enjoy what they are doing, for example their work, for its own sake and not see it only, or primarily, as a sacrifice.[36] Then there is the possibility that they may merely redirect their economic activity in ways that are of no consequence for the problem of efficiency. This could be the case if, as is often suggested, taxes make people move their economic activity out of the open economy and into the shadow sector or if they substitute do-it-yourself production or barter for market activity. It has been suggested that such responses should be seen as part of the disincentive problem,[37] but that is a result of a mis-specification of the issue whereby, so to speak, everything we happen to dislike is regarded as an economic evil. These responses may be problematic for ethical or distributional reasons, or because the tax base is eroded, or otherwise, but although that might be serious enough in its own right, it is irrelevant for the problem we are concerned with here. Hidden economic activity is still economic activity that creates income and is a problem here only if it is less productive than open economic activity. Finally, even if disincentives make people not only redirect their economic activity but change the magnitude of, for example, the labour force they are willing to supply or the quality of the work they do, there is the possibility that different people react differently to the same disincentives. What discourages some, may encourage others; there are, in the technical jargon, simultaneous substitution effects (unproductive activity is substituted for productive activity, e.g. leisure for work) and income effects (productive activity is stimulated, presumably resulting in additional income).[38]

[36] In a survey undertaken at the Institute for Social Research at the University of Michigan (Juster & Stafford, 1984), an attempt has been made to measure the value people attach to various activities (such as work and leisure), leaving aside the value they attach to the result of the activity (such as the pay they get from working). The survey finds that the gainfully employed consistently attach a higher intrinsic value to their work than to most leisure activities, that this is true for most occupational categories, that very few report attaching low value to their work, and that income has virtually no power in explaining high or low intrinsic work value. Jencks, Perman & Rainwater (1985) find that earnings are the most important single determinant of 'job desirability', but that non-monetary job characteristics together are more important than earnings. Of course, the attachment of intrinsic value to work does not prevent it from being seen as a sacrifice on the margin (such as on Friday afternoon).

[37] By Lindbeck (1981b).

[38] The term *dis*incentives is, strictly speaking, an ideological term which is not appropriate in a positive theory. There are no such things as pure disincentives, i.e. factors which only discourage economic activity. Most changes in the economic environment can, at the same time, have opposite influences on economic behaviour. A neutral terminology could refer to all such factors as incentives.

Finally, there is the question of how individual responses add up to an effect on aggregate income. If income and substitution effects cancel each other out, there will be no aggregate effect no matter how strong the individual effects are.[39] But even if substitution effects outbalance income effects so that, for example, less labour is supplied, there will not necessarily be any effect on aggregate income. This could be the result if the labour that is not supplied is marginal or unproductive, so that it would cost as much or more to employ it as it would produce, or if there is unemployment so that the labour that might have been supplied could still not have been put to productive use.

We have here a logical system of *causes* (disincentives arising from redistributive policies), *effects* (income going lost), and a *mechanism* connecting cause and effect (behavioural response). This system is so complex that it is impossible to say a priori how it works itself out in real life situations. If, for example, a new tax is introduced, will people want to work more in order to preserve the same disposable income as previously (the income effect) or less because they receive less reward for their effort (the substitution effect)—or rather:.how will these conflicting instincts work on different people (given, that is, that they are aware that their tax burden has increased, something that is not altogether obvious with the intricacy of modern tax systems)? If the tax is used to finance a new transfer or service, how will people react to the combination of

---

[39] Some economists suggest that only substitution effects should be considered in a discussion of disincentive problems and that income effects are not relevant, e.g. Lindbeck (1981b:31), because 'there is no inefficiency, or "distortion", involved in the fact that some people react to changes in (lump-sum) income by adjusting not only consumption and saving but also leisure and other non-market uses of time'. According to this view there will always be inefficiencies when there are substitution effects, even if income effects are stronger. This is entirely a matter of definition, and in my view the suggested terminology is not good. While the exclusion of income effects may make the one-sided concept of disincentives meaningful, this is to confuse the underlying issue. If a new tax encourages some people to work more and others to work less and these two factors balance each other out there is no welfare loss because there is as much aggregate income after the tax is introduced as there was before. It may be distributed differently, but that is another matter. Of course, if the tax revenue could be collected with no substitution effect, all the better, but if it cannot be collected without both income and substitution effects, the possible disincentive problem arising from the new tax must be seen as a function of both effects. To know the effect of a policy, we must include all effects. To exclude systematically half of the effects a priori is to assure, by way of definition, a certain outcome of any theoretical treatment or empirical investigation of a problem.

new benefits and new burdens? Is the economy flexible enough to make it possible for them to adjust according to their preferences? If so, will the intensity or quality of their work be affected in addition to how much they work? How long do such adjustments take; do they happen immediately or over some months or years? Since questions such as these cannot be resolved theoretically, attempts have been made to answer them empirically.

Empirical results

The social sciences do not have sufficiently sophisticated tools and models to measure the net outcome of all these processes. Empirical research on disincentive effects related to the welfare state has, therefore, settled for partial analyses, and in particular concentrated on the problem of identifying behavioural responses to changes in transfers and taxes. There are good reasons for this priority. It is obvious that the welfare state creates disincentives in the economic structure and it is, therefore, reasonable to suspect that it may also cause income to be lost. But for this to occur, economic actors have to react to the disincentives in a special way; they have to supply less input to production than they otherwise would. Although this will not in all circumstances result in less aggregate income than we would otherwise have had—that depends on how the input that is not supplied could have been used—it is a necessary condition for income to go lost. If we know how people respond to disincentives we will know if income *could* have gone lost, and if we find input which would otherwise have been available to be withheld—that is, if substitution effects outbalance income effects—we will have a pretty good clue that income has gone lost.

The problem which has been confronted in empirical research on disincentives is the effect of such changes in transfers and taxes as are associated with welfare state expansion, on labour supply and household savings. Results of available research are summarized in Appendix C.

The issue of household savings appears not to be very important in relation to the present problem. Little or no effect has been found. Changes in taxes probably do not have much impact. Changes in social security may influence people to save more while they are young in order to be able to retire early with some but not sufficient social security contributions, or to save less because their income in old age is secured. There is some indication that the latter effect may, all in all, be stronger than the former, but this is far from being established. Furthermore, it is a long step from household savings to the supply of capital for investment; even if households save less it does not follow that less capital is available.

The situation is different in the case of labour supply. This is a factor of production which individuals control directly; if people decide to take more leisure, less labour will immediately be supplied. There is ample evidence that labour supply is sensitive to changes in transfers and taxes. In fact, a first main result of recent research is that labour supply has proved to be more elastic to changes in the net wage rate than was previously assumed.

Three types of policy change are relevant: increases in the level of taxation, increased progressivity in the distribution of a given tax burden, and increases in transfers. On theoretical grounds, one should expect different individual responses to these policy changes. If the level of taxation goes up, we should expect both income effects of increases in the average tax rate (more work in order to compensate for the reduction of disposable income, an expected response by individuals who have no more income than they 'need') and substitution effects of increases in the marginal tax rate (less work since the opportunity cost of leisure goes down, an expected response by individuals who have more income than they 'need').[40] If the distribution of a given tax burden is made more progressive (the marginal tax rate goes up while the average tax rate remains the same), we should expect no income effect (there is no reduction in disposable income to be compensated) but only a substitution effect (since the opportunity cost of leisure goes down on the margin). If transfers are increased, we should again expect no income effect (there is no reduction in disposable income) but a substitution effect (we get 'free' income and can afford more leisure). Exceptions can be mentioned—for example, increased social security benefits may have the income effect of encouraging more people to enter the labour market in order to obtain social security

---

[40] A policy of increasing the average tax rate without affecting the marginal tax rate might be expected to have only income effects, but since a higher average tax rate will generally result also in a higher marginal rate, this is of little practical concern.

entitlements—but this is the general pattern of theoretical expectations.

These are the individual responses. As to how this adds up to an aggregate influence on total labour supply, the following can be hypothesized. There will be no effect of increasing the tax level since income and substitution effects pull in opposite directions and more or less balance each other out. For both increased progressivity and increased transfers there will be a reduction of labour supply since here there are only substitution effects. These expectations are not affected by introducing several policy changes at the same time. If both level and progressivity of taxation are increased, we should still expect a reduction in labour supply since the income effect of the rising average tax rate cannot be expected to balance out the substitution effects of both types of policy change. Similarly, if increased transfers are financed by increased taxes, the opposite effects of increased taxes balance each other out and the substitution effect of transfers remains. These hypotheses are based on the assumption that all income and substitution effects are of about the same magnitude. This may not be realistic but nothing can be said about that on theoretical grounds. Again, additional modifications may be added, but this is the general pattern.

A second main result of empirical labour supply research is to confirm these expectations. Systematic effects on total labour supply of changes in the level of taxation have not been established, but the expected results of changes in both progressivity of taxation and transfers have been confirmed as to the direction of the effect. Appendix C contains some examples of attempts to quantify the effects. These are highly tentative and should be treated with the utmost caution, but they do suggest that the labour supply effects may be considerable. The relative strength of the various income and substitution effects is unresolved. So is the interaction, if any, between the level of transfers and taxes and the effect of policy changes. We do not know, for example, either theoretically or empirically, if the kinds of effects that are established tend to be stronger in high tax/transfers systems than in systems with a lower level of transfers and taxes.

One might say that as empirical results go, this is pretty meagre, and that a very considerable research effort has done no more than establish what was already obvious. Be that as it may; obvious or not, we now know that labour supply is sensitive to some policy changes which are associated with welfare state expansion and that a reduction of labour supply must be expected to follow from some of these changes. What remains is to interpret this fact.

Interpretation

Does the expected reduction of labour supply indicate a problem of economic inefficiency arising from the redistributive policies of the welfare state? The answer to this question depends to some degree on how the labour that would have been supplied if it were not for the influence of the welfare state, could have been used. Had it resulted only in higher unemployment, and consequently no additional income, there would be no economic loss following the reduction in labour supply and hence no inefficiency. But this would depend on special circumstances. More generally, it must be seen as a problem in an economy if policies encourage available factors of production, such as labour, not to be supplied for use, and we must assume that there is a loss of income (other things being equal) associated with this. More important for the interpretation is the distinction between cost and welfare loss and between economic and non-economic inefficiencies.

What we know is that progressive taxation and income transfers are not free. These policies not only redistribute a given aggregate income but must, in addition, be expected to have some impact on how much income there will be in the next round. Implicit in 'progressive' changes of these policies is a response in the population whereby some income is given up because leisure is substituted for work. Hence, there is a trade-off between redistribution and aggregate income. However, trade-offs are not the same as inefficiencies and the loss of income is not the same as a welfare loss. If we choose leisure instead of work, because we would rather have more free time than more income, we are only adjusting our economic activity to our preferences and possibilities and are in no way the unwitting patsies to market imperfections.

The theory of inefficiency we are concerned with here has *two* elements: it predicts a certain *outcome* (a loss of optimal income) produced by a certain *mechanism* (economic distortions arising from redistribution). In order to confirm the theory we must both identify the predicted outcome and demonstrate that it is caused by economic distortions and not by some other mechanism. It is not enough to show that some potential income is lost; we must show that optimal income is lost and that it is lost because redistributive policies have trapped us into a situation where we are compelled to choose more leisure and less work than we would ideally have preferred. We must show not only that the adjustment between income and leisure after redistribution is different from the adjustment before redistribution, but also that the new adjustment represents a welfare loss caused by economic distortions. When seen in this perspective, the effects of progressive taxes and of income transfers will be interpreted very differently. Both policies have a cost, but the nature of this cost is totally different.

In almost all transfers, a reduction of labour supply of recipient groups is implicit and *intended*; it is a part of the policy. These policies reflect a collective choice in favour of more leisure. The purpose of social security is to make it possible for the elderly to retire without economic hardship. The purpose of early retirement schemes is to make it possible for workers who are burnt out to retire or to secure income for workers who would anyway be forced out of work. Part of the purpose of unemployment compensation is to give the unemployed time to search carefully for a new job. The purpose of sick-pay is that workers can stay home from work when they are sick. The purpose of maternity leave is to make it possible for working mothers (and, increasingly, fathers, through paternity leave) to avoid economic loss during the time around birth and to stay at home when children are ill.

Major transfers, by redistributing income to the non-working population, are simply a way of organizing a part of our potential income to be taken out in the form of leisure. An expansion of transfers is a choice to take out relatively more of potential income as leisure. Of course, choosing leisure still has a cost: we will have less income than we could have had. But as long as the combination of income and leisure reflects our preferences, we have the optimal income and there is no welfare loss. This is true however much leisure we choose and however much potential income we give up. There is no more welfare loss in a choice of giving up income for leisure in the labour market than in giving up cash for bread in the supermarket.

The collective choice of leisure and income that is implicit in a certain transfer policy may or may not correspond to the preferences of the population. It is perfectly reasonable to expect that with economic growth and more affluence, people will want to take out relatively more potential income in the form of leisure. The expansion of transfer policies can be seen as a 'natural' manifestation of this preference,[41] and the cost, in the form of potential income forgone, as an expression of the value we set on leisure.

On the other hand, there may be imperfections in the political system which cause the collective choice to deviate from what the population had really wanted. We may not be aware of the costs of the policy choices we make, politicians may make decisions on their own without a mandate from the population, or the political system may fail to clear means and ends. These are the kinds of problems I have discussed in the two previous chapters. The result of all transfer decisions could be that we end up with more leisure and less income than we would ideally have preferred. But, if so, this would be a direct result of problems in the *political* system of decision making and not an indirect side-effect arising from political interventions in the *economic* system. It would be a case of a welfare loss caused by another mechanism than that of economic distortion.

If transfer policies are legitimate and the decision making behind them under control, there can be no economic inefficiency as a result of these policies. If these conditions are met, the population has the combination of income and leisure that it wants. The policies might still be costly, as measured in potential income forgone, but there would be no welfare loss in this cost. The discussion of economic inefficiency does not add anything to our understanding of the rationality of transfer policies beyond what we have learned in previous chapters. The issues of legitimacy and political control have already been dealt with. The inclusion of problems caused directly by political imperfections in this discussion of economic inefficiency would be to identify the same problem under two different labels and to count it twice.

It has been estimated that all transfer policies in the United States have resulted in a reduction of labour supply by 4.8 per cent compared to a system without transfers and that the expansion of

---

[41] In fact, actual labour supply, as measured by hours of work or labour force participation, has in most industrial nations remained stable or risen during the 1960s and 1970s. This is caused mainly by a strong rise in female labour supply, which has compensated, or more than compensated, a decline in male labour supply, in particular that of elderly men. But this does not exclude the possibility that labour supply could have been even higher had it not been for the possibly adverse effects of certain redistributive policies.

transfer policies during the 1970s in Holland and the United States
may have resulted in an annual reduction of labour supply of 1 per
cent or more.[42] These figures may well be correct and thereby
confirm that transfer policies are not free and may be quite costly.
But they express only a difference between actual and potential
labour supply and are, hence, no estimate of a welfare loss. A good
part of this difference, possibly all of it, must be assumed to arise
because of a preference for more leisure (and when seen in this
perspective the figures are perhaps not at all high).

With progressive taxation, all this is different. Here, both outcome and mechanism are demonstrated so that there is clearly a
problem of inefficiency caused by distortions in the economic system. A reduction of labour supply is neither an intended nor an
anticipated consequence of redistributing income with the use of
progressive taxes. While a good transfer system should make it
possible for people to substitute leisure for work and thereby
implies a reduction of labour supply, a good tax system should have
no such consequences. A labour supply response to changes in the
structure of taxation is a side-effect which arises only because of
economic disincentives. The income forgone as a result of progressive taxes is not a part of the policy choice but a result that is
imposed upon us afterwards, as a consequence of decisions taken
for other reasons. Not much can be said for certain about the
strength of the labour supply response to progressive taxes, except
that it may be considerable, but all the income that is forgone as a
consequence of (changes in) the progressivity of taxation must be
counted as a welfare loss in the economic understanding.

A final methodological note is in place here. This interpretation
of inefficiency rests on the distinction between the concepts of cost
and welfare loss. This distinction is consistent with the usual understanding of inefficiency in economic theory. It is also a distinction
which comes naturally to the analysis of public policy within the
framework of rational choice and the subsequent political process
approach, as explained in Chapter 1. The distinction is, however,
not always made in discussions of the economics of redistribution,
the result being that any cost is taken as a political problem. I see the
failure to make the distinction as a result of applying the more

---

[42] By Danziger, Haveman & Plotnick (1981), and Wolfe *et al.* (1983),
respectively.

limited decision-making approach whereby the political problem is seen only as one of cost-effectiveness rather than of the correspondence between preferences and outcome. This limited perspective encourages the whole difference between potential and actual income to be interpreted as a welfare loss and, therefore, tends to exaggerate the inefficiency problem.

Welfare Loss?

The welfare state may be a Good Thing, but it may also be an Expensive Thing. Experience until now shows that we have had to pay for the welfare state by giving up some of the income we might otherwise have had. We do not know how much income we have had to give up. There may be sacrifices we are not aware of, as, for example, the possibility that the growth of the public sector has had a negative impact on economic performance. We are only starting to understand the nature of behavioural responses to welfare state policies. But we know enough to say that the welfare state has come with a price tag.

A part of the price we pay represents no problem within the framework of rational choice that is applied here. If we just give up some potential income because we would rather have more leisure, there is no welfare loss. This is the general nature of the trade-off between income and transfers. We have used transfers to be able to choose more leisure as we have become more affluent.

But there are also problematic price components; more income is given up than has been directly intended by transfer and tax policies, reflecting various forms of inefficiencies resulting from the expansion of the welfare state. There is the possibility of inefficiencies which arise because of imperfections in the system of political decision making. It might be, for example, that parties go too far in outbidding each other in their competition for voters, with the result that politicians become 'too generous' in their decisions on transfers so that we end up with more leisure and less income than we would have wanted. To judge from the two previous chapters such imperfections may well exist, but are hardly rampant. As for inefficiencies caused by economic distortions, we have identified some internal inefficiency in the form of low productivity in the social services and some external inefficiency in the form of disincentive effects from progressive taxation.

How high is the price? About this very little can be said for certain, but I venture to interpret the available evidence in the following way. Internal inefficiencies in the form of low productivity may be considerable. It is only recently that we have started to get empirical estimates on this factor. Some of these results are alarming and more is likely to be found the more one searches. This problem is likely to be *more serious* than has generally been known or assumed. External inefficiencies in the form of behavioural responses to economic distortions, on the other hand, are almost certainly *less serious* than has lately come to be widely feared. This anxiety rests on a great deal of confusion about the concept of disincentives whereby both intended and unintended behavioural responses to transfers and taxes, and relevant and irrelevant forms of response, are seen indiscriminately as signs of economic inefficiency. The only effect resulting from economic distortions that is identified is the response to changes in the progressivity of taxation. We do not know what the magnitude of this effect is, but this unintended effect (the welfare loss) must be smaller than the sum of both intended and unintended effects (the total cost).

Is the price necessary? In one sense, probably not. Both in the public production of social services and in progressive taxation we are paying a price not only for what we do—produce certain services and collect certain taxes—but also for how we do it. Less costly alternative techniques are available, at least in principle, for example more private or small-scale production of services and less progressivity of taxation. On the other hand, since there is a redistributive intention in these policies which is not discussed here, their present organization may be necessary for that purpose. If this were proved to be the case, we would want to go on and ask if the price is worth the redistribution we get in return for it. These are issues we shall return to in the chapters on poverty and redistribution and in the concluding chapter.

6

Activity

Professor Staffan Burenstam Linder, the Swedish economist and politician who won some notoriety when he, in a very funny book in the Beckerian spirit a few years ago, explained the short duration of courtship between men and women, in our modern and restless affluence, before they go to bed with each other by the high cost of time, has in a more recent but less funny book described the welfare state as 'heartless'.[1] He observes that in spite of welfare state policies our societies have not found harmony but are instead plagued by *malaise* and conflict; there is increasing crime and misuse of drugs and alcohol, there is violence and suicide, family instability and loneliness, anonymity and alienation, and vandalism and ruthlessness are part of our everyday experience. This *misère*, he says, shows not only that the power of the welfare state to solve problems has been exaggerated but that the welfare state can itself cause new problems. The concentration on public programmes and the neglect of private means for improving social standards has undermined human compassion and basic securities which do not depend on money. The excess of the welfare state stifles and pacifies people and influences them to become indifferent to themselves and dispassionate *vis-à-vis* each other. While economists have usually worried that the welfare state crowds efficiency out of economic life, the concern is here added that it may crowd compassion and activity out of private life.

Quality of Life

Burenstam Linder is not alone in seeing problems in 'the quality of contemporary private life',[2] nor in blaming the welfare state. Irving Kristol's observation that egalitarian societies are not creative was

---

[1] Burenstam Linder (1970, 1983).
[2] This elegant term is by Mary Jo Bane (1983:91).

noted in Chapter 2. For James Robertson, the welfare state is a link in a long chain of development, the thrust of which has been to 'drive human activity out of the informal sector . . . into the formal sector . . .'.[3] This happened with economic activities, through market forces, and later with social activity, because informal networks such as the family were weakened. According to David Gress, 'The innumerable laws, rules, and regulations governing work-economic activity, and interaction with the authorities, tend to create an attitude of dependency. More and more often the subject is not a citizen with rights and duties, but a client, a recipient of aid and services waiting to be told what to do rather than doing what he wants and not waiting for official permission'.[4] Assar Lindbeck explains that, because of high public expenditures and taxation, '. . . public authorities increasingly take care of intimate personal services, while households increasingly take care of things . . .'.[5] Nathan Glazer sees a decline in the role of voluntary agencies in the areas of social, health, and educational services because of their '. . . problems due to governmental assistance'.[6] And Bent Rold Andersen has noted that observers of the Scandinavian welfare state tend to '. . . maintain that egalitarianism has gone beyond economics to become uniformism, and that in both education and cultural and political life . . . superiority takes second place to mediocrity'.[7]

Conceivably, redistributive policies could in several ways come into conflict with more qualitative aspects of how we live. One possibility is a weakening of economic incentives which encourage activity and compassion. If, for example, retirement income is secured through public social security, there might be less reason to maintain within-family systems of income transfers between generations and some of the economic bonds which tie family members together could thereby be cut off. This is possibly desirable from certain points of view but could still have negative side-effects on

---

[3] Robertson (1982).
[4] Gress (1982:41).
[5] In the *Wall Street Journal* (9 September 1981).
[6] Glazer (1983:84).
[7] Rold Andersen (1984:109). It serves to Rold Andersen's credit as a social observer that he dismisses the idea that Scandinavian 'egalitarianism' is a product of the welfare state. Instead, he points out that 'egalitarianism' is part of the cultural heritage in Scandinavia and that the welfare state is a product of Scandinavian civilization rather than the other way around.

the quality of family life, as if the elderly gained economic security at the price of loneliness. If child care is 'nationalized' in public kindergartens and day care centres, parents might be encouraged to make use of this service beyond their inclination because they pay for it anyway through their tax bill, and hence give more priority to themselves and less to their children in their use of time, and thereby contribute to reducing the importance of the family as an institution of child rearing.

The provision of public social services could leave family, social networks, neighbourhood, church, and agencies of private charity without social functions to fill, or such institutions might by political intervention be refused responsibility in relation to social concerns if they were seen as coming into conflict with the goals of the welfare state—for instance, if charitable gifts are distributed differently from public transfers. This could contribute to a withering away of what have been called 'mediating structures',[8] and this again could have the double effect of depriving individuals of arenas where they can engage in private activity and interaction, and of leaving them in a state of helplessness in a society without strong, small-scale, 'human' institutions between the little man in the street and big government up above. Again, there may be good reasons for shifting social responsibility from private to public institutions but this does not mean that there may not also be unintended side-effects from such shifts. Government can succeed in giving people things at the price of undermining their possibilities for doing things themselves.

From results of experimental psychology it has been suggested that individuals need a feeling of predictability in and influence over their environment in order to be creative. If these needs are not met, people tend to react by losing their power of initiative and action. If it is true, as is often said, that the welfare state is a maze of intricate rules, regulations, taxes, and benefits, which most people do not understand and cannot penetrate, and that this makes people experience that how they live depends as much on what 'someone else' does as on what they do themselves, it follows that social policies could deprive people of a feeling of control over their own lives, overwhelm them, and leave them behind in a state of bewilderment, or in the psychological jargon, 'learned helplessness'.[9]

[8] By Berger & Neuhaus (1977).
[9] See Magnusson (1980), drawing on work by Seligman.

If these and related assertions are true, they are also serious. The argument starts from the simple and reasonable assumption that a life of activity is a good life; it is believed to be what people seek and to reflect a dignified and rewarding existence. It is good if people are active and care about each other; it is good if family members stick together; it is good if neighbours lend each other a hand in practical affairs; and it is good if people get together in voluntary co-operation to do things they have a common interest in seeing done or to solve common problems. Activity is a part of our welfare; if activity is discouraged there is a welfare loss.

Furthermore, this is a particularly grave form of welfare loss. It is one thing to suggest that we may have to give up some income to have more equality, but a very different matter to say that redistribution may affect our very attitude to life and to those who are close to us, and our will and ability to take care of ourselves and to help others; or that equality and security can be had only at the cost of less content, meaning, and quality in the way we live. If we value both income and equality, it is meaningful to give up some income in order to have more equality. But initiative, spontaneity, activity, compassion, and self-reliance are closer to being absolute values which we would normally not want to trade against more relative values. It does not really make sense to ask how much quality of life we are willing to give up in order to have more equality.

And then in the background of this discussion lies the issue of freedom. Freedom and activity are closely related concepts; we want to be free in order to do what we like. A lack of freedom can be seen as a barrier which prevents us from doing what we want to do. More or less outspokenly, the question raised by those who see the welfare state as infringing upon the quality of private life is the following: is the welfare state 'structurally repressive', making it difficult for us to live as we want to live? Can we envisage, ultimately, 'welfare state man', relieved of material worry but enslaved by the way this has been done?

'In effect, our discussion of income redistribution and equality', writes Kristol, 'is not so much a discussion of economics as it is a discussion in political philosophy. What kind of civilization do we want to live in? What kind of social, political, and economic order do we want? What kind of life do we want?'[10] If, indeed, this is the problem we are up against, if choosing social policy is to choose a way of life, we are dealing with fundamental qualitative choices and not merely optimal solutions to quantitative trade-offs.

What People Do

I take the level of activity as an indicator of quality of life, realizing, of course, that this is only one of several aspects which could be included under that broad heading.

Social research has long had a bias in favour of public as opposed to private life and in favour of what people *have* as opposed to what they *do*. We are, however, gradually beginning to get a better picture of what goes on in the informal and private spheres of societal life. It can be said as a general rule that the more this is studied, the more activity is discovered. The 'rediscovery' of the role of voluntary agencies in the modern welfare state has already been mentioned in Chapter 2. The family, it is being found, is 'still' an important arena of production and not just an emotional community. If all productive work, both in the market and within the family, is measured in the use of time and added up, it turns out that women on average work more than men,[11] yet we have tended to think that it is more common for women than men not to work, because what goes on within the family has been ignored or considered non-work. A German study of household activity finds '. . . that private households are the biggest transportation, food and laundry business in the country (and) that about one third is engaged in agriculture (own field or kitchen garden) and in home building and much in repairs of several sorts. Many more old, sick and handicapped persons are taken care of in households than can ever be admitted to institutions. Two thirds of the households are engaged in neighbourhood help and exchange'.[12]

These are examples of new research which suggest that there may be a great deal more vitality in contemporary private life than some

[10] In Campbell (1977:62).
[11] Wærness (1975, 1982).
[12] Zapf (1984:271–2).

critics believe. Below I shall introduce more empirical evidence on private activity. These data are systematically selected to 'test' the theory that social policies crowd quality out of private life. I shall want to see if we are justified in describing private life, under the influence of the welfare state, as being typically passive. This I shall do by describing the *trend* in activity during the period of welfare state expansion of the 1960s and 1970s. I shall include data on individual activity and on life within the family. By considering a wide range of activities it will be possible to see if the way individuals live their daily lives adds up to a pattern of passivity or activity. The quality of family relationships will be described through within-family old-age care. The caring for elderly by younger generation family members is perhaps the most altruistic of all family relationships and, at the same time, the relationship that is most directly affected by social policies, both social security transfers and social services. If compassion is weakening we should expect to see traces of it here. The data considered are for Sweden. This is the largest of all welfare states and the one that has been growing most rapidly. The theory under consideration does not claim that all social policies obstruct private activity, but only that this will be the case as a result of additional expansions in already large welfare states. Sweden should be a test case.

Individual activity

The Institute for Social Research at the University of Stockholm has conducted three large-scale surveys of the living conditions of the Swedish population, in 1968, 1974, and 1981. The surveys cover activity and status in the areas of economic resources, employment, working conditions, health, education, housing, family and social relations, safety, leisure, and political resources. With some very few exceptions, identical questionnaires were used in all three surveys. The samples were representative for the population of 15 to 75 years of age, sample size was about 6,500 to 6,900, and non-response between 9 and 17 per cent. The samples make up a panel whereby the same individuals were interviewed on all three occasions, except for adjustments for the older and the younger cohorts and for immigrants. These surveys thus give data for the same individuals over a broad range of areas and for a panel over a period of thirteen years. They are tailor-made for analysing changes over time, include a wide range of questions on activities, and cover the expansion period of the welfare state from the late 1960s to the early 1980s.[13]

The main findings of these surveys for trends in individual activity are the following[14] (see Tables in Appendix D):

1. More people are gainfully employed. The proportion of the population between 15 and 75 years in gainful employment increased from 64 to 69 per cent (see Table D1). This happened in spite of a substantial increase in the proportion of retired persons and was caused almost exclusively by increased labour force participation of women. On the other hand, working hours have gone down. Average weekly net working hours (including both full time and part time workers) went down from about 38 hours in 1968 to about 32 in 1981 and gross working hours (all time at work, plus time for travel to/from work) from about 45 to 38 hours. Total leisure (time left over after gross working hours and household work) has remained unchanged, increasing slightly for men and decreasing slightly for women.

2. More people take part in educational activities. The proportion of the population in education has increased somewhat, from about 8 per cent in 1968 to about 11 per cent in 1981 (see Table D2). Participation in free time courses and study circles increased markedly. At the time the survey was conducted in 1981, every third person in the sample was a regular participant in courses or study circles, and 12 per cent were frequent participants, up from one in five and 7 per cent since 1968. Participation in courses at work has increased in much the same way, from 27 to 36 per cent of workers between 1975 and 1979.[15]

3. More people take part in leisure activities. Participation has increased in almost all activities listed in Table D3; more people spend holidays away from home, and more people fill their daily leisure with activities. The level of activity has increased in outdoors recreation, entertainment, and cultural activities; only in the area of pure pastime activities has there been no increase. The proportion of the population which does not take part regularly in at least

---

[13] For a detailed description, see Erikson & Åberg (1984).

[14] Some more information is included in the summary than is reproduced in Appendix D. See Erikson & Åberg, op. cit.

[15] Statistics Sweden: *Levnadsförhållanden, Rapport 35.*

two of the activities listed in the surveys went down from 20 to 10 per cent between 1968 and 1981.

4. More people take part in political and organizational activities (see Table D4). While party membership and activity is stable, trade union membership and participation has increased strongly. Individual political activity and initiative, such as speaking at political meetings, writing to newspapers, and taking part in demonstrations has become more widespread. The proportion of the population which, except for voting, does not in some way take part in the political process as measured in these surveys is down from 37 per cent in 1968 to 22 per cent in 1981.

5. There is more social intercourse among friends and relatives (see Table D5). Only a small and declining minority does not socialize regularly with relatives or friends, and the frequency of socializing has increased substantially, in particular among friends. People simply get together more often than they used to.

These data are unique. We have here, for the first time, representative quantitative information on trends in the level of individual activity in a large welfare state, covering a wide range of areas and a relatively long period of time. This information shows that the level of individual activity is high, that it has been rising during the period of welfare state expansion, that interaction among relatives and friends has become more frequent, and that the minority of the population living in passivity and isolation has become even smaller. The level of activity has increased in several areas at the same time, which means that the total volume of activity has gone up and not only that a constant volume of activity has been shifted to new areas.

To have these data makes a lot of difference. We now know something about questions on which we could previously only speculate. What we know is that the picture of the passive and isolated individual in the welfare state does not fit the facts. People generally have an active life style. They have become more, and not less, active.

What we cannot know from these data is why people have become more active. It may be that social policies, contrary to what the crowding out theory predicts, have stimulated activity, but there are also other possible explanations. People have become more affluent and can afford more activity. Men, if not women, have more free time. From the more detailed analyses which this summary draws on, there is reason to believe that the pattern of increased activity to some degree reflects an increased emancipation and integration of women into more areas of societal life. It is, in theory, possible that individual activity might have increased even more if these developments had been the same without the welfare state, but this seems pretty far-fetched, considering the virtual explosion of activity that is identified.

Nor do we learn too much from these quantitative data about the quality of individual activity. We know that people do more things but this does not say anything directly about the satisfaction they experience from what they do. Still, there are clues that indicate an improvement of quality as well, such as the increase of social interaction and the lack of increase in pure pastime activity. And anyway, it would be a little strange to think that people should consistently compensate for lower quality in their activities by increasing their frequency.

To those who worry about the destiny of individual activity in the welfare state, we can say that their anxiety seems to have no basis in the actual behaviour of those who live under its influence. People have not been crushed by the welfare state and have not responded to its expansion by turning away from their society. They have, instead, increased their societal participation and are more active than ever. If people had lived passive lives, there might have been reason to speculate that social policy could have had a stifling effect on activity, but people live active lives. As judged by what we know, rather than what we might fear, there is, here, no problem to worry about.

Old-age care and the family

The relationship between the elderly and their children, in particular old-age care, should be expected to be sensitive to outside influences. These relationships are 'voluntary' in the sense that they depend totally on motivation, notably that of the younger generation, and all the more so as a consequence of the inter-generation independency in the welfare state. Marriage, in contrast, is bound by formal contract (although informal co-habitation is becoming more common). There are strong emotional and social safeguards in the relationship between parents and children within the nuclear family. While old-age care is generally burdensome, the raising of children is usually regarded as more rewarding. Of course, there are emotional bonds between adult children and their parents, too, but, more than other family relationships, these depend on the subjective element of solidarity.

Sweden is a society where the traditional family does not have a strong position. By international comparison, the marriage rate is low, the frequency of informal co-habitation high, and average household size small. The rate of family break-ups, the average age of mothers at first birth, the rate of children born outside of wedlock, the rate of single-parent families, and the rate of gainful employment of married women are all high.[16] Hence, the data below are on a sensitive aspect of family life in a society with a weak family institution.

Family activity in the area of old-age care in a modern welfare state, and the changing dialectics of family and public care in a period of welfare state expansion, has been analysed in a number of studies by Gerdt Sundström of the University of Stockholm School of Social Work.[17] What follows is a summary of some of the main findings of these studies. All data relate to Sweden for the period from the mid–1950s through the 1970s. The group of elderly is defined so as to include persons over retirement age (67 years in 1954 and 65 years in 1975).

The living arrangements of the elderly have undergone considerable change during this period. One of the most striking and important changes is that there are now more elderly who live on their own and fewer who live with their children. In 1954, more than 25 per cent of the elderly lived with a child or children of their own; in 1975, less than 10 per cent of the elderly lived in this way. This includes both married and unmarried elderly and both children with and without families. About 70 per cent of the elderly have living children and this proportion has been about stable. On first sight, the reduction of co-habitation between elderly parents and their children might seem to suggest that the bonds between the generations are weakening and even that the younger generation is abandoning their elderly. But a closer look behind these figures reveals

[16] The comparisons are from a forthcoming paper by David Popenoe, presented at a seminar at the Department for Sociology, University of Stockholm, 5 November 1985.

[17] Sundström (1983, 1984).

that this is not the case. The reduction of co-habitation reflects, firstly, better possibilities for both generations to choose living arrangements which correspond to their preferences, and secondly, changing objective possibilities for younger generation families to provide within-family old-age care, relative to the total volume of care that is needed.

The majority of the elderly live on their own, either alone or with a spouse. In the mid–1950s, between 65 and 70 per cent of the elderly lived in this way; by the mid–1970s the proportion had increased to about 85 per cent. The number of house-bound unmarried elderly is estimated to have increased from 53,000 in 1954 to 96,000 in 1975, but the proportion in this group living with children fell from 43 to 8 per cent and in institutions from 42 to 37 per cent. Only a small minority of all elderly live in institutions, about 5 or 6 per cent. This has remained roughly unchanged.[18] There has been an increasing role for public and professional agencies in old-age care but this has mainly taken the form of improved old-age pensions and new services for the non-institutionalized elderly.[19] The growth of the welfare state has not been accompanied by an increasing institutionalization of the elderly; the proportion of the elderly who live in institutions, in the large welfare state of Sweden, is on about the same level as in most other industrial nations, including, for example, the United States, with its relatively small welfare state. The issue of institutionalization, therefore, is not important for the present discussion. The elderly have moved out of younger generation families and into families of their own, not into institutions.

The first preference of most of the elderly is to live close enough to their children and other kin to have frequent contact, but not to live with them. Elderly people with higher incomes, and consequently more freedom of choice, co-reside less frequently with children than do those with lower incomes, but more often live geographically close to them. Higher standards of living, probably better health for many elderly people, better housing, and better

---

[18] According to public statistics (Statistical Yearbook of Sweden) the number of beds in homes for the aged in 1955 corresponded to 4.2 per cent of the population of 65 years and older, in 1975 to 4.6 per cent, and in 1980 to 4.2 per cent.

[19] The number of elderly and disabled helped by home-help services increased from a figure corresponding to 7 per cent of the population of 65 years and older in 1960 to 26 per cent in 1980 (Statistical Yearbook of Sweden).

home-help services have gradually made it possible for more of the elderly to live in this way. In 1975, 40 per cent of the elderly reported that they managed completely without help, as compared to 29 per cent in 1954. Survey data from several developed countries show that the elderly overwhelmingly want to live and manage on their own, and that many of those who live with their children would have preferred to live on their own had that been possible. These preferences are shared by the younger generation. Both from the perspective of the elderly and their children, co-habitation is often a second-best solution when other possibilities are not open.

The changing pattern of co-habitation is to some extent a result of changes in the demographic composition of the population. Because of the ageing of the population there are now, in relative terms, more elderly and fewer younger people. This means that the pattern of co-habitation would have had to change, even with no change of behaviour in individual families, and helps to explain the increasing role of professional and public care-giving. Also, since co-habitation between elderly parents and grown children occurs most frequently with unmarried children, rising marriage rates have contributed to fewer grown children living with their parents.

Care-giving within the family has almost exclusively been the domain of women. Because of increasing labour force participation of married women, and for other reasons, the female 'pool of care-givers' in younger generation families has been reduced. The number of women aged 45 to 59 per 1,000 aged went down from 923 in 1950 to 591 in 1975. The number of elderly who live with their children has remained unchanged in relation to both the number of unmarried women in this age group and the number of married women in the same age group who do not work outside of the home. This indicates that when controlling for changing possibilities for co-habitation, the frequency has not gone down.

Co-habitation with children is most frequent among the oldest of the elderly and among the elderly who are in poor health. This is the opposite of what one would expect if the reduction in the frequency of co-habitation had been caused by a declining willingness in the the younger generation to care for their elderly.

Living with children is not the same as being cared for by children. The majority of the elderly who live with children, live with unmarried sons, which suggests that it is perhaps the old who care for the young more than the young who care for the old, and that it is possibly grown children living with parents that should be discussed rather than elderly living with children. In 1954, when 27 per cent of the elderly lived with children, only seven per cent lived with married children. In 1975, the equivalent figures were down to 9 and 1 per cent. In both 1954 and 1975, 7 out of 10 co-residing children were sons, almost all of them single. Among the oldest of the elderly, however, that is, those with the greatest need for care, there are more co-residing parents who live with daughters than with sons.

Informal care for the elderly by children or other family members does not depend on the two generations living together. Co-habitation is, to some extent, a question of distributing the care-giving burden among children. Elderly who live on their own and who have more than one child tend to receive help from several of their children, whereas, with co-habitation, one child tends to take the entire burden. While co-habitation between elderly parents and grown children has gone down, the frequency of contact between them has gone up. The proportion of the elderly who live in social isolation has gone down. The increased frequency of contact between relatives reported in Table D5 in Appendix D holds true also for contacts between the elderly and their relatives.

The increasing importance of public services for the aged has given informal family help a new dimension. Because of bureaucratic and other problems it is not always easy to make use of the opportunities offered by the public care system, in particular for elderly people who often do not have the necessary skills or stamina to find out what their rights are or to deal with a welfare bureaucracy. The probability of acquiring public care has, therefore, proved to be greater for those elderly who have the support and help of an informal network, family or otherwise, than for elderly who do not have such informal resources but who may have the same or more need for public care. Among the aged who live alone, the childless are the ones less likely to have public home-help service, and those with children living nearby the ones most likely to have such help. This is the opposite of what one would expect if public home-help services were distributed as a substitute for lack of private care.

In summary: there have been significant changes in the living arrangements of the elderly and in the patterns of old-age care, but these changes do not reflect a declining standard of old-age care.

The need for old-age care has increased. Private families and public services share in meeting these needs and supplement each other in so doing. The role of professional care has increased, but informal care in the family sector is still the dominant form of old-age care. Public old-age services have increasingly been brought to the elderly in their home. This has strengthened the family status of the elderly. They have achieved greater independence without suffering neglect. More of the elderly are now able to maintain their own family life and live independent lives, even when house-bound or otherwise disabled. Although less co-habitation, there is more contact between the elderly and their kin. Since these developments correspond to the preferences of both elderly and younger generations and imply more freedom and independence in their interaction, one might assume that there is also an improvement in the quality of interaction between the generations.

The family is not a strong institution in the Swedish society, yet, when taking into consideration demographic factors, family resources, and preferences, families continue to provide old-age care for their members on the same scale as previously. The elderly have become more dependent on government but they also have more income[20] and better services. They are less dependent on family, but this is because they have wanted more independence and now have the means to achieve it. There are no signs in this material of a decline in family activity, of less vitality or compassion in the sensitive relationships between the elderly and younger family members, or of a decline in the quality of the family life of the elderly.

I here add a methodological note. It should be observed that a description of relationships between family members is not a test of the strength of the family as a societal institution. The latter depends on several factors, including, at least, demographic factors (e.g. the age and sex composition of the population, fertility, marriage and divorce rates, geographical mobility), the distribution of income and other family resources between types of households, and within-family relationships. There is evidence that these factors together have, for some time, pulled in the direction of what Victor

---

[20] The observed trend of equalization of the distribution of income in Sweden during the 1970s is explained, to a large degree, by a rise in the relative income level of the elderly. See Åberg, Selén & Tham (1984).

Fuchs calls 'the fading family'.[21] Several authors have emphasized the persistent strength of the family,[22] but this appears to be based mainly on observations of what individual families do with the resources they happen to have. It is perfectly possible for individual families to be as strong as ever and the family institution still to be weakened. The controversy over 'the decline of the family' is probably to some extent a misunderstanding, resulting from one group speaking about individual families and another group about the family institution. The evidence presented here supports the thesis that individual families remain strong. This suggests that, if the family institution is in decline, the problem does not lie in the motivation of family members *vis-à-vis* each other, but rather in objective resources and demographic factors. Those who warn that the welfare state may weaken the family seem most often to believe that this occurs via its influence on motivations (although the causal mechanism is usually not explained clearly). This theory finds no support here.

Social policies may have an influence on some of the more objective factors which influence the strength of the family as an institution. The expansion of the welfare state represents new employment possibilities for married women; this may influence fertility. Family support makes wives more independent of husbands; this may encourage divorce.[23] American experiences indicate that AFDC and other support programmes for unmarried mothers may have contributed to the rising number of young single mothers, because some teen-age girls or young women from deprived families believe, rightly or wrongly, that these programmes will give them sufficient income for an independent life and see pregnancy as their only possible escape from their depressed situation.[24] However, these influences (or their significance) are contested. Increased divorce, as a result of a relative economic security for single mothers, can be seen as a sign of increased freedom for wives who do not want to continue their marriage.[25] Although the frequency of households headed by single women in the United States doubled between 1968 and 1983,

[21] Fuchs (1983).
[22] See e.g. Bane (1976); Caplow *et al.* (1982); Lein (1984).
[23] As shown by Bishop (1980).
[24] According to Fuchs (1983).
[25] As argued by Jencks (1985).

regional differences in this trend have been found not to correlate with differences in support programmes for single mothers, indicating that the explanation does not lie in the generosity of support policies.[26]

Welfare Gain?

It has been speculated that the welfare state may influence individuals to adopt a life style of passivity and indifference, but this appears not to be the case. People are more active and involved in society and with each other than before and families have maintained their vitality and their essential functions for family members and kin. Empirical evidence on individual and family activity does not support the theory that the welfare state has come in the way of quality in contemporary private life.

We cannot know how people would have organized their lives in the absence of the welfare state. In theory it is possible that they would have been even more active and families stronger, but this does not seem likely. There is more reason to interpret this material as indicating that the expansion of the welfare state has stimulated activity. For the elderly, in particular, this is quite apparent. Income is redistributed in their favour and social services provided. This has contributed to raising their standard of living and to their increased independence and improved family status.

There are several ways that new social policies can stimulate activity. Firstly, there is the possibility that our economic and social environment is influenced so that more opportunities for activity are offered. Obvious examples are educational opportunities and social service jobs. In addition, on the fringe of social policy proper, there is, for example, the subsidization of leisure, sports and cultural activities, the public responsibility for parks and recreational facilities, and the opening up of beaches, hiking areas, and areas of fishing and hunting, so that private property does not give the right to exclude non-property-holders from the enjoyment of natural facilities.

Secondly, the ideology of 'egalitarianism' may have had some

[26] Ellwood & Summers (1986), based on original research by David Ellwood and Mary Jo Bane.

influence on attitudes. The attempt to create a society of non-exclusive institutions may have made conventional distinctions between those who 'belong' and those who are 'outsiders' less legitimate and imposing and made it more difficult to protect exclusiveness and more easy for those who have been excluded to demand access. Examples of this may be the increasing demands on the part of the handicapped for full participation in society, and not merely compensations, and the appearance of a modern theatre audience of being a cross-section of the population.

Thirdly, the redistribution of income may have a direct stimulating effect on private activity. If successful, income redistribution transfers money from higher to lower income groups. Since income is, *inter alia*, a resource for activity, it is likely that the rich give up less possibility for activity than the poor gain. Since the rich do not spend their entire disposable income on consumption, they can, in large measure, maintain their activity unchanged even if they have to give up some of their income. Beyond a certain level, what additional income can buy is not new activities but 'only' better quality in more or less the same kinds of activity: opera instead of cinema, good restaurants instead of pubs, large cars instead of small ones, and so on. This may make a difference for satisfaction but less so for activity. For the poor, however, some marginal additional income may have a good deal of effect. This could be the difference between simply managing the necessities and having some surplus income to spend for recreation or pleasure. Social activities are almost never free, if only for indirect costs such as equipment and transportation or baby-sitting. Some of the additional income redistributed to the poor will, of course, be spent on regular consumption, but it is still likely that successful income redistribution increases their possibilities for activity more than it reduces those of the rich.

Fourthly, redistribution in the form of social services is, to some extent, a question of bringing resources to families and, thereby, of helping them to maintain their vitality. The best example of this is home-help services for elderly and other more or less dependent groups. These services are usually of limited scope, perhaps only a few hours of help per week, but this is often what makes it possible for clients to continue to live on their own and for older and younger generation family members to live in close contact with each other but still in independence.

Finally, the expansion of the welfare state has in several ways been more important for women than for men and has influenced the status of women and contributed to their emancipation.[27] The interplay between the changing status of women and the development of new social policies is essential for understanding both the increasing level of individual activity and the persistent strength of the family. The growth of the welfare state has encouraged more women to increase their activity outside of the family. This has contributed to giving women a stronger position in society, but has also represented a new strain on the family. This strain has, however, been counteracted by social policies which have brought new services to the family. Because of this, and because women, in spite of their increasing activity outside of the home, have continued to accept their traditional family responsibility, the family remains the most important institution in the care for dependents.

More women than men are recipients of income transfers through the welfare state (although often smaller transfers). There are more women than men in the population of elderly. In at least some countries with universal child allowance programmes, all *mothers* receive a regular child allowance cheque. Many elderly women today have an income of their own for the first time in their life upon reaching retirement age, and many mothers have the child allowance as the only money they can themselves control.[28]

More women than men have jobs in the welfare state. It is, above all, the increasing number of jobs in the social sector which has made it possible for more women to enter the labour market. This has given many women new economic independence and a basis for increased participation in political and organizational life and in other activities. Women continue to have lower paid jobs than men and less important positions in unions, parties, and other organizations but their situation has improved, and the welfare state has contributed to this.

---

[27] For a more detailed discussion, see Wærness & Ringen (1986). See also Hernes (1984). The concept of emancipation is, of course, controversial. It is, for example, not obvious that much is gained for women by being 'emancipated' into low status jobs while traditional family burdens are maintained.

[28] The significance of this way of organizing child allowance payments was illustrated when the Norwegian Minister of Finance a few years ago suggested an integration of child allowances and taxes so that most families would not receive a child allowance cheque but a deduction in taxes. This created an uproar from women which forced the Minister to withdraw his proposal and it has not come up again.

Women more than men benefit from social services which have relieved families of some of their care burdens or which support their care giving, such as day care for children and home-help services for the elderly. This is not so much the case, perhaps, among the clients—elderly men are more dependent on the help of others than are elderly women—but certainly among the adult generation which is the provider of family care. It is over-whelmingly women who carry the practical burden of family care and this continues to be the case even though they increasingly have work outside the home.[29] Public care services have helped to make it possible for women to manage the double burden of job and family.

This 'crowding in' theory—assuming it is right, as suggested through these arguments, that the expansion of the welfare state has stimulated private activity—has a double significance, in part substantively and in part theoretically.

If we include activity in our concept of welfare, we have here identified a welfare gain. Some economists, for example Gunnar Myrdal in *Asian Drama*, have contested the trade-off between redistribution and economic efficiency and argued instead that redistribution can be productive through its mobilization of human capital and other mechanisms. This may be true in underdeveloped economies and it may be true if we compare a system with a welfare state to a non-welfare-state situation, but it appears from what we have seen in the previous chapter that it is too much to hope that marginal additional redistributions in systems which already have a relatively large welfare state can be expected to add to economic efficiency. If, however, we include other components of living conditions than income in our concept of welfare, social policies may still turn out to be productive in the sense that additional aggregate values are created. There may be some economic welfare loss in redistribution but on the other hand there may also be welfare gains of a more qualitative nature.

In his *Economics of Welfare*, which was first published in 1920, Pigou argued that it followed from the theory of falling marginal

---

[29] According to estimates by Tåhlin (1984), women in Swedish households do more than 80 per cent of all household work and men less than 20 per cent. The trend in the distribution of household work is that women take a slightly smaller share and men a slightly larger share, but men still do very little and it may be that their share is increasing not because they do more but because women do less.

utility that the redistribution of income from the rich to the poor was to the benefit of society as a whole because it would give more additional utility to the poor than the disutility it would cause the rich.[30] In *An Essay on the Nature and Significance of Economic Science*, published in 1932, Robbins dismissed the possibility of interpersonal comparisons of utility and thereby rejected Pigou's argument. It is true that for the same person there is falling marginal utility of additional income, but since people can have different preference structures it does not from this follow that a given income increment gives more utility to a poor man than to a rich man. Occasional papers in defence of interpersonal comparisons of utility continue to be published[31] but welfare economists have, for the most part, stuck to Robbins' position.

This controversy is relevant and interesting only if we take the subjective concept of welfare as given. In Chapter 1 I have argued for an objective concept of welfare. If this is accepted the whole issue of interpersonal comparison can be dismissed. It may not be possible to compare subjective utility, but there is no theoretical problem in comparing objective living conditions. If we furthermore adopt a broad measurement of living conditions and include activity as one of several relevant components, we find that Pigou was right. There are aggregate benefits in redistribution in addition to the direct income benefits for those who are on the receiving end. He was not right on his own terms, but that was because he was wrong in his choice of welfare concept. Had he been right in the choice of concept, the conclusion that was later proved to be wrong would have been right.

---

[30] Marshall had previously (in *Principles*, p. 2) argued that in terms of 'the fullness of life' some income to or fro mattered a great deal for the poor but not much for the rich, and before him, Sidgwick (in his *Principles*, p. 519) that, 'The more society approximates to equality in the distribution of wealth among its members, the greater on the whole is the aggregate of satisfactions which the society in question derives from the wealth that it possesses.'

[31] For a discussion, see Sen (1982:Ch. 12).

7
Poverty

To ask about poverty in the welfare state is to question the elementary effectiveness of social policy. It is to ask not only if there is unfairness in these societies but if there are segments of the population who suffer extreme deprivation; it is to ask not only if there are some who lag behind in the general trend towards better standards of living, but if we have proved unable or unwilling to let all groups share in our overall affluence, if only in a minimal way; it is to ask not only if there are imperfections in social policies, but if they have failed in their most elementary intention; it is to ask not only about unintended side-effects of redistribution but to challenge the very idea of redistribution on its own most basic terms. It is important to raise the issue of poverty, because of the historical significance of the problem, because its elimination has been the first priority of the welfare state, and because this offers an opportunity for discussing social policy on a basis of consensus. While there is disagreement about the responsibility of government with regard to overall inequality, its responsibility in relation to poverty has been accepted for generations and is not seriously contested today. If poverty prevails, the welfare state is a failure.

How Much Poverty?

Since poverty was 'rediscovered' in Britain and the United States in the early 1960s we have seen an upsurge of empirical research which has aimed to answer the seemingly simple but in fact elusive question, 'How much poverty is there?' The principal characteristics of the main body of this research are the following: It is based on what has been called the 'relative concept of poverty', it uses the 'income poverty line' to divide the population into the poor and the non-poor, and it measures the extent of poverty with the 'head count method', that is, the number of poor relative to the entire population, also called the 'incidence of poverty'.

While previous studies, notably those of Rowntree, had shown that poverty was diminishing, this new wave of research found it to have remained on a high and relatively stable level. Comparable estimates for the Common Market countries set the proportion of the population living in poverty in the mid–1970s to between 4.8 per cent (the Netherlands) and 23.1 per cent (Ireland).[1] In a comparison of Australia, Belgium, Britain, and Norway around 1970, the incidence of poverty is between 9.1 and 24.9 per cent,[2] and in a comparison of Sweden and the US for 1974 it is 3.0 and 8.2 per cent respectively.[3] The *Luxembourg Income Study*, which has compared the distribution of income in Britain, Canada, Germany, Israel, Norway, Sweden, and the United States around 1980, using minutely co-ordinated micro-data sets, finds poverty to be between 4.8 and 16.9 per cent (in Norway and the United States respectively).[4] Estimates by the Department of Health and Social Security in Britain set the incidence of poverty in 1981 to 5.3 per cent of the population, up from 4.3 per cent in 1976.[5] A recent Swedish study finds that between 3.8 and 5.9 per cent of the population was below the poverty line in 1979,[6] and a recent Norwegian study finds the incidence of poverty in 1981–2 to be around 5 per cent.[7] 'It is a sad reflection', write George and Lawson in the introduction to their *Poverty and Inequality in Common Market Countries*, 'that after twenty-five years of unprecedented economic growth and massive government expenditure in social security, poverty is still prevalent . . .'.[8]

In this chapter I am concerned only with the problem of measurement. I shall not discuss explicitly the effect on poverty of welfare state policies—the effectiveness of redistribution will be dealt with in the next chapter—but only the correctness of the conclusion that poverty has prevailed at a relatively high and stable level through the last couple of decades of welfare state expansion. Much hinges on this conclusion. It represents a devastatingly negative verdict on redistribution, and not much can be claimed for the welfare state

[1] Commission . . . (1981).
[2] Beckerman (1979a).
[3] Hedström (1981).
[4] Smeeding *et al.* (1985).
[5] According to Atkinson (1985).
[6] Gustafsson (1984a).
[7] Stjernø (1985).
[8] George & Lawson (1980:xi).

unless it can be refuted. Of course, one could still claim some
success if it could be shown that poverty would have been even
more widespread without the welfare state, but that is not enough.
While this argument may have some merit with regard to the total
structure of inequality, it is not credible with regard to poverty. The
welfare state was introduced into societies of mass poverty. The
elimination, or at least reduction, of poverty is its first and most
elementary goal. Success clearly requires more than the keeping of
this basic problem at bay, in particular since the expansion of the
welfare state during the post-war period has, for the most part,
occurred under the favourable circumstances of economic growth
and rising average standards of living. If 4 to 5 per cent, or more, of
the population continue to live in poverty, the problem is nowhere
near being eliminated. Remember, as a point of reference, that
Rowntree found just under 10 per cent poverty in York in 1899. If
we are to believe the results cited above, nothing much has really
happened to the extent of poverty during this century. Poverty
remains an integral aspect of our socio-economic system in much
the same way as it has been historically and is not even pushed back
to being a residual problem. The strategy of redistribution is futile
and the hope of progress through growth has proved to be a myth.

   The research behind the alarming findings on poverty has lately
come under criticism for side-stepping some of the complexities of
the concept and measurement of poverty and thereby producing
estimates which may not be theoretically sound or empirically
realistic.[9] I join this revisionism. I shall discuss the concept of
poverty and show that the distinction between absolute and relative
poverty, which has been of the utmost importance for justifying the
results of recent studies, is a misunderstanding. I shall, however,
accept the broad sociological concept of poverty and, thereby,
evaluate the research in question on its own terms. Instead of
rejecting the results by rejecting the concept on which they are
based, I shall accept the theoretical concept of poverty but argue
that this concept and its implications have not been taken in earnest
in the empirical measurement of poverty. This will lead me to
dismiss the income poverty line as a method of measurement, under
the concept of poverty which is accepted, and, thereby, to a rejec-

   [9] See e.g. Sen (1979b, 1980, 1983); Atkinson (1985). See also an exchange
between Townsend (1985) and Sen (1985b).

tion of the kinds of findings cited above.[10] Furthermore, I shall offer an alternative method of measurement which I believe to have a stronger theoretical justification, and I shall, by applying this method, show that the income poverty line typically results in an overestimate of the extent of poverty. I shall not produce strictly alternative estimates of the incidence of poverty—I doubt that it is at all meaningful to measure the extent of poverty in a single figure—but only show that methods which have been widely accepted have led to an exaggeration of the problem. This is not to say that poverty has been eliminated, but only that there is not a sound theoretical and methodological basis for claiming that 4 or 5 per cent or more of the population in contemporary welfare state societies typically live in poverty. I do not know how much poverty there is—the question may well be unanswerable—but, as measured by the head count method, there is less poverty, and its incidence has been reduced more during the 1970s, than is generally claimed in the research I have taken as my point of departure.

The Concept of Poverty

To be poor is to be deprived. But poverty is a demanding concept which must be used with care if it is to remain relevant and meaningful and not become just another word for inequality or social problems. Poverty must be limited to certain types and degrees of deprivation. To be poor is to be deprived. But deprived of what? And how deprived?

Degrees and types of deprivation

There are degrees of deprivation which may be objectionable but still not sufficiently grave to be regarded as poverty. Finding it difficult to make ends meet is not in itself to be poor. This is a

[10] There are other criticisms which I shall not take up here, notably against the head count method, which ignores the important question of how poor the poor are and how income is distributed among the poor, and which has long since been said to have 'little but its simplicity to recommend it' (Watts, 1968). In principle I agree, and this only strengthens my own argument, but I will still stick with the head count method in order to criticize recent poverty research on its own terms. In this way I will, in effect, be saying that even if this unacceptable simplicity is accepted, the empirical results which depend on it cannot be taken as authoritative.

problem for many who are not poor. To live in poverty is to be *seriously deprived*; it is to have to make do without what is *necessary*. More will be said later about the meaning of necessities.

As to types of deprivation, there are some which may be extremely serious in their own right but which must still conceptually be separated from poverty. To be in bad health, for example, is to be deprived of something which matters both directly for one's well-being and is at the same time a resource of importance for achieving other goods, but this does not mean that to be in bad health is to be poor. Bad health and poverty may be associated with each other empirically but conceptually they are separate problems. The concept of poverty is limited to 'material' deprivations.

Direct and indirect concepts

One possible understanding of poverty is to say that people are poor if they subjectively feel deprived. I have discussed subjective and objective welfare in Chapter 1 and there dismissed the subjectivist approach. It can be added only that the inadequacy of the subjective concept of welfare becomes apparent in a discussion of poverty. It is easy to see that some people can feel poor without being poor—for example, children of the upper class who experience downward mobility into the middle class—and that others can be poor without feeling poor: for example, 'guest workers' from a poor country who feel well off on a miserably low salary in a rich country because they compare their present situation to their former situation in their home country. The feeling of satisfaction is of course not unimportant for people, but it does not determine poverty.[11] To be poor depends on how you live, not how you feel.

A second possibility is to say that people are poor if they do not have the necessary resources, capabilities, or rights to achieve what is defined as a minimum standard in their way of life. A third possibility turns this around and says that people are poor if they, in

[11] This subjective concept has not been much used in empirical poverty research, but van Praag, Hagenaars & van Weeren (1982) have shown that a subjective approach can be used to determine the poverty line, albeit with some strange results, such as finding the incidence of poverty in Italy to be between 9 and 17 per cent and in Denmark between 23 and 35 per cent. More recently, Mack & Lansley (1985) have used a similar approach in a survey of poverty in Britain.

fact, have a way of life which is below the defined minimum standard, irrespective of what has determined this way of life. These two conceptions can be called *indirect* and *direct* respectively; in the first case, poverty is defined indirectly through the determinants of way of life, in the second case, directly by way of life. This distinction is, as we shall see later, of considerable importance. If there are indirect and direct concepts of poverty, there should also be indirect and direct measures of poverty. Under the indirect concept we should measure poverty by income or other resource indicators; under the direct concept by consumption or other way of life indicators.

Both these understandings of poverty reflect an objective concept of welfare, they are close to each other without being identical, and they are both influential in the theory of poverty. I shall make no choice between these two understandings, but instead define poverty as a combination of the two: as a low standard of living, meaning deprivation in way of life because of insufficient resources to avoid such deprivation.[12] This, too, will be explained more carefully later.

Subsistence minimum and relative deprivation

Empirical research on poverty has applied two main concepts, the subsistence minimum concept and the relative deprivation concept.

The subsistence minimum concept was developed by Seebohm Rowntree in his first study of poverty in York in 1899.[13] By his definition, families were counted as poor if their 'total earnings are insufficient to obtain the minimum necessities of merely physical efficiency'. He was highly restrictive in what he considered to be necessities. This included only the simplest possible diet (as stipulated by experts) and minimum requirements in clothing, housing, and heating. No 'luxury' was allowed, not even a newspaper, union membership, a stamp for a letter, tobacco or beer, no gifts or charities, and, of course, no expenses for leisure activities or pure pleasure; only what was necessary to maintain physical health and even then the simplest and most economical alternative possible.

---

[12] I here use three concepts: *resources* (which are determinants), *way of life* (which is a result), and *standard of living* (which covers both resources and way of life).

[13] Rowntree (1901).

Rowntree found, as we have seen, that 9.9 per cent of the families in York were poor in 1899 (and that an additional 27.8 per cent lived in 'secondary poverty' by which he meant that their income was above what was strictly required but that their consumption still did not include the minimum necessities because of the way the income was used) and that the incidence of poverty had fallen to 1.7 per cent by 1950.

A modern use of the subsistence minimum concept can be found in the 'official' poverty index used for statistical purposes by the Census Bureau in the United States.[14] The poverty line is determined by the same type of method as the one used by Rowntree, and set at three times the cost of a basic food basket as stipulated by the Department of Agriculture. This procedure differs from Rowntree's only in what commodities and quantities are included in the basic food basket and in the surplus income allowed in addition to what is assumed necessary for foodstuffs. In Rowntree's original study, expenditure for foodstuffs made up 56 per cent of total expenditure at the poverty line income; in the US poverty index it is set at 33 per cent.

Using this standard, the Census Bureau has calculated the incidence of poverty in the United States to about 20 per cent in the early 1960s, 11 to 12 per cent in the mid–1970s, and up again to about 15 per cent in the early 1980s.[15] The very considerable difference between these US figures and Rowntree's figures for York depends on many factors, but part of the explanation is that the poverty line in the US index is set at a more 'generous' level than the one applied by Rowntree.

The relative deprivation concept came into use in Britain as a reaction against the work of Rowntree, and in particular his and Lavers' 1950 study which came to be regarded as outdated. The pioneering work in this new approach was *The Poor and The Poorest* by Brian Abel-Smith and Peter Townsend, published in 1965. While Rowntree had defined poverty in relation to physical efficiency, the problem now came to be understood in terms of what might be called 'social efficiency'. One is, of course, indisputably poor if one lacks what is necessary for physical efficiency, but even when this is not the case one might still be poor if one is not able to

[14] HEW (1976).
[15] Danziger, Haveman & Plotnick (1986:Table 3.1).

sustain a way of life which is regarded as a necessary or decent minimum in the kind of society in which one happens to live. This resulted in the poverty line being set at a considerably higher level that the one used by Rowntree and, consequently, in much higher figures for poverty. Abel-Smith and Townsend concluded that, as estimated from official statistics, 10.1 per cent of British households were poor in 1953–4 and that this figure, far from falling, had risen to 17.9 per cent in 1960. In a later study, Townsend estimated that in 1968–9, between 7.1 and 25.2 per cent of British households were poor, depending on how the theoretical concept was operationalized.[16]

While the meaning of poverty under the subsistence minimum concept is fairly straightforward, its meaning under the relative deprivation concept needs to be explained more carefully. According to Townsend, 'Individuals, families and groups in the population can be said to be in poverty when they lack the resources to obtain the types of diet, participate in the activities and have the living conditions and amenities which are customary, or are at least widely encouraged or approved, in the societies to which they belong. Their resources are so seriously below those commanded by the average individual or family that they are, in effect, excluded from ordinary living patterns, customs and activities'.[17] The (former) Supplementary Benefit Commission in Britain writes, 'Poverty, in urban, industrial countries like Britain is a standard of living so low that it excludes and isolates people from the rest of the community. To keep out of poverty, they must have an income which enables them to participate in the life of the community. They must be able, for example, to keep themselves reasonably fed, and well enough dressed to maintain their self-respect and to attend interviews for jobs with confidence. Their homes must be reasonably warm; their children should not feel shamed by the quality of their clothing; the family must be able to visit relatives, and give them something on their birthdays and at Christmas time; they must be able to read newspapers, and retain their television set and their membership of trade unions and churches. And they must be able to live in a way which ensures, so far as possible, that public officials, doctors, teachers, landlords and others treat them with the

[16] Townsend (1979:273).
[17] Townsend (1979:31).

courtesy due to every member of the community'.[18] The Council of the European Communities has defined poverty as the situation of '. . . individuals or families whose resources are so small as to exclude them from the minimum acceptable way of life of the Member State in which they live'.[19] And David Donnison has put it briefly in this way: 'I believe that poverty means a standard of living so low that it excludes people from the community in which they live'.[20]

The common denominator of these explanations of the concept of poverty lies in the term *exclusion*. The meaning of poverty under the relative deprivation concept, as it has been explained by the advocates of this concept, is to be excluded from the ordinary way of life and activities of one's society.

The subsistence minimum and relative deprivation concepts of poverty differ from one another in several ways, but there has been some misunderstanding about the nature of this difference. One misunderstanding is that the relative deprivation concept is 'modern' and the subsistence minimum concept 'old-fashioned'. It is true that subsistence minimum was the early concept to be used in empirical poverty research, but it is not yet outdated, as witnessed by its present use in the United States. It may be that Rowntree's application is outdated, but the concept has proved to be sufficiently flexible to be applied differently in a different time and society. It is also true that relative deprivation is a recent concept in empirical research, but the understanding that the problem of poverty must be seen in relation to the circumstances of time and place is very old. Already Adam Smith, in *Wealth of Nations*, explained the meaning of poverty in this way. 'By necessaries, I understand not only the commodities which are indispensably necessary for the support of life but whatever the custom of the country renders it indecent for creditable people, even of the lowest order, to be without. A linen shirt, for example, is strictly speaking not a necessity of life. The Greeks and Romans lived, I suppose, very comfortable though they had no linen. But in the present time . . . a creditable day-labourer would be ashamed to appear in public without a linen shirt, the want of

[18] *Annual Report* 1978, p. 2.
[19] Commission . . . (1981:8).
[20] Donnison (1982:7).

which would be supposed to denote that disgraceful state of poverty.'[21]

Alfred Marshall, in *Principles of Economics*, did not give a precise definition of poverty, but came close, when in the introductory chapter, he wrote of poverty in terms of the material conditions of a 'complete life' and of living in poverty as of living in 'degradation'.[22] Being the Victorian gentleman he was, he no doubt had a spartan understanding of the material resources required for 'a complete life', but his concept of poverty was all the same related not merely to survival but to some quality of life.

Rowntree was probably more restrictive in his concept of poverty than he needed have been in view of how the problem was understood at the time. This was, in part, because of his determination to use a concept which would assure that he could not be criticized for having exaggerated the problem he was investigating, a laudable scientific caution which is perhaps not characteristic of all recent poverty research.

Another misunderstanding is that under the subsistence minimum concept, poverty is seen as an 'absolute' problem which can be defined once and for all and in the same way irrespective of time and place, while only under the relative deprivation concept is poverty seen as 'relative' in relation to the society in which it occurs so that the meaning of poverty can change as social and economic circumstances change. This has been the rationale for setting the poverty line at a higher level in 'modern' than in 'conventional' studies. In fact, however, the subsistence minimum concept is every bit as relative as the relative deprivation concept (in spite of labels).[23] This is best seen in the difference between Rowntree's application of the concept and its present application in the United States. It is true that there is a good deal of stability in the official poverty line in the US because it is not adjusted from one year to another except to correct for inflation, but this has nothing to do with absolute or relative concepts. The concept is clearly relative in that the level of consumption taken to be necessary is determined on the basis of

[21] As quoted by Atkinson (1975:189).

[22] 'It may make little difference to the fullness of life of a family whether its yearly income is £1000 or £5000; but it makes a very great difference whether the income is £30 or £150: for with £150 the family has, with £30 it has not, the material conditions of a complete life.' (Marshall, 1949:2)

[23] The arbitrariness of the distinction between absolute and relative poverty has been argued previously by Rein (1970b).

nutritional standards and patterns of consumption in present American society, and it can be relativized as much as anyone might want by simply including more consumption items as necessary. Nor has the subsistence minimum concept ever been regarded as implying an absolute and unchangeable minimum standard. One of the principles of the *Beveridge report*, for example, was that of flat rate benefits based on the notion of a subsistence minimum, but Beveridge did not see this as an absolute and unchangeable standard but as a level which could be adjusted to changes in the general standard of living.[24]

Even Rowntree's application of the concept is itself an expression of a relative understanding of poverty. It is formulated in terms of efficiency—that is, the ability to function, which is precisely what relative poverty is about. True, Rowntree's understanding of ability to function was strict and by today's standard far from generous, but his concept is none the less relative. He further relativized his concept of poverty by distinguishing, as Charles Booth had done previously in separating the 'poor' from the 'very poor'[25] and as Townsend would do later by estimating the incidence of poverty on the basis of different 'standards', between 'primary' and 'secondary' poverty. Finally, the relative nature of his concept can be seen from the commodities he included in his list of necessities. In the 1899 study he included tea, a commodity without any nutritional value, which can only be regarded as a necessity because of social convention in England. When he repeated his study in 1936 and 1950, he retained his theoretical concept but adjusted the commodities included as necessities, thus accepting that as society changes the meaning of necessity changes and that changes in the standard of living influence the meaning of poverty. In the 1936 study, the poverty line was set at a level 40 per cent higher (in real terms) than in the 1899 study.

There never was such a thing as an absolute concept of poverty and there is no alternative to a relative understanding of the problem. To dismiss the absolute concept of poverty is to tear down strawmen, to reject theories which do not exist, and to argue for the obvious. In the world of poverty only death is absolute; beyond that, all poverty is a matter of more or less and the question is not

[24] According to Harris (1975).
[25] Booth (1903); first original volume published in 1889.

whether to apply a relative concept but, always, how much to relativize poverty. To say that poverty is relative is in itself to say nothing about where the poverty line should be set.

The difference between the subsistence minimum and relative deprivation concepts does not lie in one being old and the other new or one being absolute and the other being relative, but in their assumptions with regard to what is considered necessary, that is, how the twin questions 'Deprived of what?' and 'How deprived?' are answered. The subsistence minimum concept is an *indirect* concept of poverty. To be poor is to be deprived of income. The level of income to be used as the poverty line is determined by what consumption is regarded as such that no one should be expected to make do without. Necessities are determined by individual needs. The relative deprivation concept is a *direct* concept of poverty. To be poor is to be deprived in way of life. People need a certain standard in their way of life in order to avoid exclusion and to be able to participate in and be accepted into normal activities in one's society. Necessities are determined by social requirements.

Poverty and inequality

If poverty is seen as a matter of relative deprivation, it necessarily becomes associated with inequality at the bottom of the distribution. The more inequality there is, the more people will be deprived relative to the average standard of living and the more people will consequently be poor, other things equal. But the relationship between poverty and inequality is a complex one that depends on how high or low the average standard of living is and on the structure of inequality. If the standard is high and the distribution not too inegalitarian, even those near or at the bottom of the distribution may have been pulled out of poverty; they may still be deprived compared to what is 'normal' in their society but no longer live in poverty. There might be considerable inequality without poverty, for example if those below the average are close to it and some of those above are very rich. Falling behind the rich may be annoying, but to be poor in the relative deprivation understanding is not just to have less than the rich but must mean to fall behind relative to the average standard of one's society. On the other hand, there might be only moderate inequality and still considerable poverty, for example in the hypothetical situation where everyone is equally poor or where many are poor and no one is rich.

In much of the research based on the relative deprivation concept, poverty has been defined operationally so as to become almost inseparable from inequality. It is, for example, common to set the poverty line at 50 per cent of the median income. This is convenient and practical, but it has the consequence that the measured incidence of poverty will, by definition, remain unchanged as long as there is no change in the distribution of income, irrespective of how much the level of income of both the poor and the non-poor rises or falls. If everyone overnight miraculously doubles their income, there will still be as much poverty, and there will be no more poverty even if everyone from one day to another should lose half of their income.

The justification for tying income so closely to inequality has been mostly political. The conventional concept of poverty has, in affluent societies, been said to 'obscure reality' and to 'divert attention from the larger structure of inequality'.[26] 'Casting the issue of poverty in terms of stratification leads to regarding poverty as an issue of inequality . . . Our concern becomes one of narrowing the differences between those at the bottom and the better-off . . .'.[27] 'That (widespread and lasting support for impoverished groups) will be easier to achieve if the British can be persuaded to adopt the egalitarian, relative definition of poverty . . .'.[28] But, from a theoretical point of view, this very close association between poverty and inequality is highly problematic. For one thing, it does not follow from the relative deprivation concept. This concept does imply that poverty cannot be seen as independent of inequality but it is a big step from there to seeing poverty as an issue of inequality, and a step which is not justified in the theoretical concept. There is, for example, nothing in the relative deprivation understanding of poverty to prevent the poverty line from rising (or receding) as the average standard of living goes up (or down), but less rapidly. Furthermore, it simply does not make sense to say that poverty has nothing to do with absolute standards of living. If we accept this uncritically, we will soon be classifying families as poor who own a comfortable home, a car, TV and stereo sets, and go to restaurants

[26] Westergaard & Resler (1976:123).
[27] Miller & Roby (1970:143).
[28] Donnison (1981:183).

regularly and abroad on holiday annually, only because they have or do less of this than is usual in their society. Even though a Norwegian may be poor in Norway with a much higher standard of living than is typical of the poor in, say, Tanzania, the poor Norwegian is still less poor than the poor Tanzanian, and although a Norwegian may be poor today with a much higher standard of living than was typical for poor Norwegians two or three generations ago, he is still less poor than they were. Poverty does not disappear automatically as a result of rising standards of living, but nor is it unaffected by rising standards of living.

Amartya Sen, who has discussed the theory of poverty against the backdrop of famine and thereby opened our eyes to some of the strange things that have been said about poverty in the name of relative deprivation, has rightly observed that '. . . there is an irreducible core of *absolute* deprivation in our idea of poverty, which translates reports of starvation, malnutrition and visible hardship into a diagnosis of poverty without having to ascertain first the relative picture'.[29] However much we accept the relative deprivation concept, we should, if we use it critically and with common sense, see that poverty cannot be a simple function of inequality but must depend, at least in part, on absolute standards of living. The problem of poverty is relative, but it would be a strange kind of dogmatism to trap oneself into a definition of poverty where no consideration is taken of the absolute standard of living involved. Poverty is a question of both absolute and relative deprivation.

The choice of concept

If there is one thing that has been demonstrated through nearly one hundred years of empirical poverty research, it is that there is no such thing as 'true poverty'. Our question—How much poverty is there?—is in principle an empirical one, but it has become clear that how much poverty you find depends almost completely on how you define poverty and the tools you use to measure it. Fiegehen, Lansley, and Smith, for example, have estimated the trend in poverty in Britain from 1953–4 to 1973 in two different ways. By using the 'absolute standard' they found the percentage of house-

---

[29] Sen (1981:17).

holds in poverty to have gone down from 6.5 per cent to 0.3 per cent while the alternative estimate based on the 'relative standard' showed poverty to have been reduced only moderately, from 6.5 per cent to 4.3 per cent.[30]

In the present study, the problem of poverty is discussed in relation to the effectiveness of the welfare state. To make fair judgements about political effectiveness we must take goals for given and evaluate policies in relation to their goals, such as they are formulated. One of the goals of the welfare state is to guarantee all citizens a minimum standard. This is why the trend in poverty is an important indication of the effectiveness of redistributive policies. The minimum standard can be understood either as subsistence minimum or as relative deprivation. If poverty is understood as subsistence minimum in the formulation of policy goals, and I measure it as relative deprivation (or the other way around), I may be saying something about poverty as I understand the problem but not as it is understood in the formulation of policies, and consequently not about the effectiveness of these policies.

As discussed in Chapter 1, welfare states differ in their goals. In small welfare states, the minimum standard tends to be seen as a question of subsistence minimum—of no one falling out of society—whereas in large welfare states it tends to be seen more as a question of relative deprivation—of everyone being integrated into society. It is, hence, understandable that subsistence minimum has been accepted as the most relevant concept of poverty in the United States whereas in Europe the relative deprivation concept has won some 'official' acceptance, for instance in the anti-poverty programme of the Common Market. This also helps to explain the difference in orientation between European and American poverty research, as exemplified by Townsend's work in Britain, which concentrates on the definition and measurement of poverty, and the work around the Institute for Research on Poverty in the United States, which concentrates on the effects of anti-poverty policies for low-income groups, defined more pragmatically.[31] This study is concerned primarily with redistributive policies in the large welfare state. The promise of this type of welfare state is not only that all

---

[30] Fiegehen, Lansley & Smith (1977:27–9).

[31] Compare, for example, Townsend's *Poverty in the United Kingdom* and Danziger & Weinberg's *Fighting Poverty*.

citizens shall have the means for a decent level of consumption, but that no one shall be excluded from a decent way of life. There is a perfect correspondence between this ideology and the meaning of poverty understood as relative deprivation. This concept of poverty is, therefore, the appropriate one for the present purpose.

This is not to say that poverty is thereby measured objectively—no such objectivity is possible—or that this concept is always the right one. I am only saying, that in view of how policy goals happen to be formulated, relative deprivation is the right concept of poverty in a discussion of the effectiveness of the large welfare state.

The Measurement of Poverty

While we have two competing definitions of poverty, the literature offers only one method of measurement: the income poverty line. The poverty line has been the basic tool in empirical research, whether the concept has been subsistence minimum or relative deprivation and whether the objective has been to estimate the incidence of poverty, to calculate the 'poverty gap' (the total income transfer needed to bring all those who have an income below the poverty line up to the poverty line), or to analyse the composition of the poverty population (e.g. the distribution of income among the poor or the socio-demographic composition of this group). The difference between studies based on the subsistence minimum concept and those based on relative deprivation lies more on the conceptual side than on the measurement side. They use different concepts of poverty, but the same method of measurement, only applied somewhat differently. Poverty has been given a new meaning but is still measured as if nothing had happened on the conceptual side.

The income poverty line has several attractions. It is an intuitively simple measure, it enables such estimates as the incidence of poverty and the poverty gap, and it helps to make results easy to present and interpret and, thereby, to give poverty research a political impact. But the method also has several weaknesses, and while the attractions are mostly practical and political, the weaknesses are theoretical and have the effect of bringing arbitrariness into the measurement of poverty. This is the case whether the underlying concept is subsistence minimum or relative deprivation, but it is particularly true for the measurement of poverty defined as relative deprivation.

Direct and indirect measures

The main problem is that the income poverty line is a method of measurement which fits the subsistence minimum concept but not the relative deprivation concept. Subsistence minimum is an indirect concept of poverty and the income poverty line is an indirect measure. Relative deprivation is a direct concept of poverty but no direct method of measurement corresponding to this concept has been developed.[32] Instead, the indirect method of measurement has been retained, and poverty research has run into problems arising from the lack of correspondence between concept and measurement.

For Rowntree and others who have used the subsistence minimum approach it has been a cumbersome but, in principle, simple task to determine the poverty line. All one needs to do is to decide on a list of necessities, calculate the cost of purchasing the items on the list, and then set the poverty line at a disposable income equivalent to this cost. The main criticism against this approach is that poverty is defined in relation to a more or less arbitrary mode of consumption which the researcher in question, or the experts he consults, decides is a necessary minimum. This criticism is justified, but this arbitrariness is still considerably less than the arbitrariness of the poverty lines which have been suggested under the influence of the relative deprivation concept.

While the subsistence minimum concept at least gives some rationale for where to set the poverty line, the relative deprivation concept gives no guidelines at all as to exactly what income separates the poor from the non-poor. Additional criteria are, therefore, needed in order to determine the level of the poverty line. The most common of such criteria have been the policy definition method, by which the poverty line is set at a level which has been expressed through the political process as a minimum income (for

[32] A step towards direct measurement was taken by Townsend (1979) in the estimate of an 'index of deprivation' based on a series of way of life indicators. This index, however, was not used to measure poverty directly but instead to determine the level of the poverty line, and proved as such to be not very successful.

instance the minimum benefit in a public pension system) and the relative income method, by which the poverty line is defined as a fraction of the average income level (for example at 50 per cent of median household disposable income per unit of consumption). These criteria, however, are not part of the concept of poverty or derived from it but are taken out of thin air and result in measurements which are not theoretically justified. Because the concept of poverty does not determine a poverty line and because the criteria for doing this do not follow from the concept, there is no unbroken chain of logical deduction between the theoretical concept of poverty and the operational method of measurement.

Under these circumstances it should come as no surprise that the combination of the relative deprivation concept and the income poverty line method has resulted in some odd statistics on poverty. Not only does every researcher have his own poverty line, so that each study comes up with different figures for what is in principle the same phenomenon, but also most of the statistics have some strange characteristics of their own. With the use of the relative income method, for example, measured poverty will change only if, and whenever, the distribution of income changes, and measured poverty will be the same in two countries with the same distribution of income even if the level of income is twice as high in one country as in the other. The use of the policy definition method can result in even more intriguing paradoxes. If, for example, the poverty line is tied to the minimum benefit in the public pension system, measured poverty will go up overnight if the minimum benefit level is raised, even though more income will thereby be transferred to those at the bottom of the income distribution. Effective anti-poverty policies will result in more measured poverty! Or, in a comparison between two nations, measured poverty can be higher in the nation which has the highest average level of income and where the distribution is less inegalitarian, if this nation has a more generous minimum benefit.[33]

Conclusions such as these simply do not make sense. Instead of accepting them on face value only because we are told that they are the result of a relative as opposed to an absolute concept of poverty, we should look behind the results and ask what has gone wrong in

[33] Which is precisely why Beckerman (1979a) in his study for the ILO concluded that the incidence of poverty was higher in Norway than in Belgium.

the process that has generated such absurd conclusions. When Rowntree started his research, he chose a concept of poverty which corresponded to the way the problem of poverty was generally perceived at the time and developed a method of measurement which was logically derived from his theoretical concept. Since then our societies have changed and with them the nature of poverty and our perception of it. New concepts are justified. The relative deprivation concept is a reasonable understanding of the problem today, at least when seen in relation to the ideology of the large welfare state. On this score, contemporary poverty research has the same quality as Rowntree's had. But what the contemporary approach does not have is a method of measurement derived from its own concept. It has, instead, continued to use a method which is derived from the very concept it has rejected and which is not justified in its own concept. Some studies have tried to get around the problem of arbitrariness by using several poverty lines at different levels, but many arbitrary poverty lines is hardly less arbitrary than few arbitrary poverty lines. Studies based on the relative deprivation concept and using the income poverty line method have had to take criteria for determining the poverty line out of thin air. Their results are more to be seen as statements of opinion than as scientific estimates of the extent of poverty.

Income and poverty

A second problem with the income poverty line is that it measures poverty with the single indicator of income. Income, of course, is a relevant and important factor in poverty. But to know a person's or a family's income is not necessarily enough to determine if they are poor, and certainly not if poverty is defined as relative deprivation. This has been pointed out previously by, for example Kincaid, who has made the point that '. . . lack of money is only one element in a complex of deprivations which make up the experience of poverty . . .'[34] and who has emphasized 'political poverty', that is the lack of ability on the part of the poor to exert political influence and thereby to improve their situation through the political channel (or in other words their exclusion from political participation). According to Atkinson, '. . . an important objection to the use of the

[34] Kincaid (1973:172).

official poverty standards is that they are based purely on money income and ignore other aspects of deprivation. No account is taken of poor quality housing, schools or health care, which may or may not be associated with low money incomes. No account is taken of the limited availability of community facilities, parks, playgrounds, transport, and of other environmental inequalities'. [35]

If poverty is defined directly by way of life, as in the relative deprivation concept, it should be obvious that the indirect indicator of income is insufficient, (since no one, presumably, would argue that way of life is totally determined by income). But even if poverty is defined indirectly it is highly problematic to rely for measurement on the single indicator of income. The same income does not buy everyone the same consumption. Income is useful only in markets, but what we get out of markets depends not only on our income but also on other resources which influence how we are able to use our income, for example, education, knowledge, and information. The market is not the same for all. Consumption can be acquired outside of the market, for example by home production, or through 'connections'. It has proved exceedingly difficult to measure income accurately. As early as 1962, Richard Titmuss, in *Income Distribution and Social Change*, demonstrated conclusively not only that income is a problematic indicator of welfare but also that income-as-we-are-able-to-measure-it is usually an inaccurate indicator even of what it is supposed to measure, that is of economic resources. There are non-monetary incomes which are difficult to incorporate realistically. For data, one usually has to rely either on surveys or tax return information and both these sources have serious shortcomings, in particular for recording high and low incomes. Other economic resources than income, particularly wealth, are often either ignored or at best measured superficially. Measured income usually reflects only the immediate economic situation which may often differ a good deal from the normal, long-term or permanent situation.

Of course, no one would want to say that poverty has nothing to do with income. Low consumption is strongly influenced by low income, and low consumption is part of what it means to be excluded from normal life in an affluent society. But consumption is not determined by income, and poverty understood as relative

[35] Atkinson (1975:191).

deprivation is more than low consumption. Income matters, but income alone does not decide inclusion or exclusion.

Poverty as Accumulated Deprivation

In the preceding paragraphs I have accepted the relative deprivation concept as an appropriate definition of poverty in relation to the ideology of the large welfare state, but rejected the income poverty line as a method of measurement under this concept. What now remains is to suggest an alternative and more direct method of measurement.

The criterion of poverty under the relative deprivation concept is exclusion from one's society or community. If this were interpreted literally our task would be to identify those who live in exclusion, but that would be neither practical nor convincing. It would be difficult to find meaningful operational criteria and there are types of exclusion, such as social isolation, which do not necessarily have anything to do with material deprivation. It is, instead, more fruitful to take exclusion as a slightly figurative expression and to understand the meaning of relative deprivation poverty as a standard of living which can be characterized as a state of general deprivation where ' . . . different types of deprivation mesh one into another, to create for those who must endure them a total situation shot through and through by one level of want after another', and where the different dimensions of poverty '. . . constitute an interrelated network of deprivations'.[36]

A state of general deprivation cannot be measured with either resource indicators or way of life indicators alone. Several indicators of various forms of deprivation are needed in order to identify a network of deprivations. Resource indicators alone can only say something about the probability of deprivation in way of life. Low income, for example, at least as we are able to measure it, may represent only a temporary and atypical situation which does not force the person in question to change his life style—he may for a while live off savings—and there may be ways of avoiding a life in deprivation in spite of low income, such as to live on someone else's income. To ascertain poverty we need to identify directly the con-

---

[36] Coats & Silburn (1970:50).

sequences we normally expect to follow from low income. On the other hand, to rely on way of life indicators alone, that is, to go all out for direct measurement, is also insufficient since people may live as if they were poor without being poor, as can be the case with misers or with the eccentric beggar who has £1 million in the bank. A 'different' way of life which is the result of 'different' preferences and free choice is not a result of deprivation and must, therefore, be excluded from the measurement of poverty. We need to establish not only that people live as if they were poor but that they do so because they do not have the means to avoid it. Poverty, in other words, is the result of an *accumulation of deprivation* in both resources and way of life. This is an operationalization of the problem of poverty which is faithful to the demanding nature of the concept and which takes in earnest the way the advocates of the relative deprivation concept have themselves explained and argued their understanding of the problem.

It is now established that the measurement of poverty should take into consideration both absolute and relative deprivation and use both resource and way of life indicators. These requirements can be combined by starting with low income defined by some 'relative standard', thereby acknowledging the relative nature of poverty and that low income is a necessary condition of poverty. We can, for example, say that the poor must be found among those who have an income below half of the median in the total population. This is to say that no one is poor unless their income is low and that they can be poor even with an absolute income which is not miserably low, if it is only decidedly behind the average income level in the population. But, in addition, we need to ask what absolute standard of living those who belong to the low-income group have so that we can remove from the measure of poverty those who have a low income (as we are able to measure it) but who for one reason or another still do not live in poverty, and thereby make sure that the relativization of the concept does not bring us beyond an absolute standard of living that it makes sense to speak of as poverty. This we can do by introducing additional indicators which are defined according to some 'absolute standard' of deprivation. The poor, then, are those who have a low income, relatively speaking, and a deprived way of life, absolutely speaking.

Appendix E contains an analysis of accumulated deprivation along these lines in Sweden in 1968 and 1981. The results can be summarized in four points (indicators and concepts are defined in the Appendix).

1. Low-income groups are defined in the usual way in relation to median income and turn out to have the expected size. For example, in the population 15 to 74 years of age, excluding students and school pupils, 7 per cent of all persons in 1968 and 5 per cent in 1981 belong to families with a disposable income per unit of consumption of less than half of the median for all families, and 3.6 and 3.1 per cent respectively belong to the lowest income group (below 40 per cent of the median).

2. The probability of deprivation as measured by other resources and way of life indicators is estimated in various income groups. As expected, this probability is generally higher in the low-income groups than in the rest of the population, but, contrary to what we would expect if income were a good indicator of poverty, the probability in the low-income groups of other forms of deprivation is generally not very high, and not very much higher than in the rest of the population. This shows that low-income groups are not homogeneous with regard to other material resources and aspects of way of life, and confirms that income alone is not a sufficient indicator of poverty.

3. Between 1968 and 1981, although the incidence of low income has not changed very much, the probability of other forms of deprivation has gone down a great deal in all income groups. For most indicators, the probability of deprivation has gone down more in the low-income groups than in the rest of the population, which means that their situation has improved in both absolute and relative terms and consequently that poverty must, by any standard, have gone down.

4. The incidence of accumulated deprivation is much lower than the incidence of low income. Although the incidence of low income has remained relatively high in 1981 compared to 1968, the incidence of accumulated deprivation is a great deal lower. The probability in the lowest income group of a small cash margin is down from 38 to 26 per cent, of low personal capability from 29 to 13 per cent, of crowded and low standard housing from 28 to 15 and from 54 to 10 per cent respectively, of not having been away on holiday last year from 75 to 53 per cent, and so on. The accumulation of more than two indicators is estimated with income (economic

resources), personal capability ('non-economic' resources), and housing quality (way of life). In 1968, 3.6 per cent of the population belonged to the lowest income group and 0.75 per cent were deprived as measured by all three indicators; in 1981, 3.1 per cent was still in the lowest income group but only 0.15 per cent were deprived on all three indicators.

I make modest claims for these estimates. I do not say that they show how much 'true poverty' there is—other indicators and different definitions could have been used. How much poverty you find depends, to repeat, above all on how you define the concept and what tools you use to measure it.

But I do claim this: the relative deprivation concept is relevant in relation to the ideology of the large welfare state but the income poverty line is not an appropriate method of measurement under this concept. The measurement of poverty is here approached with a method that follows from the relative deprivation concept of poverty. The use of this method reveals that low-income groups, as defined in the conventional way, are not homogeneous, either in other resources than income or in way of life. Their members are not similar to each other, nor distinctly different from the members of non-low-income groups. When other resources and way of life indicators are included in addition to income, in an attempt to single out a more homogeneous group of persons who live in a state of general deprivation, this group turns out to be a great deal smaller than conventionally defined low-income groups, and its size to have been reduced considerably over the period described.

There is, perhaps, nothing surprising in this, any more than it is surprising that poverty is found to be, more or less, stable, if the tool of measurement is a relative income poverty line. If we define poverty as low income and bad housing we should expect to find less poverty than if we define it by low income only, and if bad housing is defined according to some 'absolute standard' we should, over a period during which we know the quality of housing to have improved, expect to find less bad housing. But surprising or not, the use of this method and the estimates thereby produced show that the conclusion that poverty has prevailed at a relatively high and stable level in spite of the expansion of the welfare state—and the devastatingly negative verdict over the welfare state implicit in this conclusion—can be refuted.

All this is purely descriptive. It is shown that the extent of poverty has gone down but nothing is said about the causes of this development. I have not proved that the welfare state has reduced poverty but only dismissed estimates which have been taken as proof that it has not.

8

Equality

The redistributive ambition in the welfare state is to create, by way of social policies, a society of less inequality than there would have been had the policies in question not been enacted. Redistribution is thought to be necessary because the market, if left unchecked, would generate a more inegalitarian distribution than is acceptable in a democratic society, and it is thought to be useful because the result would be less misery for those who would otherwise be poor, and less division, tension, and conflict to the benefit of all. The question before us here is whether the strategy of redistribution is effective in reducing inequality.

The Meaning of Redistribution

Social scientists have studied this question in great detail but come up with strikingly different answers. Harold Wilensky, in his now classic comparative study, *The Welfare State and Equality*, published in 1975, concluded that '. . . taxes and benefits taken together have a highly egalitarian effect on income distribution'.[1] But John Goldthorpe and collaborators, in their massive *Social Mobility and Class Structure in Modern Britain*, found that over the last three or four decades up to the mid–1970s, in spite of continuous economic growth, transformation of the occupational division of labour, and large scale educational and other political reforms, '. . . no significant reduction in class inequality has in fact been achieved' and commented that the implications of their findings '. . . count as rather grave ones for . . . the strategy of seeking to

Terminology: For convenience, in this chapter I use the terms 'rich' and 'poor' freely in reference to the top and bottom parts of the income distribution. Distributions that are pro-poor are said to be 'progressive' and those that are pro-rich to be 'regressive'. Social services financed over public budgets are occasionally said to be 'free'.

[1] Wilensky (1975:94).

attack social inequalities via legislative and administrative measures of a piecemeal kind . . .'.[2]

In a study of income distribution in Sweden on the basis of data for 1979, Assar Lindbeck has found that taxes and cash transfers have the effect of radically modifying income inequality so that the resulting distribution of income is very different from the distribution of pre-tax/transfer (market) income. 'The most striking conclusion from this study is perhaps that purchasing power, and hence probably also "economic well-being", in a Welfare State like Sweden, is not tightly connected with the contributions of households in the official production system . . .'.[3] But, in Britain, Julien Le Grand, in a study of non-cash transfers, has concluded, 'Almost all public expenditure on the social services . . . benefits the better off to a greater extent than the poor (and that) it is difficult to avoid the implication that the strategy of promoting equality through public expenditure on the social services has failed'.[4]

Although these studies are not strictly comparable—they are undertaken in different countries, apply to different aspects of inequality, and use different methodologies—they address basically the same question: have the policies of the welfare state succeeded in reducing inequality in these nations? Wilensky and Lindbeck interpret their evidence as implying that they have, Goldthorpe and Le Grand that they have not.

One of the reasons for disagreement among social scientists about the effectiveness of the welfare state is that the concepts of inequality and redistribution are not always understood in the same way. If we disagree about what inequality or redistribution is, we may, of course, easily disagree about how much inequality there is or how effective redistributive policies are. There is room for different interpretations of these concepts in response to at least five questions.

Firstly, inequality of what? One possible answer here is opportunity; there is equality in society if everyone has the same opportunity in, for example, education and employment. This is the concept of equality in Goldthorpe's study. A second possible answer is result. Equality of opportunity is not enough; what matters

[2] Goldthorpe *et al.* (1980:252).
[3] Lindbeck (1983:253).
[4] Le Grand (1982:3, 132).

is the results which people end up with. Even if everyone has the same opportunity for education, there is no equality if they still end up with very different incomes. This is the concept of inequality in, for example, Lindbeck's study. Equality of result can further be interpreted in two different ways, in terms of living conditions or of utility. In the first case, equality is a question of the distribution of objective conditions, in redistribution analysis usually income, and in the second case of subjective satisfaction. The latter of these interpretations has not had much impact on empirical redistribution research since it would require the measurement of the utility and dis-utility which different people derive from the outcome of redistributive policies, and that has not been possible in a meaningful way beyond the kinds of legitimacy studies discussed in Chapter 3.

Secondly, redistribution by way of what policies? The ideal answer would be all policies. In a democracy, no policy should be enacted if it is not believed to be to the benefit of the population. All policies potentially have distributive effects since they may benefit some people more than others. A frequent question, for example, is of who benefits from environmental regulations. Although all policies can be discussed from a distributional point of view, the idea of estimating empirically the net redistributive effect of all public policies has (as yet) been regarded as too wild an ambition to be accepted as a practical challenge.

A slightly less ambitious answer is all fiscal policies, that is, all policies which have the form of public revenues or expenditures. This answer has the advantage of limiting attention to policies which imply a flow of money (or things that can be bought for money) back and forth between government and population and hence offering a common denominator for measuring the redistributive impact. The problem is that for some fiscal policies it is difficult to determine meaningfully between whom the money flows, the classical example being defence expenditure. But this ambition is still not so wild as to have been dismissed altogether, and it has been demonstrated that it is possible to do a reasonably meaningful job of estimating the redistributive impact of the entire public budget.[5]

---

[5] See e.g. Gillespie (1965); Ruggles & O'Higgins, and O'Higgins & Ruggles (1981).

In order to avoid some of the problems of this very broad approach, attention can be limited further to the household sector, that is, to fiscal policies where it is reasonably clear that the money flows between government and private households. Exactly where to draw the dividing line between the household sector and other sectors is far from obvious, but, for example, corporate taxation would typically be excluded through this limitation. This is the most common approach in redistribution research and can be described as an attempt to measure the redistributive impact of household transfers and taxes.

A final possible answer is one policy at a time. It can be argued that since different kinds of policies have different kinds of distributive effects, the very idea of analysing the effects of many or all policies at the same time is suspect, because it requires radically simplifying assumptions which may distort the results. Julien Le Grand, for example, in *The Strategy of Equality*, has for this reason limited his inquiry to one type of policy, public expenditure on social services, and has suggested that the difference between his results and what some broader studies have found may be a result of methodological problems in broader studies.

Thirdly, redistribution between whom? The classical problem of distribution is between the factors of production, mainly between labour and capital, land being an additional important factor in less advanced economies and know-how increasingly so in advanced economies. This issue is presently not central in empirical redistribution analysis, which—again—is for the most part limited to the household sector, but it occasionally comes in indirectly to the extent that the distribution of wealth is taken into consideration.

Within the household sector, a first possible answer is between population groups, for example, between income groups or socio-economic groups defined in terms of status or position, or between groups in different stages of the life cycle, for example, the young or middle aged (the gainfully employed) and the elderly (the retired). A second possiblity is to disaggregate further and to analyse inequality not between societal groups but between actual income units, either families/households or individuals. All these possibilities are represented in current research.

Fourthly, redistribution by way of what effects? A first distinction here is between primary and secondary policy effects. To illustrate:

If a new income tax is imposed on high-income households, this will
have the primary effect of making these households as much worse
off as they will have to pay additional taxes, and consequently of
equalizing the distribution of income in proportion to the distribution of the tax. But if high-income households modify their economic behaviour in response to the new tax burden—they may, for
example, work more or try to conceal some of their income from
taxation—there will be a secondary effect on the distribution of
income through their 'behavioural response' so that the new distribution is perhaps less inegalitarian than the old distribution but
not to the same extent as would follow from the primary effect.
Experimentation techniques have made it possible to take secondary effects into consideration, but empirical estimates of redistribution have, for the most part, been limited to primary effects.[6]

A second and related distinction is between direct and indirect
effects. Policies may affect inequality directly by changing the
streams of money or other economic resources between government and households, but they can also influence inequality indirectly by affecting the possibilities of households for acquiring
income of their own in the market. That can be the case with, for
example, economic policies which boost demand and create new
jobs or with anti-inflationary policies which increase unemployment. Redistribution studies are limited to direct effects, the simplified model being that first the market works out a certain
distribution of market income and then redistributive policies are
introduced, after the fact, to create a less inegalitarian distribution
of purchasing power or of consumption than that of market income
(cf. my distinction between redistributive and regulatory policies in
Chapter 1).

Finally, a fifth question is, redistribution compared to what? If
our question is how much redistribution is brought about through
the policies of the welfare state, the ideal answer is the distribution
after the influence of the welfare state compared to what the distribution would have been without the welfare state. However,
since this alternative distribution is unknown and since a situation
without any welfare state is unrealistic, two other methods of
comparison have been suggested. One is to compare the actual

---

[6] On the methodology of 'dynamic simulation', which in principle allows incorporation of secondary effects, see e.g. Orcutt, Caldwell & Wertheimer (1976).

distribution to a more or less realistic potential distribution, for example the distribution of income in a situation with progressive taxation compared to a situation with flat rate taxation.[7] The other method is to compare today's distribution to a previous distribution.[8] This 'counterfactual problem' is, as we shall see, one of the most difficult problems to tackle in the empirical analysis of redistribution.

These five questions represent the hurdles which need to be negotiated in order to reach an answer to the question posed at the beginning of the chapter. The researcher faces two problems. Theoretical choices have to be made with respect to all five questions. These choices form assumptions which influence the way redistribution is studied and the conclusions of the analyses. Such choices having been made, a practical methodology needs to be found for measuring the redistributive impact in a way that is faithful to the theoretical assumptions which are established. This has proved to be difficult. The main obstacle is the counterfactual problem to which no fully satisfactory solution has been found.

For the present purpose, some of the questions are already answered in the frame of reference of this book, as explained in the two introductory chapters. We are concerned with equality of result, interpreted as objective living conditions. Attention is limited to the effects of transfer and tax policies. The main emphasis will be on the redistribution of income between income units in the household sector. This more or less answers the first three questions, although more will need to be said about the concept of income and what precisely transfer and tax policies are. For the moment, the questions of the counterfactual and, related to that, of the interplay between primary and secondary effects remain open. We shall return to these questions later on by way of discussing what the implications might be of their various possible answers.

The Standard Method

The standard method of redistribution analysis is to compare the distributions of income 'before' and 'after' transfers and taxes and

---

[7] See e.g. Frantzén, Lövgren & Rosenberg (1975).
[8] See e.g. Gillespie (1978).

to take the difference between these distributions as a measure of the direction and degree of redistribution.[9] This result will henceforth be referred to as 'measured redistribution'. The main transfer and tax concepts are:

direct transfers (cash benefits, e.g. social security),
indirect transfers (in-kind benefits, e.g. health care and consumer subsidies),
direct taxes (e.g. personal income tax), and
indirect taxes (e.g. VAT).

The main income concepts are:

market income,
gross income,
disposable income, and
final income.

Market income is the sum of wages and salaries, income from self-employment, income from capital, occupational pensions, and private transfers (e.g. alimony, charities).[10] Gross income is the sum of market income and direct public transfers. Disposable income is gross income less direct taxes. Final income is the sum of disposable income and the income equivalent value of indirect transfers, minus indirect taxes.

This is a simple but ingenious and flexible model. The difference between the distributions of final income and of market income indicates the redistributive impact of the entire system of transfers and taxes. If we want to know only how redistributive direct transfers and taxes are, we can compare the distributions of disposable income and market income. The redistributive impact of any single policy component can be read out of the difference between the distributions of the income 'above' and 'below' this component, for

[9] According to Danziger, Haveman & Plotnick (1981:982–3), 'The redistributive effect of transfers is generally measured by comparing pretransfer and posttransfer income distributions'. According to Lindbeck (1983:227), 'The most used (method) is to make comparisons of various types of distributions—such as the distribution of factor income versus disposable income'.

[10] Instead of market income, many studies use factor income (market income less occupational pensions and private transfers). The distinction between market and factor income is of little practical importance in the present discussion and I will, in the following, for simplicity use the term market income in both cases. The British CSO estimates (see Table F1) use the term 'original income' instead of market income in order to avoid the implicit suggestion that this is the way income would have been distributed in a free market.

example disposable income as compared to gross income, for the impact of direct taxes. In principle, we can find out how much any policy item matters by simply retracting it from the model and seeing how this changes the distribution of the relevant income concept. For example, to measure the redistributive power of central taxes, we need only to see how the distribution of disposable income if central taxes are excluded from the estimates compares with the distribution of disposable income when central taxes are included along with other direct taxes.

Table F1 (in Appendix F) reproduces data on income redistribution in Britain in 1984. Such figures are produced annually by the Central Statistical Office by estimates pioneered by Leonard Nicholson.[11] The table illustrates the logic of the standard method, and the way of presenting the results can be taken as representative for this type of study.

The table demonstrates that the distribution of market income is highly inegalitarian, the households in the bottom quintile having average market incomes of only 2 per cent of the average for all households, while the average for top quintile households is 236 per cent. Direct transfers do a great deal to modify this inequality so that, in gross income, bottom quintile households are up to 32 per cent of the average for all households and top quintile households down to 205 per cent. Direct taxes are progressive, but less so in relation to gross income than direct transfers are in relation to market income. Indirect transfers are moderately progressive in relation to disposable income, and indirect taxes moderately regressive. The end result is that bottom quintile households have about half and top quintile households not quite double the average final income of all households. Equality there is perhaps not, but less inequality certainly.

The assumptions of an analysis such as the one presented in Table F1 are the following: Inequality is studied in terms of the distribution of income between income groups of households. The concept of income is a broad one which includes not only cash income but also the income equivalents of indirect transfers and taxes, for example of social services such as free education and health care. The policies covered are fiscal policies only and among them only

[11] Nicholson (1964).

transfers and taxes within the household sector.[12] Only direct and primary effects are taken into consideration. The base line of comparison is, in principle, the situation without any welfare state, the distribution of market income being an indication of how income is distributed 'before' transfers and taxes, and the distributions of the subsequent income concepts indicating the effects of tempering the market distribution with redistributive policies. As is commonly known, however, this last assumption is not followed up realistically in the method, since the distribution of observed market income under the influence of the welfare state is almost certainly different from the distribution of income we would have had without a welfare state. This will be explained more carefully below.

Given the assumptions of the standard method, there is now broad agreement about what its application has revealed about redistribution in the welfare state. Numerous studies of this kind have been conducted in a large number of countries over the last ten to fifteen years, and their methods, data, and conclusions have been compared in detail.[13] In spite of differences between countries in transfer and tax policies, general conclusions on measured redistribution have emerged which apply to most welfare state nations. In broad terms, these conclusions can be summed up in five points.

1. The entire system of transfers and taxes is redistributive in favour of the poor in the sense that there is less inequality in the distributions of disposable and final income than in the distributions of market and gross income.

2. This redistribution is caused primarily by the effects of direct transfers. The most important form of their redistribution is between households in the economically active population and households in the economically passive population, the largest net receiving group being old-age pensioners.

3. Taxes have, all together, little or no impact on the distribution of income. Direct income taxes are generally moderately pro-

---

[12] On standard method coverage, see Table F2, footnotes.

[13] See review articles by e.g. Ringen (1980); Danziger, Haveman & Plotnick (1981); Saunders (1984); Uusitalo (1985). For a more recent collection of conference papers covering a number of countries, see *Journal of Social Policy* 1985/3. For recent comparative studies, see Ringen (1986); Smeeding, O'Higgins & Rainwater, forthcoming.

gressive, payroll taxes (employees' social security contributions) flat or moderately regressive, and indirect taxes moderately regressive.

4. Indirect transfers all together tend to be distributed moderately in favour of the poor but this effect is considerably less than that of direct transfers. Some indirect transfers, such as higher education, tend to be pro-rich (or pro-middle-class). Conclusions about indirect transfers are controversial because of methodological problems in establishing them.

5. Comparative studies are scarce, but the similarity of findings for countries with different transfer and tax systems is a recurring theme in the literature. Reviews of the literature from several countries have emphasized similarity more than difference.

In other words, these studies have found the *degree* of redistribution to be considerable and the main *mechanism* of redistribution to be direct transfers. Very few will probably be surprised to hear that the welfare state has some effect in the direction of equalizing the distribution of income, but we shall later have reason to discuss whether the standard method accurately represents the degree of 'true redistribution'. It may be somewhat surprising that the primary mechanism of redistribution is transfers and that taxes do not matter much; more will be said about this, too, later on. It is certainly surprising that there is little difference between systems, which is to say that, although the welfare state matters, the *type* of welfare state does not matter. If this is true, the implication is that among welfare states, such as they can be observed today, no more redistribution is produced in large ones than in small ones and that, after redistributive policies have been developed to some scope, their further expansion should not be expected to produce additional redistributive effectiveness. Needless to say, this is a conclusion of great importance for the present study, considering its emphasis on the large welfare state. It might be added that this conclusion stems mainly from the observation that independent studies in many countries have, broadly speaking, come to the same kinds of conclusions. Since these studies are usually not directly comparable, what we have is perhaps more an impression than a conclusion. But the evidence from standard method studies is still relatively firm on this point. Even in the United States, with its relatively low level of redistributive policies, it has been observed, as we have seen, that 'most easy gains have been made', and such evidence as has until recently been available from careful comparative studies supports the impression. Hence, a comparison between Britain and the United States finds that '. . . although the details of tax and expenditure programs in the US and the UK differ considerably, their overall redistributive impact appears to be remarkably similar'.[14]

We shall return to all of these issues later. For the moment, if we accept the conclusions from standard method studies on face value, should we on this evidence say that the welfare state has been a success in terms of redistributing income?

This question has, for the most part, been answered affirmatively. Danziger, Haveman and Plotnick have summarized the evidence on the effects of direct transfer programmes in the United States around 1980 and concluded that these programmes have reduced income poverty by about 75 per cent and income inequality by about 19 per cent.[15] In a later study, they have shown that changes in anti-poverty policies contributed both to the decline of the American poverty rate from the mid–1960s to the mid–1970s, and to its subsequent increase into the early 1980s.[16] In Britain, O'Higgins has concluded, for the period throughout the 1970s and into the early 1980s, '. . . that state welfare plays a valuable, if limited, role in increasing the share of resources going to lower income groups' and that although social welfare spending '. . . has not brought about greater overall equality over the period studied . . . it has combated and significantly modified the impact of pressures towards increased inequality'.[17] In Denmark, Hansen has demonstrated in an analysis of data for 1977 that there is considerably less inequality in the distribution of income after transfers and taxes than of pre-tax/transfer income and that the net redistribution is in the scale of about 10 per cent of total income.[18] In Sweden, Gustafsson in an analysis for 1981 has found that direct transfers and taxes reduce income inequality by almost a half.[19] And in a summary of available evidence from a number of countries,

---

[14] O'Higgins & Ruggles (1981:322).
[15] Danziger, Haveman & Plotnick (1981:1019).
[16] Danziger, Haveman & Plotnick (1986:68–9).
[17] O'Higgins (1983:14; 1985a:303).
[18] Hansen (1986:14).
[19] Gustafsson (1984b:55).

Uusitalo concludes that the impact of transfers and taxes on reducing income inequality '. . . has been significant'.[20]

Yet it is not absolutely clear that this is a fair or non-controversial interpretation of the evidence. For those who have thought that progressive taxation was the road to equality, the evidence is disastrous, as it is for those who have taken it for granted that the large welfare state is more redistributive than the small one. For those who have thought that free or subsidized services would bring equality, it is disappointing. Only those who have seen direct transfers as the principal element in the strategy of redistribution can be reasonably satisfied, and this might be a slightly trivial conclusion since cash transfers, for the most part and by definition, go to individuals or households who have little or no income from other sources, such as the elderly, the disabled, the ill, and the unemployed. The welfare state, the cynic might say, has achieved redistribution only with the help of policies which, once enacted, are unavoidably redistributive; other policies which have been intended to be redistributive but whose impact depends on how they are implemented have all turned out to have little or no effect.[21]

On the other hand, it may have been unrealistic to expect much redistribution from taxes and social services. Taxes are needed to raise revenue, and a high level of taxation must necessarily be borne by the mass of the population on near-median income levels. The higher the level of taxation, over a certain point, the more it usually becomes necessary to use indirect taxes and the more difficult it is to maintain a progressive profile of total taxation. The primary purpose of free services is to meet needs (e.g. for health care) or demands (e.g. for education). A good distribution in terms of needs or demands is not necessarily redistributive in terms of income. And although it may be trivial to demonstrate that income maintenance transfers are redistributive, this is nonetheless how they work, and they are, of course, far from trivial for those who depend on them.

---

[20] Uusitalo (1985:174).

[21] Direct transfers aim mainly to redistribute income from the economically active to the economically passive populations (vertical redistribution). Progressive taxation is a main instrument for reducing inequalities among the economically active (horizontal redistribution). These conclusions suggest that the welfare state is effective in reducing vertical inequalities but ineffective in reducing horizontal ones.

In conclusion so far, then, it can be said that, as judged by standard method evidence, the welfare state is not a redistributional failure but nor is it an unconditional success story. In order to pin it down more precisely between the extreme possibilities of total success and total failure, the rest of this chapter will first, through a critical discussion of the standard method, offer a more careful interpretation of the available evidence, in particular with regard to the degree of redistribution. This is a much needed discussion, for although everyone is aware that the standard method is based on a selection of certain assumptions among several that are theoretically possible, and that this selection influences its conclusions,[22] the tendency in the literature is at best to pay lip service to these problems and to accept uncritically the findings of standard method studies as authoritative. Thereafter, new evidence from international comparisons of income redistribution will be introduced. This material will enable us to say more about how different from or similar to each other industrial nations are in this respect, and more about the mechanisms of redistribution.

The Degree of Redistribution

There are a number of problems in the standard method which need to be observed in order to interpret correctly the results of studies using the method. The problems where the choice of assumptions are most consequential are the following three.

First, the counterfactual problem: what is the alternative distribution against which the distribution after transfers and taxes should be compared in order to determine if there is less inequality? There is no disagreement about the ideal answer to this. The actual distribution of disposable or final income under the prevailing system of transfers and taxes should be compared to the potential distribution of the same income concepts under a system where transfers and taxes are different and where everything else is equal. The redistributive effect of a system of high transfers and taxes should be measured in the difference between the distribution of income resulting from this system and the distribution that would

---

[22] See e.g. O'Higgins (1980a); Le Grand (1983); Uusitalo (1985).

have resulted from a system with lower (or no) transfers and taxes, controlling for all other differences.

However, such alternative distributions are necessarily unknown. It is, therefore, not possible to implement the theoretical ideal in empirical studies. Some proxy which is practically observable is needed for the potential distribution which cannot be observed directly. The choice of proxy in the standard method is observed market income in the prevailing system. The problem with this choice is that the distribution of market income is itself influenced by public policies, both by economic policies which regulate the market and by transfers and taxes through the behavioural response of economic actors to these policies. The result of these influences is that observed market income in a system with relatively high transfers and taxes is more inegalitarian than any realistically possible alternative income distribution in a system with lower levels of transfers and taxes, and hence that the distribution of income after transfers and taxes is compared to an unrealistically inegalitarian base line distribution.

This has some important consequences for measured redistribution. The redistributive impact of direct transfers is overestimated since this distribution is compared directly to the unrealistically inegalitarian distribution of market income. It may be that the redistributive impact of taxes and indirect transfers is also overestimated, but this is less certain since these distributions are compared, not to market income, but to gross or disposable income. This overestimation of the impact of direct transfers is one of the reasons why standard method studies have been taken to show that direct transfers are the main mechanism of redistribution and that taxes matter comparatively less. Taking the counterfactual problem into consideration thereby brings this conclusion about the balance between the impacts of transfers and taxes into doubt. Furthermore, the redistributive impact of the entire system of transfers and taxes is overestimated, since the actual distribution of post-tax/transfer income is compared to a pre-tax/transfer distribution which is more inegalitarian than the potential distribution under a realistically alternative system. This brings into doubt the general conclusion from standard method studies about the degree of redistribution in the system.

Second, there is the problem of allocating social services; who benefits from the production and distribution of free services? The standard method assumption is that social services are a form of in-kind income and consequently that the consumer has the entire benefit. However, a good case can be made that there are benefits for non-consumers as well. Everyone benefits from a high educational level through its impact on economic performance and cultural life, and non-consumers of health care benefit from the assurance of knowing that health care will be available if and when they should need it. While the standard method, by allocating all social services to consumers, finds them to be moderately progressive, the allocation resulting from the alternative assumption would show them to be either less progressive, distributively neutral, or regressive.

Finally, there is the limitation to the household sector. Here again, the ideal is clear: since all public expenditures and revenues ultimately affect private households and benefit some more than others, they ought all to be included in the analysis of redistribution. This is not easy to do, but experiments have shown, and it can be argued logically, that the result of including a broader range of expenditures and revenues would be to reduce measured redistribution compared with what is found in standard method studies that are limited to the household sector.

This brief summary is documented in more detail in Appendix F. It is there shown that, at all three of these decisive junctures, the standard method is based on assumptions which from a theoretical point of view are second-best choices and which have the effect of increasing measured redistribution compared to the expected result, given any of the alternative theoretical assumptions. Additional methodological issues discussed in Appendix F generally have the same effect. To these interpretations should be added an important qualification. Given the availability of 'generous' direct transfers and free services, there are a great many people, notably among the elderly, who are almost totally dependent on public transfer income and whose way of life depends on the serivces they have become accustomed to. Clearly, should the direct transfers and services which are now available be eliminated or seriously cut back, many of these people would fall into poverty. But this is not the same as to say that they would have been poor in a different system with less 'generous' social policies (although there is every reason to suspect that there would have been more poverty) because people would have had to adapt differently to a different system and, in some way or other, to have had more income from other sources. What can be said, however—and here services may be as important as cash transfers—is that they would, in a different system, have had a different life style, which may be as significant as having a different income. Whereas they now depend on public transfers and free services, they would, in a different system, have been more dependent on earnings, savings, or private transfers, and on services bought in the market or provided by family or charity. One possible consequence of this, as discussed in Chapter 6, could have been a life style of less independence. In the final analysis, the welfare state redistributes not only income but also life styles.

The choice of assumptions in the standard method is mostly dictated by necessity. The theoretically best choices do not lend themselves to practical implementation in empirical studies. The use of second-best assumptions is, therefore, no criticism of the standard method. But the consequence of these choices is, all the same, that a systematic bias is introduced into standard method results whereby the redistributive impact both of transfers and of the entire system of transfers and taxes is overestimated.

The Mechanisms of Redistribution

This section addresses the question of the importance of the *type* of welfare state for redistributive effectiveness. Does a higher level of transfers and taxes produce more redistribution?

This question is approached by comparing standard method results for countries with different levels of transfers and taxes. The difference in measured redistribution is taken to express a difference in redistributive effectiveness.[23]

The cross-national comparison of income distribution and redistribution has long suffered from a lack of adequate data. Many nations have good income statistics for their own purposes but these

---

[23] One should here bear in mind the shortcomings of the standard method. A difference in measured redistribution between two countries may be influenced through the secondary effect of redistributive policies on the distribution of market income. We therefore do not escape the counterfactual problem by moving from analyses of single countries to comparisons of several countries. But it may be hoped that the importance of the counterfactual problem is less in the analysis of differences in measured redistribution between several countries than in the analysis of redistribution in single countries.

statistics are usually not directly comparable to each other. Most available international comparisons are based on already-published statistics which are not strictly comparable and are, therefore, as their authors have been careful to warn, highly uncertain.[24] In order to have more reliable comparisons, attempts are now being made to produce comparable statistics from co-ordinated data rather than to rely on tables produced independently of each other in different countries and for other purposes. This was first done for pairs of nations[25] and has recently been brought further within the *Luxembourg Income Study (LIS)* in the establishment of a data bank of comparable income data for seven Western industrial nations.[26]

The results reported below are from the LIS data bank and from a separate comparison between Norway and Sweden based on tables estimated for this specific purpose from their respective income surveys by the Norwegian Central Bureau of Statistics and Statistics Sweden.[27] As far as international comparability goes, these are unique data. They are derived from national micro-data sets of good quality. These data sets have been rearranged according to common standards and definitions which constitute the best possible common denominator for all data sets. Identical procedures have been used in the analysis of all data sets. In this way a very high degree of comparability has been achieved so that these analyses can with confidence be taken to reveal real differences between countries and to be almost free of spurious differences which are caused by a lack of comparability in the data. Sensitivity tests have shown that the co-ordination and rearrangement of micro-data sets makes a considerable difference, in terms of measured inequality,

[24] See e.g. Sawyer (1976); Stark (1977).

[25] See e.g. Smolensky, Pommerehne & Dalrymple (1979); Ruggles & O'Higgins and O'Higgins & Ruggles (1981); Nygård (1984).

[26] The Luxembourg Income Study is an international research project that was started in 1983 by a group of economists and sociologists for the purpose of comparative analysis of income distribution and redistribution. The first phase of the project was financed by the Government of Luxembourg, hence the project name. The data bank is located at the *Center for Population, Poverty and Policy Studies* in Luxembourg. Financial support was later received from the Ford Foundation and by national grants to individual members of the project. The results of a first round of analyses of the LIS data bank were presented and discussed at a conference in Luxembourg in July 1985. Revised versions of the conference papers, on which the present summary is based, will be published in Smeeding, O'Higgins & Rainwater, forthcoming.

[27] For a fuller summary of LIS results and a more detailed analysis of the Norway-Sweden comparison, see Ringen (1986).

compared to analyses of already-published statistics.[28] Because of the quality of these rearranged data, the results derived from their analysis should be regarded as more firmly based than results of previous studies using an inferior methodology and conclusions from more or less impressionistic comparisons of the results of non-comparative studies.

These analyses are limited to cash income since it has at this stage of the research not been possible to include indirect transfers and taxes while maintaining sufficient comparability.

Difference and Similarity

The Luxembourg Income Study represents the first opportunity we have to compare the distribution of income in several industrial nations with the use of data which are truly comparable. The result of this comparison is to shatter the impression of similarity and, instead, to lead us to emphasize how different these nations are both in the distribution of income and the level of transfers and taxes.

A selection of LIS statistics is reproduced in Table G1 (in Appendix G). These statistics show that there are very considerable differences in the distributions of market and gross income as well as of disposable income between the seven nations that are included (Britain, Canada, Germany, Israel, Norway, Sweden, and the United States). Germany has the most inegalitarian distribution (the gini coefficient for disposable income is almost twice as high as in Sweden, the country with the least inegalitarian distribution). The difference is even greater if we compare only distributions among elderly families. The relative standard of living of elderly families is between almost on a par with the national average, in Israel, and only two-thirds of that level, in Britain. The incidence of measured poverty[29] is between 5 per cent, in Norway and Sweden, and 17 per cent, in the United States, and the incidence of low income among single parent families is only slightly above the 'expected' 2 out of 10 in Israel as compared to almost 6 out of 10 in the United States.

---

[28] Ringen (1986).
[29] I here use the term measured poverty to distinguish it from poverty as discussed in Chapter 7.

It is further shown that there is as much difference in transfer and tax levels as there is in inequality. On average for all families, public transfers contribute between 8 and 28 per cent to gross income, in Israel and Sweden respectively. Direct taxes are between 15 and 30 per cent of gross income. As one would expect, taxes are generally higher in countries with higher levels of transfers (although this correlation is not perfect, Israel being the most notable exception). In consequence, the redistributive potential as expressed in the level of transfers and taxes is vastly different between these nations.

Finally, the LIS analyses confirm the conventional standard method conclusion that the system of transfers and taxes has an equalizing influence on the distribution of income: disposable income is less inegalitarian than market income. But it is not confirmed that this is mainly because of transfers and that taxes do not matter. Since disposable income is less inegalitarian than gross income, these estimates show that the system is redistributive not only on the transfer side but also on the tax side, and, therefore, generally that the income tax is progressive in relation to the distribution of gross income (Germany being the only exception). The balance between the effects of transfers and of taxes is analysed in more detail in the next paragraph.

Given these differences in both redistributive potential and inequality, there is reason to hypothesize that the two are related, the assumption being that the higher the redistributive potential, the more redistribution. This works out in the following way. There is a positive correlation between the level of transfers and taxes on the one hand and their redistributive impact on the other. The European countries in the comparison all have a higher level of transfers than do the non-European countries and, at the same time, achieve more redistribution via transfers, as expressed in the difference between the degree of inequality (measured by the gini coefficient) of gross and market income. The same correlation is found between the tax level and the redistributive impact of taxes, as expressed in the difference between the distributions of gross and disposable income, although this is perhaps less perfect, with Germany contradicting the general rule. Hence, in these comparisons, we find that the redistributive result is closely and positively associated with the redistributive potential. This suggests considerable effectiveness in the system, on both the transfer side and the tax side, in relation to the redistributive goal.

This redistributive effectiveness does not, however, translate into a positive correlation between the redistributive potential and 'final' inequality, as measured in the distribution of disposable income. Transfers and taxes do influence inequality by redistributing market income, but final inequality is also influenced by other factors, such as those which determine the distribution of market income in the first place. Because of redistribution there is less inequality than there would otherwise have been, but more redistribution in one country than in another does not necessarily mean less final inequality. Germany, for example, has the most inegalitarian distribution of disposable income, but this is not because of a lack of redistribution in its transfer and tax system. The reason is, instead, that redistribution starts from a more inegalitarian distribution of market income in Germany than in any of the other countries.

A systematic correlation over these seven nations, between transfer and tax levels on the one hand and the distribution of disposable income on the other, shows that Sweden is a case of its own—the highest levels of transfers and taxes and the least inegalitarian distribution—but that there is otherwise no systematic pattern.[30] For example: Germany, Britain, and Norway have about the same level of transfers but very different degrees of inequality. The same is true, although to a lesser degree, for Canada, Israel, and the United States. Israel has about the same tax level as Sweden, but much more inequality. Britain and Norway are close to each other in inequality, in spite of a much higher level of taxation in Norway.

In spite of the relative lack of association between the level of transfers and final inequality, we do find that the higher the level of transfers and taxes is, the stronger their redistributive impact. These simple correlations, therefore, support the hypothesis that the redistributive potential of a system matters for its redistributive effectiveness. However, the LIS material does not allow more than a cursory and suggestive analysis of this question. The most important finding of the Luxembourg Income Study is the degree of difference between the industrial nations, a finding which contradicts and refutes the previous impression of similarity.

---

[30] This holds true also if inequality is correlated with the sum of transfers and taxes and if it is measured by the poverty rate instead of the gini coefficient.

Level and profile

The neighbouring countries of Norway and Sweden are probably more similar to one another in economic and political structure than any other pair of nations in the Western industrial world. They are both small, simple, stable and traditionally egalitarian societies, affluent, archetypal large welfare states, long dominated by social democratic politics and strong centralized trade union movements.[31] The difference in income distribution and redistribution between these two countries might reasonably be taken as a kind of 'minimal' expected difference between any of the industrial nations.

Since the comparison between Norway and Sweden is between only two countries, since these countries are similar to one another in economic and social structure, since their statistical agencies use almost identical procedures for recording income statistics, and since the rearrangement of the data used in this comparison has benefited from the experience of compiling the LIS data bank, these data have some advantages over the LIS data regarding comparability. The technical differences between these data and the LIS data are mostly of little or no practical significance, but there is one important exception. In the data used in the comparison between Norway and Sweden, employers' social security contributions are incorporated, by estimates based on the wage data in the respective surveys. It is assumed that employers' contributions are shifted on to labour. These contributions are, therefore, counted as part of personal income and personal taxes and added to other incomes on the income side and to other taxes on the tax side.

Norway and Sweden have different tax systems. In Norway, employers pay a social security contribution of 16.8 per cent of wages (with some regional differentiation) and employees a roughly flat rate payroll tax of about 10 per cent and a progressive income tax. In Sweden, employers pay a social security contribution of 38.7 or 43.9 per cent, and employees an income tax which has no earmarked payroll tax component. (These figures are for 1982.) If employers' social security contributions were ignored,

---

[31] This basic similarity is reflected in, for example, almost identical levels of average gross income, almost identical distributions of market income, and almost identical demographic structure as measured by the distribution of family size across income groups. See Ringen (1986) and Table G2.

which is common in income distribution studies, the comparison between these two countries would be based on a non-uniform tax concept because of formalistic reasons which are irrelevant in the present context. This is the case in the LIS comparisons, as it is in most other available international comparisons. By incorporating employers' contributions we compare taxes defined identically in both countries. The reasons for assuming *all* of the employers' social security contributions to be shifted on to labour are that this appears to be the least arbitrary procedure,[32] that social security benefits are included on the transfer side, and that public expenditures are, in the standard method, taken as given at their present actual level. If employers' social security contributions were reduced and public expenditures remained constant, government would have to take additional revenue from some other source, such as direct taxes on households or indirect taxes which would eventually be shifted on to consumers. Employers would now be able to pay employees higher wages, employees would of course claim this 'available' wage, and they should be expected to be able to substantiate this claim by arguing that they would otherwise end up with a lower standard of living because of a restructuring of the tax system. The standard method estimates income and tax components in the present system, and does not compare the present system to an alternative one. Since social security contributions are earmarked for (mostly cash) benefits to households, it is, given this method, reasonable that they are fully incorporated in the estimates.

The comparison between Norway and Sweden is summarized in Table G2 (in Appendix G). This comparison confirms the impression of difference that we have seen in the previous paragraph. Even between these two basically similar countries there are clear differences both in the distribution of disposable income and in the level of transfers and taxes. Sweden has a less inegalitarian distribution and higher levels of both transfers and taxes. The most

---

[32] Holmlund (1983) has estimated that about half of the increase in social security contributions in Sweden (which are all carried by employers) from 1951 to 1979 was shifted on to labour. But this is not to say that the same proportion would be shifted on to labour from a *reduction* in social security contributions today or that the same proportion is shifted on in the Norwegian system where both structure and rates are different.

significant difference is in the level of taxation.[33] On average for all families, disposable income in Sweden is only 56 per cent of gross income, as compared to 69 per cent in Norway. Public transfers contribute 19 per cent to gross income in Sweden and 14 per cent in Norway.

It is further seen, again in accordance with the LIS results, that the system is redistributive on both the transfer side and the tax side. As usual in standard method results, most of the redistribution appears to be through transfers, but the income tax, too, is clearly progressive and the distribution of disposable income a great deal less inegalitarian than the distribution of gross income.[34] These are both high tax systems and the progressivity of the income tax in

[33] This reflects a difference between the two nations in the balance of public and private consumption. Public expenditure relative to GDP is about 10 percentage points higher in Sweden than in Norway. This is explained mainly by the higher level in Sweden of public expenditure for social service, 21 per cent of GDP as compared to 12 per cent in Norway. (Figures for 1982, according to OECD: *National Accounts 1971–1983*, Vol II.)

[34] In other words, following up on footnote 21, the system is shown to be effective in reducing both vertical and horizontal inequalities. These conclusions on tax and transfer levels and the redistributive profile of direct taxes depend rather strongly on the incorporation of employers' social security contributions. Without employers' social security contributions, the transfer level relative to gross income is 13.6 per cent in Norway and 21.0 per cent in Sweden and the tax level 24.1 and 29.8 per cent respectively. This methodologically inferior but more common way of comparison makes the two countries look less different from each other and gives the appearance that most of the difference is found on the transfer side, which is more in accordance with conventional standard method results. The exclusion of employers' social security contributions affects the conclusions on distributive profiles as in the table below, here illustrated with estimates for Sweden where the effect is the greater because of their higher level. The distribution of disposable income is not affected (cf. Table G2). The distributions of market and gross income are less inegalitarian and the income tax less progressive. The general conclusions stand but the system is less redistributive. The income tax in particular is less progressive, both because its own profile is less progressive and because gross income is less inegalitarian. However, its progressivity is maintained. This is in accordance with the LIS results and shows that the progressivity of the income tax in the estimates does not depend on the incorporation of employers' social security contributions.

Quintile	1	2	3	4	5	Tot.
Market income	0.8	6.5	21.8	29.1	41.8	100.0
Transfers	47.9	33.5	10.3	4.6	3.7	100.0
Gross income	9.5	12.3	20.3	24.2	33.8	100.0
Income tax	6.4	11.8	15.9	23.6	42.1	100.0
Disp. income	14.8	14.3	17.3	22.5	31.1	100.0

these systems is not necessarily representative for all welfare states, although it does apply to all the LIS countries except Germany. But these comparisons at the very least show that redistribution through taxation is possible and suggest that this is the rule rather than the exception. The conclusion from previous studies that taxation tends not to have much redistributive impact is, therefore, not universally, and probably not even generally, valid. It should be remembered, though, that indirect taxes are not included here and that their inclusion would probably counterbalance somewhat the progressive profile of the income tax.

As to the redistributive effects of the level and profile of transfers and taxes, the comparison shows the following. The distribution of market income is about the same in both countries. This means that any difference in subsequent income concepts can be ascribed to the effects of transfers and taxes. Consequently, since the distribution of disposable income is less inegalitarian in Sweden than in Norway, we can conclude that the Swedish system has a stronger equalizing impact on the distribution of income than has the Norwegian system. The system with the highest levels of transfers and taxes also has the greatest redistributive effectiveness.

A closer look at the distributive profiles of transfers and taxes in the two countries reveals that the Swedish system is more effective than the Norwegian one in spite of a more progressive distribution in Norway of both transfers and taxes. In Norway, the lowest income quintile receives 53 per cent of total transfers and carries only 1 per cent of total taxes, as compared to 48 and 3.5 per cent in Sweden. But in spite of this, the lowest quintile has only 11 per cent of total disposable income in Norway as compared to almost 15 per cent in Sweden. Independently, transfers and taxes have a more equalizing profile in Norway than in Sweden, but the total system is still more redistributive in Sweden than in Norway. The explanation of this apparent paradox lies in the difference between these two countries in the *level* of transfers and taxes. The level of transfers, and in particular of taxes, is so much higher in Sweden than in Norway that this more than compensates for their slightly flatter distributive profiles.

To illustrate this further, potential distributions of gross and disposable income are simulated in the bottom section of Table G2 by applying, in both countries, the Swedish level of transfers and taxes and their Norwegian distributions, and assuming that market income remains unchanged. This results in more or less the same distribution of gross and disposable income in both countries (since market income has about the same distribution), and hence shows that it would have had more redistributive effect to increase transfers and taxes in Norway to their Swedish level than to adopt in Sweden the more equalizing Norwegian distributive profiles.

In other words, the difference in the redistributive effectiveness between these two systems is explained exclusively by the higher level of redistributive policies in Sweden. This, of course, is not to say that distributive profiles are without importance for redistribution, but only that there is in addition an independent effect on redistributive effectiveness of the level of transfers and taxes given their profile.

These findings are of considerable importance for the present discussion. Previous conclusions are contradicted in two ways. The level of redistributive policies is of importance for redistributive effectiveness, which is to say that the *type* of welfare state does matter. Since the difference in level is, in this comparison, found mainly on the tax side, it is here suggested that direct taxes have a greater impact than follows from their distributive profile alone and thereby than has generally been assumed to be the case on the basis of standard method evidence. Again, the importance of taxes in redistribution is underlined.

Conclusion

Standard method studies have generated a number of specific conclusions about income redistribution via transfer and tax policies. Direct transfers are strongly progressive and indirect transfers moderately so. Direct taxes may be moderately progressive but total taxation does not have much impact on the distribution of income. These conclusions apply to present-day welfare states across the board, with little or no difference depending on the level of transfers and taxes. Taken together, these specific conclusions show the redistributive effectiveness of transfer and tax systems to be considerable and warrant the overall conclusion that the welfare state has proved to be reasonably successful in relation to the redistributive ambition.

The result of this chapter's review of the standard method and the introduction of new evidence from comparative studies is that all the specific conclusions are found to be wrong but that the overall conclusion is still right.

Because sufficient attention has not been paid to the counterfactual problem, most interpretations of standard method results have overestimated the progressive profile of direct transfers. Because indirect transfers are unrealistically taken as in-kind income, they are mistakenly estimated as having a progressive profile. Because comparative studies have not been based on a uniform and proper concept of direct taxes, the progressivity in the distribution of direct taxes has been underestimated. For want of truly comparable data and reliable international comparisons, the difference between welfare states has been underestimated. The degree of difference between them and the importance of the level, as compared to the profile, of transfers and taxes for redistributive effectiveness has not been recognized.

These 'mistakes', however, do not all pull in the same direction as far as the overall conclusion is concerned. The overstatement of the progressivity of transfers lean towards its rejection, but the understatement of the progressivity of direct taxes and of the impact of the level of transfers and taxes lends it support. The net result is that the overall conclusion is not only substantiated, but strengthened. These findings show that there is redistributive effectiveness in the welfare state, not only due to policies which are by definition redistributive but also from policies whose effects depend on how they are implemented. It is here suggested that new redistributive efforts may reasonably be expected to pay off in more redistributive results. These latter conclusions, it is true, depend heavily on the results from the comparison between Norway and Sweden, two large welfare states in traditionally egalitarian societies which are not necessarily representative for other industrial nations. We should, perhaps, be careful in generalizing from these results, but at the very least they do show that there is, in the strategy of redistribution, a potential for effectiveness.

9
The Power of Reform

This study is concerned with two questions. First, does the welfare state work? And second, what does the answer to this question say about the possibility of political reform?

The idea behind the study is simple enough. The welfare state, once a futuristic vision, has now been tried. Its expansion in the industrial democracies during the 1960s and 1970s brought political reform to its peak of ambition. Because of the economic turmoils of the 1970s, this experiment in politics was set to the test of performing under hostile circumstances. The subsequent experience has been studied and recorded. By sorting out the evidence, it should be possible to establish what the various effects of welfare state policies are, and, thereby, to contribute to our understanding of the power of reform.

The welfare state is defined as a set of public policies, the immediate goal of which is to equalize the distribution of welfare. The policies in question are intended to redistribute welfare without fundamentally regulating the processes which in the first place generate inegalitarian distributions. Regulatory policies are not considered. This strategy of redistribution corresponds perfectly to the logic of reform: political goals are established but limitations imposed on the use of means so that only piecemeal ones are allowed.

Redistribution is analysed in the context of a democratic polity and within a framework of the theory of rational action. This leads to taking *choice* as the criterion against which policies are judged in order to determine how well or poorly they perform—a policy works if it does what those who choose it intend it to do—and to seeing *citizens*, ideally, as the choosers of policies. From here follows a broad analysis of political process, as distinguished from an analysis of merely political decision making. The question is not only if optimal means are chosen in order to advance given goals, but, more generally, if the process of choosing goals as well as means is free from 'imperfections' so that what we get is what we want. The welfare state is said to work to the extent that its goals and means correspond to popular preferences and intentions, to the extent that means are effective in relation to goals, and to the extent that the implementation of redistributive policies does not result in unanticipated costs.

The rationale for reform is that the limitation to cautious means is a protection against unacceptable side-effects which it is feared that more radical policies might produce. There are two major, and contrary, criticisms of this theory. Reform is, on the one hand, held to be ineffective because only weak means are allowed, and, on the other hand, to be self-defeating because even piecemeal interventions, as they expand and accumulate, invariably produce the dreaded side-effects.

The main methodological problem in the study has been to reconcile the very broadly formulated questions and the intention to answer them on the basis of empirical evidence. Appendix H contains a short discussion of some methodological issues and explains briefly the techniques which have been used to achieve the reconciliation. In this concluding chapter, the main conclusions of the study are stated briefly. Methodological problems involved in reaching these conclusions are discussed in the respective chapters and appendices and are not repeated here.

The Welfare State

The issues analysed can be sub-divided, roughly, into questions relating to political process, questions of redistributive effectiveness, and questions of economic efficiency. Within these areas, and between them, there is a clear consistency in what has been found.

Political consistency

Certain problems of legitimacy and of governability are identified. A trend of falling confidence in the policies of the welfare state is observed, suggesting that the popular reaction to the experience of the expanding welfare state is some degree of uncertainty and criticism. Public budget deficits in most OECD countries reflect difficulties in clearing goals and means. These difficulties are found to be associated with the growth of welfare state spending in a way which suggests that the decision making on spending and taxing is not altogether under political control. I have gone out of my way to set these problems in perspective, so as not to exaggerate their scope, but there remains, nevertheless, an increasing lack of correspondence between the policies that are enacted and both the preferences of the population and the intentions of politicians. Because of imperfections in the political process, there is an element of arbitrariness in the welfare state which adds up to a set of related problems of the kind Janowitz has discussed under the heading of 'social control'.

Given the problem of legitimacy, the problem of governability should come as no surprise. If more people start to have less confidence in the system of social policy, it should be expected that this will be reflected in political decision making. Citizens will, in political activity, hesitate less in expecting or demanding more benefits without more taxes or lower taxes without less benefits, and may, in economic activity, feel more justified in trying to find ways to beat the system for their own benefit and to push burdens on to others (although there is no hard evidence to show that more critical attitudes towards the welfare state are followed up with more free-riding behaviour). Politicians will sense a change of mood in the electorate and let this influence the decisions they make, or they may feel compelled to outbidding each other in the process of competitive politics in ways they are later not able to follow up with consistent decision making. Once the economic environment no longer permitted new expenditures to be financed from growth there proved not to be sufficient power in the system to reconcile ends and means. Tax payers and voters demanded better value for money. Politicians tried to adapt their decisions to these expectations but proved unable to avoid 'overspending' and, thereby, came to boost rather than to contract budget deficits which were already regarded as too large. It is not difficult to see that this can form a vicious circle: politicians perform poorly because they lose popular confidence; people lose confidence in politicians because they perform poorly.

There is some tendency to blame imperfection in public policy on incompetent politicians. Rose and Peters, for example, have taken incompetence to be an element in 'political bankruptcy', and survey material on public opinion has been interpreted as reflecting a widespread perception of political incompetence, for example by

Lipset and Schneider. A lack of political control, as defined in Chapter 4, does reflect a shortcoming in political decision making and is hence a problem 'on the level of politicians'. But incompetence is, at the most, only one of several factors contributing to this problem. It is true that politicians in a situation of low growth and rising deficits revealed some inability to make decisions on spending and taxing which were consistent with their own interpretation of what decisions were necessary. But in addition to possible incompetence, and a more difficult decision making situation, this must also be seen as a result of an insufficient basis in public opinion for consistent decision making. The public is asking politicians to do more than is within their power and then washing its hands and blaming politicians for their inability to perform according to impossible expectations. Incompetent politicians are not unlikely but it is not likely that new problems are caused by politicians becoming more incompetent. Part of the blame, at least, for the lack of political control over the welfare state must be shifted to the 'level of the public'. To a considerable degree, the problem of governability has its roots in the problem of legitimacy.

The problem of legitimacy is, in turn, associated with the problem of efficiency. There is reason to interpret the relative decline in popular support for the welfare state as reflecting disillusionment with its performance rather than reconsideration of its goals. The public continues to want government to be active in the area of social policy, but is increasingly uncertain about government's ability to do this in an efficient manner. As will be explained below, the welfare state performs fairly well in terms of redistributive effectiveness, but at the cost of some economic inefficiencies. It appears, therefore, that the public is justified in its disillusionment and that this reaction has its origin more in side-effects and unanticipated costs than in ineffectiveness in relation to intended goals. This brings the problem of economic inefficiency into centre stage in this entire discourse on the welfare state. Ineffectiveness does not appear to be much of a problem, but inefficiency is. Economic inefficiency is a problem in its own right because income is wasted or unintentionally forgone. In addition, it gives rise to political problems. Inefficiencies result in popular criticism of the welfare state, erode the population's loyalty towards it, and make the system difficult to govern. To give it in a nutshell: root out economic inefficiencies and the other problems solve themselves.

Redistributive consistency

The welfare state is found to be not without redistributive effectiveness. Cash transfers are, to a large degree, received by households who have little or no income from other sources and, thereby, contribute to a more egalitarian distribution of post-transfer than of pre-transfer income. The comparative analyses in Chapter 8 show that post-tax income is more egalitarian than pre-tax income and, hence, demonstrate that although direct taxes do not necessarily have a progressive effect in all systems (this has, for example, been suggested for the United States and is, in the data used here, shown to be the case for West Germany), they are at least potentially progressive and can hence be an effective tool of redistribution. The general conclusion is that direct transfers and taxes are redistributive on both the transfer side and the tax side.

As for indirect transfers and taxes, the conclusion is less straightforward. Most indirect taxes are, by their nature, regressive, or at best proportional, including the large, general indirect taxes, such as the value added tax. This counteracts the progressive profile of direct taxes and can make total taxation regressive, depending on the distributive profiles of the respective types of taxes and the sharing of the total tax burden between direct and indirect taxation.

The effect found in indirect transfers depends altogether on what is assumed redistributed, and between whom. Direct transfers redistribute money. This obviously occurs between income units. Indirect transfers redistribute consumption. It is not obvious what this really implies, nor that redistribution between income units is, in this case, the most relevant or important perspective.

Some redistribution studies have regarded indirect transfers as in-kind income, the cost of producing free (or subsidized) services being taken as an income (actually, expenditure saved) for consumers. This tends to show their distribution between income groups to be moderately progressive (although some services, such as higher education, are regressive).

An alternative assumption is that the intention has not been primarily to redistribute consumption, but access. The theory, of course, is that free services are equally available to all. This assumption turns the conclusion around. There is ample evidence that high- or middle-income groups in most cases make more use of free services than do low-income groups, even if differences in needs are controlled for. Under this assumption we would conclude that indirect transfers have a regressive impact.

A third assumption is that neither income nor access is sought to be redistributed, but some benefit which we derive from free services. If so, it is sufficient to say that the benefit lies in part in consumption and in part in access (as when those who do not use health services appreciate the security of knowing that they are available) in order to reach a third conclusion. Since the in-kind income assumption—whereby free services are distributed only among consumers and in proportion to actual consumption— results in a conclusion of moderate progressiveness, the benefit assumption—whereby services are, to some extent, distributed beyond consumers to the entire population, irrespective of actual consumption—would result in the conclusion that free services do not matter much one way or the other for the distribution of welfare between income groups.

Of these assumptions, I have argued, the latter two are the more reasonable. To be hospitalized in intensive care without having to pay the bill out of one's pocket then and there is a good thing, but it is not to receive an income transfer corresponding to the cost of hospitalization. Hence, the conclusion is that free services are not an effective way of counteracting inequalities between income groups. Direct transfers have this effect, but indirect transfers do not add to it. 'Jenck's law' stands: '. . . if we want to redistribute income, the best strategy is probably still to redistribute income.'[1]

But this does not end the story of redistribution via free services. Set aside income inequalities and assume instead that free services are primarily for those who combine a need for help and an inability to cope with the strain and difficulty of purchasing help in the market, even if they should have the necessary income—for example the handicapped, the ill, and the elderly. Assume, further, that the purpose has been not so much to influence the economic status of the members of these groups as to make it possible for them to live a life with certain qualities, such as independence and security. This may well be the case for a number of services, notably the care services, although not for all, such as free education. For this purpose, free services are found to be an effective policy. In the analysis of old-age care, it is shown that care services contribute to

[1] Jencks (1979: 311).

increased independence in the way of life of those who rely on the help of others and, thereby, to improvements in the quality of life of dependents, of those who would otherwise have had to accept the care burden, and of the relationships between these groups, for instance between the elderly and their younger generation kin. In this way, indirect transfers supplement the effects of direct transfers. The latter give these clients of the welfare state increased economic resources; the former help them further to live free and autonomous lives.

All in all, the findings on indirect transfers are mixed. These policies hardly contribute to reducing inequalities of economic status, and may have the opposite effect. On the other hand, they contribute to improving the quality of life of dependents. Although, in a limited income perspective, indirect transfers are not redistributively effective, they cannot—if a broader concept of welfare is applied—be brushed aside as ineffective. The best conclusion may be that of a dilemma. The same policies are regressive in terms of income and progressive in terms of quality of life.

The thesis that poverty has remained at more or less the same level in spite of economic growth and redistributive efforts is rejected on theoretical, methodological, and empirical grounds. Instead, the proportion of the population living in poverty is shown to be low and to have been reduced. This, of course, is consistent with the conclusion of redistributive effectiveness in direct transfers. What has long been a difficulty in the interpretation of results from two important branches of empirical welfare research is thereby cleared away. While those who have studied redistribution have emphasized the significance of direct transfers for pulling low-income households out of poverty, those who have studied poverty have tended to see no change in its incidence and to interpret this as evidence of a lack of effectiveness on the part of the welfare state. An attempt has been made to resolve this paradox by suggesting that the trend in poverty would have been even worse without the welfare state, but considering the massive redistribution of income to low-income households, this is not credible. The paradox is, in fact, an illusion. Poverty research has been wrong in its conclusion that little or no change has occurred in the extent of poverty, because it has not applied a method of measurement which is consistent with its own theoretical concept. While the relative deprivation theory defines poverty directly by the way people live, the income poverty line method measures it indirectly by considering only economic resources. Recent poverty research, in particular in sociology and in particular in Britain, has insisted on the relative deprivation concept of poverty but has continued to use the income poverty line measure. It is shown, in the present study, that if poverty is measured in a way that corresponds to the relative deprivation definition, the incidence is found to have gone down during the period of welfare state expansion. This brings the conclusion on poverty into tandem with that on redistribution.

In the discussion of the concept of welfare in Chapter 1, I have argued for a broad and direct method of measurement. These analyses of redistributive effectiveness highlight the significance of moving from a narrow income measure of welfare to a broader approach in which way of life is considered directly. This is seen with regard to indirect transfers, where a totally negative conclusion is avoided by taking into consideration not only their effects on the distribution of income, but also on how recipients of care services in fact live. It is further seen in the analysis of poverty, where it is only through direct measurement that poverty can be analysed in a way consistent with the relative deprivation understanding of the problem.

The consequences of direct measurement are of some importance in relation to the counterfactual problem: what would the situation have been without the welfare state? It is, in the final analysis, difficult to establish the effect of the welfare state on the distribution of income compared to the distribution as it would have been without the welfare state (or with a different welfare state). People would most likely have adjusted to, say, a lower level of public transfers by having more income from other sources. It is theoretically possible, although not probable, that the actual distribution of income under the present welfare state is no different from the potential distribution under an alternative welfare state. What is totally improbable, however, is that our way of life would have been the same. If we, in order to have the same income (or consumption), would have needed more income from work, more savings, or more transfers from private charities, we would also, necessarily, have lived differently. By considering way of life, and not only income, we see that, even in the unlikely case of the welfare state having no impact on the distribution of income, it would not be justified to conclude that it had no impact at all on the welfare of the population.

Economic consistency

There are considerable costs involved in redistribution. The current public production of social services is shown to be more costly than has been demonstrated to be possible under some alternative form of production (which may or may not be in private agencies). Behavioural responses to both cash transfers and increasing marginal tax rates have the effect of reducing labour supply compared to what might otherwise have been expected, and this must be assumed to be associated with a loss of income. Some empirical studies suggest that these effects may be considerable.

But costs are not inefficiencies. If public policies are considered to be a choice, and not just a technocratic implementation of optimal means, it follows that there is no inefficiency (or 'welfare loss') in costs which are an anticipated part of a policy. The concept of economic inefficiency has two components; it specifies a result—an unanticipated cost—and a mechanism—economic distortions. In order to establish that redistribution gives rise to economic inefficiency thus understood, it is not enough to demonstrate that there are costs associated with such policies (which is, anyway, trivial since there are always costs in making choices; to choose is to prefer something and to give up something). We must show that the policies in question interfere with economic processes and, through this mechanism, result in unanticipated costs.

The excess cost in the present form of public production of services and the labour supply effects of increasing marginal tax rates are cases of genuine economic inefficiency arising from political interventions in the system of economic allocation. Future income is given up unintentionally as a result of the way we use and distribute our present income. In addition, new transfers may indirectly cause inefficiency if they have to be financed with new taxes which push up marginal rates of income taxation. Since there are redistributive effects from social policies, economic theory would predict that there are also economic inefficiencies. This prediction is confirmed.

The loss of income that must be expected directly as a result of additional transfers is, however, not a problem of economic inefficiency. The reduction in labour supply which follows from additional transfers is an intended element in the policy: social security and early retirement programmes are intended to encourage retirement, the purpose of sick pay is to make it possible for workers to stay home when they are ill, maternity (and paternity) leave programmes are intended to enable mothers (and fathers) to give more priority to home and children and less to paid work. There is no inefficiency in an intended result.

Of course, a new and more generous transfer policy may turn out to encourage more labour to be withdrawn from the market than was anticipated. But this has nothing to do with economic inefficiency. The problem here is that we do not know what choices we make, not that our choices interfere with the mechanisms of economic life. The reduction in labour supply resulting directly from transfers reflects either a rational choice of leisure (such as early retirement) instead of income, in which case there is no inefficiency at all, or an inefficiency which is caused by imperfections in the system of political decision making, and not by distortions in the economic system, in which case the problem is political and should be seen as part of the problem of political process as discussed above. The problem, if there is one, lies in the process of choice itself, not in subsequent economic processes which are unintentionally set in motion by policy choices. Politicians may be 'too generous' in making transfer income available, but, if so, this reflects poor performance in political life resulting in decisions which do not correspond to the preferences of the population, rather than poor performance in economic life resulting from political interventions in the economy. The ability of the economy to generate income is not undermined; we have simply, in the intricate political process, trapped ourselves in a situation where we end up choosing more leisure and less income than we have wanted.

The possibility of 'too generous' transfer policies is, in the economic literature, often discussed as a 'moral hazard'. There is, in the existence of transfer policies, a temptation to let them apply too broadly, for example to expand sick pay eligibility beyond those who are in fact sick. This is, of course, a real possibility, and if it occurs we have a problem, but not one of economic inefficiency. There are unanticipated costs, but the mechanism which produces these costs is not economic distortion but some imperfection in the political process. The problem is not that people respond unintentionally to the policy, but that something has gone wrong in the formulation of the intention. It would not be consistent with the theoretical understanding of the concept of economic inefficiency, nor with the perspective of rational choice in general, to include this effect in the category of economic inefficiency. In my schema of a broad analysis of political process, I have already discussed political imperfections under the headings of legitimacy and governability. If I were to including moral hazards as economic inefficiencies, I would be counting the same problem twice.

There are two theoretically acceptable ways to analyse the economics of redistribution. One is, as here, to compare effectiveness and inefficiencies. Following the perspective of choice and the political process approach, effectiveness is defined so that only intended results are counted on the plus side (positive spin-offs are considered luck and therefore not accepted as evidence of effectiveness) and only unanticipated costs on the minus side (anticipated costs are considered to be part of the policy choice). The alternative is a full scale cost-benefit analysis, which would be in accordance with a more technocratic-decision making approach to public policy. In this case, all benefits and all costs—unintended and unanticipated as well as intended and anticipated—should be taken into consideration and balanced against each other. Factors which, in the rational choice perspective, are considered luck should be included on the plus side, for example macro-economic stimulations and indirect benefits for the non-poor as well as redistributive benefits for the poor, and both anticipated and unanticipated costs should be included on the minus side.

The debate over the economics of redistribution is strongly influenced by the notion of a trade-off between equality and efficiency. This is, as we have seen, not without cause, but the trade-off is typically construed as a confused mixture of the rational choice approach and the cost-benefit approach. Only intended benefits are considered on the plus side, while both anticipated and unanticipated costs are included on the minus side. Redistributive effectiveness is balanced against income forgone. This may, on first sight, seem plausible enough, but, in fact, costs and benefits are treated inconsistently, so that either inefficiencies are exaggerated or benefits underestimated. This gives a biased picture of the problem of economic inefficiency and results in unduly dismal conclusions about the economic burden of redistribution.

The rational choice perspective excludes from the minus side of the account the anticipated costs, which are typically included in standard trade-off discussions, and consequently results in a less gloomy interpretation. Attempts have started to be made with full scale cost–benefit analyses of redistribution. Here, indirect benefits beyond redistributive effectiveness are included on the plus side. These attempts show that when all benefits and costs are taken into consideration, benefits appear to be on at least the same level as costs.[2]

The type of welfare state

Although redistribution studies for a number of countries have shown the welfare state to matter for the distribution of income, it has been believed that the type of welfare state does not matter, at least not much. This has been argued theoretically on the assumption of circularity, according to which additional transfers and taxes, once these policies have reached a certain level, have consequences mainly for the middle class so that their effects neutralize each other; what government puts into your right pocket in additional transfers it takes out of your left one in additional taxes. Empirical studies appear to have borne this out. Independent studies in countries with different types of welfare states have reached broadly similar conclusions, and early comparative studies point in the same direction, for instance the comparison between Britain and the United States by O'Higgins and Ruggles.

On the other hand, critics of the modern welfare state tend to argue that the type of welfare state makes a great deal of difference in terms of side-effects. It is not any welfare state, but notably the large type, which is said to weigh heavily on the efficient performance of the economy and to take redistribution further than the citizenry is willing to support.

These positions are hardly in harmony with each other: if the large welfare state is not more effective in redistributing income there should be no additional intended effects from which additional side-effects could arise. But this is still the prevailing view, a result, perhaps, of the fragmentation of social research which has

---

[2] See Lampman (1984); Haveman (1986); Danziger, Haveman & Plotnick (1986). These analyses list costs and benefits—micro-economic and macro-economic, for the poor and for the non-poor—comprehensively, but have not been able to quantify all the relevant factors, in particular some of the benefits.

caused redistributive effectiveness and problems of economic inefficiency to be studied, for the most part, separately from one another.

The comparative analyses of income redistribution which are reported in Chapter 8 show conclusively that the type of welfare state does matter for redistributive effectiveness, in that the degree of redistribution is positively associated with the level of transfers and taxes. The comparison between seven nations within the *Luxembourg Income Study* shows, generally, a stronger redistributive impact the higher the level of transfers and taxes. The same is found in the more detailed comparison between Norway and Sweden, where an independent effect on the distribution of disposable income from the level of transfers and taxes is demonstrated, in addition to the effect of their distributive profiles. Both comparisons show a redistributive impact not only of transfers but also of taxes, which is to say that redistribution works not only via policies which are, so to speak, by definition redistributive, given the way redistribution is measured in the standard method, but also via policies the effects of which depend on how they are implemented. Compared to the predominant interpretation of previous studies, a stronger redistributive impact is here found, both of the level of transfers and taxes, and of the tax side as compared to the transfer side. In terms of redistribution, then, the large welfare state is, in fact, more effective than the small welfare state.

The large welfare state does not appear to have a weaker political base than the small welfare state. Across nations with different social policy systems, there is a high level of popular acceptance of and support for such social policies as are in operation. Popular support has been slipping, but not more so in large than in small welfare states, if anything probably less. Nor does the problem of political control appear to be more difficult in large than in small welfare states. The question of side-effects in relation to the type of welfare state can be limited to the problem of economic inefficiency.

Inefficiencies following from economic distortions caused directly by the level of transfers have not been identified. There are costs implicit in transfers, but these are—to repeat—not classified as economic inefficiencies. Some economic inefficiency is, however, identified, both in the production of social services and as a result of higher marginal tax rates. It must be assumed that these problems are more prevalent in the large than in the small welfare state—the public service sector is larger and marginal tax rates higher because higher levels of transfers must be financed by higher levels of taxation, and possibly because of more progressive rates in the income tax—and, consequently, that the problems of economic inefficiency which are associated with these elements of social policy bear more heavily on the large type.

Those who have believed that the type of welfare state does not matter for redistributive effectiveness are found to be wrong. Those who have believed that it matters for economic inefficiency are found to be right. There is additional redistributive effectiveness in the large welfare state but also additional economic inefficiency.

The Possibility of Politics

Corresponding to the major criticisms of reformism, there are two competing criticisms of the welfare state which I have described, in Chapter 2, as 'old' and 'new' criticisms. According to the old criticism, redistributive means are too weak and the welfare state useless. According to the new criticism, redistribution can be effective only at the cost of side-effects which make the welfare state impossible.

This study finds not only that the strategy of redistribution is an effective method for modifying welfare inequalities, but also that it is more effective than has hitherto been widely assumed. The distribution of post-tax/transfer income is less inegalitarian than is the distribution of pre-tax/transfer income. It has long been recognized that transfers have an equalizing impact on the distribution of income; it is here shown that taxes matter as well. The interpretation of previous studies has led to the hunch that, although the welfare state matters, the type of welfare state tends not to matter; it is here shown that it does. The thesis of stability in poverty is rejected. Transfers are shown to benefit recipients not only economically, but also in terms of more qualitative aspects of their way of life.

The implications of these specific findings on redistribution for the general question of reformist politics are, first, that it is possible to effect change via reform, and secondly, that the harder we try the more impact we may expect to have. This is not to say that there are no problems of effectiveness—such problems are identified in, for example, indirect taxes which, for revenue reasons, are necessary for a large welfare state but which are distributively regressive—but it does mean that the welfare state and hence reform, is not trivial. The old criticism is rejected.

Several trade-offs are alleged in redistribution, the main ones being against economic efficiency, the quality of private life, and political consensus and control. The first of these is confirmed; inefficiencies are identified, both in the production of social services and arising from the structure of taxation. The second alleged trade-off is refuted; it is suggested, instead, that effective redistributive policies stimulate activity and independence in private life. The consideration of this issue, therefore, does not subtract from the effectiveness of the welfare state but adds to it. Finally, the third trade-off is confirmed; there is a political price on the recent experience of welfare state expansion in the form of falling popular support and increasing problems of political control.

It can be argued that, compared to the strength of much contemporary criticism, the side-effects which are identified in this study are relatively moderate. Not all alleged side-effects are substantiated in empirical evidence. In particular, the serious assertion that we pay for redistribution by sacrificing activity and compassion in our way of life is dismissed. The adverse effect on the political process is quite weak—nowhere near bringing the welfare state to a 'crisis of legitimacy' or out of control—and is best interpreted as a result of a justified popular response to economic inefficiencies and, hence, more as an aspect of that problem than as an independent problem of its own. By distinguishing between anticipated and unanticipated costs, a considerable part of the economic burden of the welfare state—that stemming from the labour supply effect of transfers—is seen mainly to be an anticipated consequence of the choice to have a welfare state rather than a result of inefficiencies in the economic system. Although the welfare state is costly, only some of the costs are in the nature of a welfare loss.

The remaining economic inefficiencies result from policies which are redistributively effective: we cannot expect more redistributive effect without more inefficiency and we cannot expect to have less inefficiency without giving up redistributive effect. The trade-off between equality and inefficiency is intrinsic in the redistributive effort. The size of the welfare loss is associated with the size of the welfare state, both because more income is forgone and because this further threatens the political legitimacy of redistributive policies. Therefore, although by trying harder we can have more redistribution, we must also expect more side-effects. The new criticism is confirmed as far as the existence of side-effects goes. But more and stronger side-effects are currently alleged by the critics of the welfare state than can be backed up through careful theoretical and empirical analysis. The new criticism in its strongest form—which is perhaps what deserves to be called new, since it is only the strength and impact of this criticism, and not the criticism as such, which is new—is therefore not confirmed with regard to the magnitude of side-effects. I agree with Okun that the bucket is leaky, but I take issue with him on size of the hole. It is more pertinent to describe the problem as that of a small trade-off.

Does The Welfare State Work?

I believe to be justified in saying that the prevailing critical view of the welfare state is that it is low on effectiveness and high on side-effects. On the basis of the present study, I would turn this around and say that it is high on effectiveness and low on side-effects. From this, my answers to the two questions of the study are as follows: As to the welfare state, it does work—sort of. As to political reform, to paraphrase Goldthorpe, these conclusions count as rather encouraging ones for the strategy of seeking to attack social inequalities via legislative and administrative measures of a piecemeal kind. The power of reform is not unlimited but it is quite considerable.

Appendices

Appendix A   Survey Data on Social Policy Opinion

Table A1 Opinions on government activity and spending in the United States. Late 1970s. Percentages.[a]

(a)

Government Power/Activity	No	Yes
Do you think the federal government is too strong?	28	72
Would you like a smaller government providing fewer services?	40	60
Do you want the government to impose wage and price controls?	39	61
Do you want a national health-insurance program?	33	67
Do you want the government to help people get low-cost medical care?	15	85
Do you want the government to see to it that everyone who wants a job gets one?	23	77

(b)

Government Spending	Too much	Too little/ about right
Is the federal government spending	82	17
Improving and protecting the environment	10	90
Improving national health	7	93
Aiding big cities	22	78
Improving the nation's educational system	11	89
Improving the conditions of blacks	27	73
Welfare	61	39

a Source: Ladd (1979).

Table A2 Opinions on government spending in Denmark. 1979. Percentages.[a]

Public spending is:	too high	adequate	too low	Don't know
In general	74	9	12	5
Pensions	0	37	57	6
Health	7	52	36	5
Day care	16	34	39	11
Education	9	51	34	6
Unemployment compensation	49	37	7	7

a Source: Andersen (1982).

Table A3 Opinions on social security in Norway. Percentages.[a]

	Social security should be			Other answers	Don't know
	cut back	maintained	increased		
1965	9	37	42	0	12
1973	23	51	14	1	11
1977	9	43	36	2	10
1980	8	43	23	12	14

a Source: Martinussen (1981).

Table A4 Opinions on social security and benefits in Finland.
Percentages.[a]

The pace of increase		Too fast	Proper	Too slow	Don't know
	1975	15	51	31	3
	1980	21	56	21	3
	1985	15	60	21	5

Desired expenditures		Less than now	Same as now	More than now	Don't know
National	1975	4	23	68	5
pensions	1980	2	37	58	3
	1985	4	46	47	4
Child	1975	4	44	51	1
allowance	1980	3	36	56	5
	1985	3	40	52	5
Sickness	1975	3	40	51	7
insurance	1980	2	56	38	3
	1985	5	55	36	4
Unemployment	1975	18	36	32	14
insurance	1980	18	44	32	6
	1985	13	47	32	8
Maternity	1975	3	42	41	14
allowance	1980	3	45	45	7
	1985	2	51	38	9
Housing	1975	8	40	50	2
allowance	1980	9	48	36	6
	1985	9	42	43	6

a Source: Pöntinen & Uusitalo (1986).

Table A5 Summary of opinions on social programmes in eight countries in the 1970s. Relative level of public support for social policy principles.[a]

	Old-age pensions	National health schemes	Family allowances	Unemployment compensation	Social assistance
West Germany	High	High	—	—	Medium
France	High	High	High	—	High
Sweden	High	—	High	—	—
Denmark	High	—	—	—	Low
Australia	High	High	High	—	—
United Kingdom	High	High	Low	Low	Low
Canada	High	High	High	Medium	Low
United States	High	Medium	—	Low	Low

a Source: Coughlin (1979)—here slightly simplified.

Table A6 Opinions on government spending on social programmes in Britain. 1980–1. Percentages.[a]

	Government spending should be			Government spending should be increased even if it means more tax
	reduced	maintained	increased	
Education	8	48	44	40
Sick benefits	2	42	56	50
Old-age pensions	6	63	31	26
National Health Service	11	36	53	48
Single parents' benefits	5	52	43	35
Council housing	17	54	29	20
Child benefits	34	54	12	8
Unemployment benefits	10	62	28	18

a Source: Taylor-Gooby (1982).

Table A7 Opinions on social reforms in Denmark. Percentages.[a]

	Social reforms should be		Other answers	Don't know
	cut back	maintained or expanded		
1969	23	67	5	5
1974	47	39	7	7
1978	32	55	7	6
1979	31	55	8	6

a Source: Andersen (1982).

Table A8 Opinions on taxes and spending in four countries. 1975. Percentages.[a]

'Some people say that taxes and wage deductions to pay for social security and health programs are now too high and should be reduced, even if this means a cut in services. Others say that the government should improve social security and health programs, even if this means higher taxes and wage deductions. Which of these two statements comes closest to your own opinion?'

	France	Great Britain	West Germany	Denmark
Reduce taxes even if services cut	25	38	29	37
Improve programs even if taxes raised	47	44	41	43
Don't know/no answer	28	18	30	19

a Source: Coughlin (1980).

Table A9 Opinions on social reforms in Sweden. Percentages.[a]

'Social reforms have gone so far in this country that in the future the government ought to reduce rather than increase allowances and assistance to citizens' (1964–79).
'Social transfers should be cut back' (1980–2)

	Agree	Disagree	Don't know
1964	63	33	4
1968	42	51	7
1970	58	36	6
1973	60	33	7
1976	61	32	7
1979	67	27	6
1980	49	37	14
1982	45	40	15

a Source: Holmberg (1984).

Table A10 Opinions on social programmes in Sweden. Percentages.[a]

'When you consider conditions in Sweden over the past five to ten years which of the following do you think has become better or worse?'

	1972	1978
Health care		
Better	72	65
Worse	23	20
Don't know	4	15
Care of aged		
Better	82	62
Worse	9	15
Don't know	9	23
Youth care		
Better	49	29
Worse	30	33
Don't know	21	38
Child care		
Better	65	60
Worse	17	17
Don't know	18	23

a Source: Zetterberg (1979).

Appendix B Public Expenditure and Revenue in OECD Countries

This appendix contains a summary of statistical information on public expenditure and revenue in OECD-countries from 1960 to about 1980. The information is taken from the following OECD-studies: (i) *Public Expenditure Trends*, 1978, (ii) 'Public Sector Deficits: Problems and Policy Implications' (*Occasional Studies*, June 1983), (iii) *Social Expenditure 1960–1990* (1985), and (iv) (Saunders & Klau, 1985).

Definition of public expenditure and revenue: All general government revenue and spending on goods and services, as recorded in the standardized System of National Accounts, by function and 'economic' classification. These comprise the consolidated expenditure and revenues of the central government as well as of regional and local authorities. Expenditure and revenue of government institutions which produce goods and services for sale in the market is excluded. (See i:p.11. The roman numeral references are to the above-mentioned publications.) The figures are generally averages for most OECD-countries, in some cases for the major OECD-countries.

Expenditure

Level and growth of public expenditure

The level of public expenditure is expressed as a ratio of the national income. The average ratio relative to GDP for OECD-countries around 1982 was 47 per cent, with a range from almost 70 per cent for the top spender (Sweden) to about 30 per cent for the lowest spender (Switzerland) (iv: Table 1.).

The growth of public expenditure has, since the end of the Second World War, and before, for OECD-countries typically been more rapid than the growth of the national income. From 1960 to 1982, the ratio of public expenditure to GDP increased from on average about 26 per cent to about 47 per cent. At the turn of the century, the ratio of public expenditure to GNP has been estimated to about 8 per cent for the United States, about 15 per cent for the United Kingdom and Germany (Musgrave and Musgrave, 1976) and about 12 per cent for Sweden (Höök, 1962). The period from 1960 to 1980 can be sub-divided in two different ways with regard to public expenditure growth. Firstly, in absolute terms, into two sub-periods, before and after 1975. Up to 1975, public expenditure grew at a steady annual rate of about 5 to 7 per cent. Since 1975, the growth rate has been a good deal lower, about 3 per cent (iii: Chart 1). Secondly, in relative terms (relative to the growth of national income), into three sub-periods, before 1974, 1974–75, and after 1975. Before 1974 and after 1975, public expenditure grew moderately faster than the national income. After 1975, both growth rates have slowed down. Public expenditure continued to grow more rapidly than the national income, but slightly less so than before 1974. In 1974 and 1975, there was almost no overall economic growth, while public expenditure growth continued. Consequently, public expenditure sky-rocketed relative to GDP. To some extent, this was repeated in 1979–80 when overall economic growth was again exceptionally low (iii: Chart 3).

Breakdown of public expenditure

The large components of public expenditure are public consumption and transfers to households (i: Table 2; iv: Tables 8–9). These are, except for defence, for the most part social expenditures in the form of services (health, education) and income maintenance (social insurance, pensions). There has been a strong growth in these expenditures. Social expenditures are the dominant component of public expenditure and the most rapidly growing one.

The smaller components of public expenditure are defence, transfers to producers, interest on public debt, and public investment. Defence expenditures have declined relative to GDP. Investments have been stable. Interest on public debt and transfers to producers have grown since the mid-1970s, reflecting increased public support to businesses and increased borrowing as a consequence of deficits.

Level and growth of social expenditure

The level of social expenditure in OECD countries had around 1981–2 reached a mean ratio to GDP of about 25 to 26 per cent, up from about 14 per cent in 1960 (III: Chart 5; the term 'social expenditure' includes education, health services, pensions, unemployment compensation, and other income maintenance and welfare services). From 1960 to 1981, social expenditures grew at an annual rate of almost twice the rate of growth of real GDP (iii: Table 1).

The growth of social expenditure has been considerably faster than the growth of public expenditure total. In 1960, social expenditure was on average 47 per cent of total public expenditure, by 1981 it had risen to 59 per cent (iii: 20–1). This leaves, very little room for growth above the rate of growth of the national income for other components of public expenditure than the social components (except for the years 1974–5 and 1979–81 when all public expenditure components grew relative to the national income, as a consequence of virtual stagnation of the national income). In other words, the fact that public expenditure has grown more rapidly than the national income must be explained first of all by the growth of social expenditures and only to a minor degree, if at all, by the growth of other expenditure components.

Up to the mid-1970s, the rate of growth of social expenditure was stable, at an annual rate of about 8 per cent or slightly less. During the second half of the 1970s, social expenditure growth was considerably lower, about half of what it had been previously. While the rate of growth of GDP fell from 4,6 to 2,6 per cent, social expenditure growth fell from 8,4 to 4,8 per cent (iii: Table 1). Social expenditure thus continued to grow faster than the national income, but not more so than before 1975; if anything, less.

The drop in the rate of social expenditure growth is explained only to a lesser degree by new policies to achieve an adjustment in social expenditure to lower overall growth rates. It is true that there have been some policy changes and these have not been without effects. In the US, for example, the Congressional Budget Office (1983) estimated that spending for 'human resources programs' by 1983 had been reduced by 7 per cent relative to what it would have been under the existing laws at the beginning of 1981. But more important have been, firstly, changes in the demographic structure, and secondly, that most of the increase in the eligibility and coverage of social programmes was completed during the 1960s. These elements would have caused some reduction in the rate of expansion of social expenditure even if economic growth had remained high. On the other hand, average real benefits continued to increase after 1975, although less rapidly than before, and this contributed to a continued expansion of social expenditures relative to national income (iii: 29ff).

Breakdown of social expenditure

The large components of social expenditure are education, public health, and pensions. Sickness and unemployment insurance, family benefits, and other programmes are each, in relative terms, smaller. Public health is the most significant growth component. Expenditures for unemployment compensation have been growing rapidly, but this still weighs less heavily because of the small relative size of the component (iii: Tables 3,5 and p. 29ff).

Difference between countries

The level of public expenditure is to a large degree a function of per capita national income and welfare state commitment. Countries which are 'rich' and have a strong welfare state commitment are also big spenders (e.g. Sweden, Netherlands, Denmark). Countries which are less 'rich' and/or with only a moderate welfare state commitment are more or less average spenders (e.g. UK, Canada, Finland). The United States is a lower spender than might be expected from its national income, obviously because of a weak welfare state commitment; the same may be true for Japan. 'Poor' countries are low spenders (e.g. Greece, Spain).

The growth of public expenditure is, to a large degree, a function of the growth of national income; the more rapid the growth of GDP, the more rapid the growth of public expenditure. From 1960 to 1980, the growth of public expenditure has in all OECD countries been more rapid than the growth of GNP (elasticity above 1,0). As for deviation from this general rule, it is, firstly, moderate (elasticities between about 1.1 and 1.4) and secondly, without any intuitively recognizable pattern (high elasticity countries: Switzerland, Sweden, Luxembourg; low elasticity countries: US, Austria, France, Iceland). There are both big and small spenders among both high and low elasticity countries (iv: Chart 3).

As for social expenditure, the big spenders are the same ones as those that are on the top in total public expenditure. Social expenditure growth is, however, less strongly correlated than the growth of public expenditure total with national income growth. There is a wider range of elasticity of social expenditure than of public expenditure total and there is a considerable difference in elasticity of social expenditure among countries with about the same growth rate of GDP. After 1975, the difference between OECD countries in this respect has increased (iii: background material).

Revenue

Government revenues, like expenditures, have grown more rapidly than the national income. The strongest growth rate on the revenue side has been in social security contributions. Direct taxes have also grown considerably faster than GNP, whereas indirect taxes have grown at about the same rate as GNP (i: Table 14).

The growth in tax revenue relative to national income has been fairly stable over time and tax revenues have continued into the 1980s to rise faster than the national income, at about the same rate as they did in the 1960s. The growth of absolute revenue, however, slowed down from the mid 1970s. This was caused mainly by a slower expansion of the tax base because of slower growth, and only to a lesser degree by reduced growth in effective tax rates (iii: Chart 3).

Expenditure/Revenue Balance

Government revenue is, naturally, on roughly the same level as government expenditure, but by the early 1980s tax revenues were in most OECD countries significantly lower than expenditures (ii: Table 2). Until the early 1970s, tax revenues roughly kept track with expenditures. During the period 1974–5, however, expenditures continued to rise while revenue growth fell as a result of two years with close to zero economic growth, and most OECD countries were left with sizeable government deficits (iii: Chart 3). This was not caused by a real increase in public expenditure growth but by a continuation of expenditure growth trends (albeit more moderate) while overall economic growth, and consequently growth of tax revenue, slowed down. By the early 1980s, deficits were generally in the range of 3 to 4 per cent of GDP (ii: Table 2).

It is clear that the main explanation behind the increasing budget deficit lies in the serious economic recessions of the 1970s, but deficits have been estimated to typically be larger than what can be explained by recession alone. This is done by estimating 'potential' economic growth at pre-recession economic capacity and the probable development of revenues and expenditures that would have resulted without recession. Fiscal policies are assumed unchanged, but changes in expenditures or revenues resulting from 'automatic' factors, e.g. changes in the demographic composition of the population, are incorporated. This gives a 'cyclically-corrected budget balance' which, if negative, shows how much of the actual deficit is caused by other factors than economic recession. Although such calculations are necessarily tentative, the conclusion is that the 'cyclically adjusted budget balance' in OECD countries in the early 1980s is typically negative and that possibly about a fourth of the increase in budget deficits from the early 1970s to the early 1980s must be explained by other factors than economic recession (II: Table 5).

The growth of deficit budgeting has resulted in increased government borrowing and consequently a growing burden of interest on debt. The interest bill has typically grown to becoming as large as or larger than the total deficit (II: Table 4).

Appendix C Empirical Evidence on Behavioural Responses to Taxes and Transfers

Empirical evidence on the effects of transfers and taxes on labour supply and household savings is summarized in Godfrey (1975): early studies on labour supply; Atkinson & Stiglitz (1980: pp. 48–59, 90–5): effects of taxation; Clark & Spengler (1980): economic behaviour of the elderly; Danziger, Haveman & Plotnick (1981): effects of transfers; Heckman, Killingsworth & MaCurdy (1981); Killingsworth (1983): labour supply; Lindbeck (1981b): work disincentives; Aaron (1982): effects of social security; Moffitt (1981); Moffitt & Kehrer (1981); Ferber & Hirsch (1982); Robins (1985); Stafford (1985): experiment results; Bosworth (1984): taxes; Brown (1983): taxes and labour supply; EFA (1984): labour supply, Swedish results; Blomquist (1985): taxes and labour supply; Saunders & Klau (1985): general.

The question to be addressed here is whether the material summarized in these reports demonstrate any specific effect of expansions in taxes and cash transfers on labour supply or household saving behaviour.

1. There is now a very large body of empirical literature available which is relevant to this question. Indeed, this is an area where it has now become difficult to keep track not only of the literature but also of the summaries of the literature. In a comment to the Heckman, Killingsworth & MaCurdy paper, Yoram Weiss observes that '...the economics of labour supply is an active area of research. The expansion of redistributive policies has generated demand for precise estimates of the labour supply parameters. We now witness a concentrated research effort in the area of labour economics which is comparable to the developments in the theory and estimate of the consumption function following the Keynesian revolution'.

Most empirical research on behavioural response to transfers and taxes has been conducted in the United States and thereby applies primarily to the situation in a small welfare state. There is, however, enough evidence available from larger welfare states, e.g. Britain and Sweden, to say that the main conclusions from studies in the US have been confirmed in studies in larger welfare states.

The relevant research is based on a wide range of methods and types of data. Atkinson and Stiglitz (p. 48) mention three main types: surveys of attitudes and perceived behaviour, observed labour market behaviour, and experimental evidence.

The sophistication of the research is witnessed by, for example, the fact that this is one of the very few areas where large-scale social policy experimentation has been used (as a supplement to more conventional survey and econometric methods), *in casu* the 'negative income tax experiments' in the United States. Brown distinguishes between three main types of studies by level of advancement and sophistication, and Heckman, Killingsworth & MaCurdy distinguish between 'first-generation' and 'second-generation' studies of labour supply, the latter characterized by a more consistent specification of assumptions and the use of more sophisticated models and econometric techniques than first-generation studies.

The magnitude, breadth, and quality of the research effort is such that one would expect fairly robust conclusions to have been reached. This, however, is not the case. Danziger, Haveman & Plotnick, for example, end their detailed review by observing that '...the research findings are too varied, too uncertain, and themselves too coloured with judgment to serve as more than a rough guide to policy choices' (p. 1020). Even after the recent advanced labour supply studies such as those of the second generation or those using experimentation methods, we have very little of firmly established conclusions. Heckman, Killingsworth & MaCurdy conclude (p. 108), 'Thus, it is difficult to draw hard and fast conclusions about second-generation research *per se*'. In their review of the US negative income tax experiments, Ferber & Hirsch found that, for methodological reasons, the implementation of the experiment idea had proved to be fraught with pitfalls and that '...there is little doubt that much of the data collected in these experiments are subject to error, and so far the analytical models seeking to measure the response effects have not attempted to incorporate any allowance for such errors. If they were to do so, the results very likely would be even further influenced towards confirmation of the null hypothesis, as there is ample evidence that especially the financial data are subject to considerable error' (p. 35). This is, in the present context, a most important comment since the experiment results on labour supply are often held to be the most reliable estimates available. Uncertainty is a topic that is consistently underlined in studies of behavioural response to social policies, including in the most recent reviews of the literature.

2. Different studies of more or less the same problems have come to different conclusions. Godfrey, in his early review, found that the literature was not consistent and that differences in conclusions were to a large extent associated with differences in methodology. The same is generally reported in the other studies reviewed here. In Heckman, Killingsworth & MaCurdy (p. 75), 'the message underlying our discussion is simple, ...theory matters and technique matters... (and) differences in theory and technique lead to important differences in results'. This is illustrated with the disagreement between studies on the estimated elasticity of labour supply with respect to net wages. The range of estimates in first generation studies is in most cases 'too large to be of much use for analytical or policy purposes' and 'not infrequently...inconsistent with basic theoretical predictions derived from the underlying labour supply model' (p. 80). The results of second-generation studies are probably better in terms of consistency but not more conclusive with regard to practical implications. Second-generation studies generate about the same range of estimates of labour supply elasticity as did first generation studies (Killingworth, p. 205). On the other hand, although they have come to widely different results, 'second-generation studies as a whole differ sharply from first-generation work with respect to magnitudes of labour supply elasticities. In particular, the elasticities obtained using the "new" methodology are usually greater—sometimes considerably greater—in absolute value than are those obtained using the old methodology' (Heckman, Killingsworth & MaCurdy, p. 108). The same is reported by Brown for studies of taxes and labour supply and by EFA for labour supply studies in Sweden. But, as for whether 'the results of these studies suggest any important regularities or "stylized facts" about labour supply not apparent in first-generation work...there is as yet no clear answer' (Heckman, Killingsworth & MaCurdy, p. 106).

3. The results of studies on redistributional policy and *household savings* can be summarized briefly. There are no robust conclusions indicating that tax increases and/or expanded income maintenance programmes have affected household savings in one direction or another.

Danziger, Haveman & Plotnick find that negative effects of

income transfers on private savings have in general not been established, but still '...venture the tentative conclusion that income transfer programs have depressed annual private savings by 0–20% relative to their value without these programs, with the most likely estimate lying near the lower end of this range' (p. 1006).

Aaron's study of social security is of particular interest here since it is from social security that savings disincentives are most often assumed to arise. He finds no conclusive evidence of such effects in the empirical literature. The findings in some much quoted studies by Martin Feldstein, which have concluded that there are dramatic savings disincentives from social security, are described as having been 'discredited' because of methodological mistakes (p. 41). Aaron observes that economists have applied 'the best that economic theory and statistical techniques have to offer' to determine which of the many hunches in circulation about how social security affects household savings is correct, but without much luck. 'The evidence is conclusive that so far they have failed' (p. 51). This is in accordance with Clark & Spengler's earlier review. They found the literature on the effects of social security on household savings to be inconclusive (pp. 132–6). See also Bosworth, pp. 95–6, and Atkinson, *Journal of Economic Literature* 1984:99–101.

Saunders & Klau draw similar conclusions (p. 146): 'Overall then, it would appear that empirical studies within the life cycle framework have not to date been able to establish detrimental effects of social security (old age pension) provision on household or private savings which are in any way robust. Concerns over the alarmingly high savings displacement effects of social security produced in early studies have to a large extent now been tempered by more recent work which has failed to consolidate these findings. Thus, it would appear that the effects of social security provision on savings remains ambiguous on the basis of both theoretical reasoning and empirical investigation.'

Sweden has a comprehensive and generous social security system which has been expanded considerably over the last twenty years. Benefits are now close to proportional to the recipient's pre-retirement income level. Several studies on the effects of the system, and in particular of recent expansions, on household savings are reviewed by Ståhlberg (1983). These studies indicate that there may have been a reduced household savings effect, but not all studies find evidence of this and none are able to quantify it in reasonably precise terms.

In Norway, an income-graduated public pension system was introduced in 1967. There was, at that time, some sign of stagnation in the private life insurance business, but this did not last. From 1967 to 1982, the incomes of private life insurance companies increased at about the same rate as the incomes of the public pension system, both multiplying by about 8 in current prices (Hatland, 1984:137).

4. The results for *labour supply* are slightly more complex. Whereas it does not appear that individuals or households are much affected in their saving behaviour by (change in) taxes or transfers, it has been firmly established that people do adjust their labour market behaviour to such policies. It is, however, not clear exactly how they adjust their behaviour or what the net effect on overall labour supply of the various individual adjustments might typically be.

In a summary of research on 'work disincentives' up to about 1980, Lindbeck writes (p. 82), 'When looking at the scholarly literature on public finance it is probably fair to say that the prevailing view during the postwar period has been that serious disincentives for work have not arisen so far. In theoretical analyses, this view has largely been based on standard micro-economic theory of households, according to which the effects on labour supply of isolated reductions in the after-tax wage rate are ambiguous, as a positive income effect on work counteracts the negative substitution effect. In empirical studies the assertion has been based on information which indicates, on balance, that the income effects are at least of the same size as the substitution effects, though the category of married women seems to be an exception.' He then goes on to suggest six reasons for dismissing this conclusion, but does not offer new empirical evidence.

Recent studies confirm that the various effects of transfers and taxes on labour supply tend to pull in opposite directions and thereby more or less cancel each other out. There continue to be simultaneous income and substitution effects, and men and women and young and old workers frequently react differently. New results from second-generation studies do not affect the conventional conclusion. They find, as we have seen, stronger elasticities of labour supply than did earlier studies, but have not provided new firm information on the relative strength of income and substitution effects. Brown (p. 167) finds opposite labour supply effects of taxes for men and women, a weak effect for men to increase labour supply with rising tax rates and a relatively strong opposite effect for women, but since the total labour supply of men is larger than that of women, these effects might be expected to more or less neutralize each other with respect to changes in overall labour supply. A study by Betson, Greenberg & Kasten (1982), based on experimentation data, looks at the combined effects of simultaneous changes in taxes and transfers (as opposed to the isolated effects of changes in one or the other of these components) and finds that whatever individual effects there may be, there is little or no overall effect. However, as summarized by Ferber & Hirsch, Moffitt, and Robins, the main conclusion from the negative income tax experiments in the US is that substitution effects outbalance income effects. Compared to the existing tax-transfer system, the more generous negative income tax schemes that were tested were found to reduce the labour supply of low-income families moderately for principal wage earners and substantially for secondary earners, between about 1 and 8 per cent and about 2 and 30 per cent respectively. This adds up to a 5 to 10 per cent decrease in labour supply of low-income families, which is the equivalent of about a 1 to 2 per cent decrease in total labour supply. (Observe, though, that these are the conclusions which are subject to the uncertainties quoted from Ferber & Hirsch above.)

5. Taxation can affect labour supply via either average or marginal tax rates. On the effect of (changes in) average rates, Saunders & Klau find (p. 164) that 'empirical evidence on the relative strength of the income and substitution effects is not conclusive enough at the present juncture to draw strong policy implications'. It does appear, however, that although 'prime-aged males are little affected by changes in income tax rates', the 'results for women tend to show an overall disincentive effect from taxation, with relatively large substitution effects only partly offset by income effects'.

The difference in labour supply elasticity between men and women is probably not stable. A Swedish study (Gustafsson & Jacobsson, 1983) finds a considerable reduction in the elasticity of female labour supply between 1968 and 1981, something which is associated with increasing rates of labour force participation for women. By 1981, this study no longer finds any effect, on the labour supply of married women, of the husband's income, and for all women a considerably weaker effect of own income and of children. In other words, the labour force behaviour of women becomes more like that of men.

As for the effect of progressive rates, recent studies—including second-generation econometric ones in the US (Hausman, 1981a) and Sweden (Blomquist, 1983) and experimentation results (see Bosworth, p. 146)—have demonstrated that compared to a flat rate income tax that collects the same tax revenue, a progressive income tax has the effect of reducing labour supply, possibly to a considerable degree (see e.g. Hansson, 1984b). In addition, these studies have found a 'deadweight loss' in progressive taxation, i.e. inefficiencies which arise because of the efforts tax payers make to avoid taxes. These conclusions apply to both male and female workers.

6. As for transfers, their isolated effect is generally shown to be a reduction of labour supply. Danziger, Haveman & Plotnick go through a wide range of American studies on the labour supply effects of such income transfers as were in operation in the United States during the 1970s. The studies reviewed cover old age, disability, and survivors insurance, family assistance (AFDC), and some other programmes. As pointed out by the authors, the review demonstrates that the literature is not consistent and varies a good deal in assumptions, methodology, and conclusions. In spite of this, the authors find that a negative overall labour supply effect is established from all the transfers covered, and 'have drawn upon the better studies to cautiously offer a guesstimate of how much higher total labour supply during the late 1970s would have been if all income transfer benefits were eliminated' (p. 995). Their 'guesstimate' is 4.8 per cent, of which 2.4 per cent is caused by old age, disability, and survivors insurance. (The percentage in question is 'reduction of work hours by transfer recipients as a percentage of total work hours of all workers'.)

Social security is by far the largest income transfer programme. Clark & Spengler conclude that pension systems together with health status, are the most significant factor influencing the labour supply decisions of older workers and that most studies have found that 'eligibility for social security benefits has lowered market-activity rates' of older workers (pp. 91–2). How much, however, is not clear. Aaron writes (p. 166), 'If we conclude that the retirement age should be changed, empirical research tells us that social security may be one among many instruments for altering it, but it now gives us little indication of the size of the response we can expect'. In Sweden, Wadensjö (1985) has found that expanded opportunities for early retirement result, roughly, in a corresponding withdrawal of labour supply by workers in the relevant age groups.

A recent study by a group of researchers at the Universities of Wisconsin and Leyden (Wolfe *et al.*, 1983) of labour supply effects of the development towards more generous income transfers during the 1970s in the United States and the Netherlands is of particular interest because it includes a high transfer and a low transfer country, and because it attempts to estimate the labour supply response from actual changes in transfer policies rather than from hypothetical alternatives (such as actual transfers compared to no transfers). Using highly sophisticated techniques and claiming to control for the effect of 'all other factors which might also contribute' to lower performance, the study finds a steady influence towards declining labour supply from the growth in transfers. (The study does not attempt to measure the effect of simultaneous changes in both transfers and taxes.) This holds true for both countries but the effect is stronger in the Netherlands (the high transfer country) than in the US (the low transfer country). The calculated effect is a reduction of 'labour supply with on average yearly 0.85 per cent in the United States and 1.39 per cent in the Netherlands'.

These quantifications should be regarded as tentative. On the other hand, it has been shown that 'the marginal cost of less income inequality' may be quite high even if income elasticities are assumed to be relatively low (Browning & Johnson, 1984: 201).

Another recent study (Atkinson, Gomulka, Micklewright & Rau, 1984) gives reason to believe that although changes in income maintenance programmes may affect labour supply, this may not be the case for unemployment compensation. The study is based on British data and includes a reanalysis of previous estimates on the basis of what the authors claim are more realistic assumptions. The previous studies had led to conclusions that an improvement in the level of unemployment compensation should be expected to result in a somewhat longer duration of unemployment periods. In the new study it is demonstrated that these conclusions are not robust and that alternative assumptions result in estimates which suggest that improvements in the level of unemployment compensation have not had any effect on the probability of re-employment. Swedish studies (summarized by Björklund & Holmlund, 1983:113–14) have not found changes in unemployment compensation to significantly affect the level or duration of unemployment, except possibly in a very marginal way.

7. To sum up: Empirical research has not established that households are sensitive to changes in taxes or transfers in their saving behaviour, but it is established that workers (in particular women) are sensitive to some such changes in their labour market behaviour. The most important effects are from the structure of income taxation (marginal as opposed to average tax rates) and cash transfers (not including unemployment compensation). It is likely that the effect of changes towards steeper progression in tax rates or increased cash transfers will usually result in some fall in overall labour supply. The magnitude of these effects is not determined, but may be significant.

Appendix D   Trends in Individual Activity in Sweden[1]

Table D1   Employment

	1968	1974	1981
Gainfully employed	64	67	69
Unemployed	1	1	2
Retired	13	15	18
Housewives	14	10	4
Other	8	8	8

Table D2   Education

	1968	1974	1981
In education	8	9	11
Full time	8	8	10
Take part in courses/study circles	19	27	32
Take part often	7	12	12

[1] Source: The Swedish Institute for Social Research, 'Level of Living Surveys' (Erikson & Åberg, 1984). All figures show percentage of population 15 to 75 years of age.

Table D3 Leisure activity

	1968	1974	1981
Have been away on holiday in the last year	52	60	66
Regular activities:			
fishing	36	39	40
hunting	7	7	8
gardening	49	56	62
cinemas	42	41	45
theatres, museums, exhibitions	40	45	49
restaurants	36	49	55
dancing	32	42	45
book reading	72	77	78
coloured magazine reading	73	74	69
excursion by car	71	72	68
courses/study circles	19	27	32
musical activity	14	15	16
sports	26	30	34
hobby activity	59	62	62
Summary categories of activities			
outdoors recreation	49	55	59
entertainment	59	67	71
cultural activities	80	85	87
pastime activities	92	93	92

Table D4 Political and organizational activity

	1968	1974	1981
Member of political party/association	13	14	14
Holds elected position	2	3	3
Has attended political meeting during last year	13	15	14
Has spoken at political meeting,	25	27	32
given talk/introduction	13	15	20
Has written to newspaper,	10	11	16
written article	6	6	9
Has taken part in public demonstration(s)	14	16	23
Member of trade union or business association	45	50	60
Holds elected union position	4	5	7
Has attended union meeting(s) during last year	21	22	28
Non-active[a]	37	30	22

a Not member of party or union and has not taken part in political meeting(s), opinion-forming activity, or contacted person in elected office.

Table D5 Social intercourse

	1968	1974	1981
Visit relatives regularly,	87	89	90
often	28	29	31
Have relatives in regularly,	88	90	90
often	26	28	27
Frequent socializing/intercourse with			
relatives	18	21	22
Visit friends regularly,	91	94	95
often	30	36	40
Have friends in regularly,	93	95	95
often	30	35	39
Frequent socializing/intercourse with			
friends	22	32	35
Frequent socializing/intercourse with			
both relatives and friends	11	13	14
No socializing/intercourse with relatives			
or friends	2	1	1

Appendix E   Low Income and Poverty

The result of measuring poverty as accumulated deprivation is compared to the result of using the income poverty line measure. The data are from two identical Swedish surveys conducted in 1968 and 1981 with representative panel samples of the population 15 to 74 years of age. These are the same surveys as the ones used in Appendix D. Students and school pupils are excluded from the analysis because of their transitory situation.

The income poverty lines are defined, in the usual way, in relation to median income in each year. The other resource and way of life indicators are defined in the same way for both 1968 and 1981 in relation to a judgement of what exclusion from normal life in a society such as the present Swedish one might mean in absolute terms. Results are reported in Table E.

Low Income

Three low-income groups are identified:

I Persons belonging to families with a disposable income per unit of consumption below 40 per cent of the median for all families.

II Persons belonging to families with a disposable income per unit of consumption between 40 and 50 per cent of the median for all families.

III Persons belonging to families with a disposable income per unit of consumption between 50 and 60 per cent of the median for all families.

Disposable income per unit of consumption is estimated with the following equivalence scale: 0.95 for single persons, 1.65 for couples, and 0.40 for each child. Other persons than spouses/co-habitants and children belonging to larger households are counted as independent families.

The low-income groups are compared to all other persons (those belonging to families with a disposable income per unit of consumption above 60 per cent of the median) and to the entire sample. Since poverty is a question of falling behind the average standard in one's society, and not simply of falling behind the rich, no comparisons between low-income and high-income groups are included.

The three low income groups together make up about 14 and 9 per cent of all persons in 1968 and 1981 respectively. Those below 50 per cent of the median—the most commonly used poverty line— make up 7 and 5 per cent. The size of the lowest income group, those below 40 per cent of the median, has remained almost unchanged, going down only from 3.6 to 3.1 per cent. This is about the incidence of low income we should expect from previous studies.

Low Income and Other Resources

The chosen indicators of deprivation in other resources than income include:

—Small cash margin. (The respondent cannot raise a certain amount of money in one week, Swedish kronor 2,000 in 1968, adjusted for inflation to 5,000 in 1981.)

—Non-ownership. (The respondent/respondent's family does not own either house/flat, car, vacation house/cottage, pleasure boat, or camper.)

—Low personal capability. (The respondent does not judge himself/herself to have the ability to make a written complaint against a decision by an authority.)

These are two alternative indicators of economic resources and a third indicator of personal resources which should be expected to influence one's ability to use economic resources efficiently and otherwise to cope in society.

The percentages in the table below express the probability in each income group that its members will experience deprivation as measured by the indicators included. This shows the level of *absolute deprivation* of each income group. The difference in probabilities between income groups shows the *relative deprivation* of the group with the highest probability of deprivation.

Absolute deprivation in other resources than income is generally higher in the low-income groups than in the rest of the population, expressing some degree of relative deprivation, but the difference is moderate compared to what one would expect if these groups included the poor and excluded the non-poor. The low-income

Table E Low income and deprivation[a]

	1968					1981				
Income group	I	II	III	Other	All	I	II	III	Other	All
Sample										
1. Number of observation	182	175	388	4379	5124	172	102	231	4987	5492
2. Per cent	3.6	3.4	7.6	85.5	100	3.1	1.9	4.2	90.8	100
	%	%	%	%	%	%	%	%	%	%
Resources										
3. Small cash margin	38	31	31	15	17	26	14	26	11	12
4. Non-ownership	62	55	63	29	34	35	30	21	20	21
5. Low personal capability	29	25	25	17	18	13	13	14	9	9
Housing										
6. Crowded	28	28	28	23	24	15	10	10	5	6
7. Low standard	54	53	45	18	23	10	8	7	4	4
8. Inferior quality (6 and/or 7)	63	63	60	36	39	22	15	15	8	9
Consumption										
9. Does not have phone	19	15	16	8	9	6	1	3	2	2
10. Not away on holiday last year	75	75	72	44	48	53	39	49	33	35
11. Not occasionally/often relatives in	16	12	11	10	10	16	12	8	9	9
12. Not occasionally/often friends in	13	10	8	6	6	9	2	5	4	4
Accumulated deprivation										
13. (5 + 8)	21	15	19	9	10	5	3	4	1	1

a Source: The Swedish Institute for Social Research, 'Level of Living Surveys'.

groups are far from homogeneous with regard to resources. Nor is there a uniform correlation across low-income groups in the level of absolute deprivation in other resources.

From 1968 to 1981 absolute deprivation is down in all income groups. The relative deprivation of the lowest income group compared to the non-low-income group is lower in 1981 than in 1968 for all three indicators. The probability of non-ownership, for example, has dropped by about a third in the non-low-income group, as compared to almost a half in the lowest income group.

Low Income and Way of Life

The chosen indicators of deprivation in way of life include:

—Housing. (Crowded: more than two persons per room, kitchen and one additional room not counted. Low standard: lacking one or more of running water, bath/WC, central heating, modern stove, refrigerator. Inferior quality: crowded and/or low standard.)

—Other forms and patterns of consumption.

Again, deprivation is more frequent in the low-income groups than in the rest of the population but the difference is not very large. As judged by these indicators, the low-income groups are no more homogeneous in way of life than in resources.

Between 1968 and 1981, absolute deprivation has gone down in all income groups, notably in housing.

The relative deprivation of low-income groups is, however, not universally reduced. The housing indicators show that the relative deprivation of low-income groups is greatly reduced as far as housing standard is concerned but that a new difference between low-income and non-low-income groups has arisen in the probability of crowded housing so that here the relative deprivation of the low-income groups has increased. In the combined indicator (inferior quality), absolute deprivation is down all around, but the relative deprivation of the lowest income group is up from about twice that of the non-low-income group in 1968 to almost three times as high in 1981. This only goes to illustrate how unreasonable it can be to see poverty as a question of relative deprivation only. The probability of belonging to the lowest income group is about unchanged, the probability that the members of this group have an inferior quality of housing is reduced to about a third (from 63 to 22 per cent), but their relative deprivation in housing quality compared to the non-low-income group is up from 1.75 to 2.75. The low income group has improved its absolute standard but fallen behind in relative standard. Clearly, there are fewer people who have both low income and inferior housing—who live in deprivation—but by relative standards only we would still have had to conclude that the situation of the lowest income group had deteriorated—that there was more deprivation.

Accumulated Deprivation

Three indicators are taken into consideration: low income, low personal capability, and inferior quality of housing. This is to move only cautiously away from the income poverty line method. Low income is retained as the basic indicator, one non-economic resource indicator is added, and only one way of life indicator, with self-evident relevance in relation to poverty, is included. The housing indicator stretches the idea of deprivation in housing as far as possible by being defined as crowded and/or low standard; it is enough not to have a modern stove to be classified as deprived.

In 1968, 3.6 per cent of the population belonged to the lowest income group and 21 per cent of these had both low personal capability and inferior housing, bringing the percentage in accumulated deprivation according to these three indicators to 0.75 per cent. In 1981, the lowest income group comprised 3.1 per cent of the population, but only 5 per cent of these were deprived on the two other indicators as well so that the percentage in accumulated deprivation is down to 0.15.

Appendix F Methodological Issues in Standard Method Redistribution Analysis

This discussion is based on Ringen (1980); Stephenson (1980); O'Higgins (1980a, 1980b, 1983, 1985a, 1985b); O'Higgins & Ruggles (1981); Ruggles & O'Higgins (1981); Le Grand (1982, 1983); Lindbeck (1983); Gustafsson (1984b); Pechman & Mazur (1984); Saunders (1984); Uusitalo (1985); and other works referred to in Chapter 8 and throughout the text of the appendix.

Results

Table F1 gives an example of typical standard method results. These results are based on and influenced by a selection of certain among several theoretically possible assumptions about the nature of redistribution. This appendix discusses what some of these assumptions are and what the effect on measured redistribution would have been of applying alternative assumptions.

Table F1 Income redistribution in Britain 1984. Average quintile shares of income per household in proportion to average for all households.[a]

Quintile[b]	1	2	3	4	5	All	Composition[c]
Market inc.	0.01	0.31	0.88	1.38	2.43	1.00	83.4
Direct trsf.	1.93	1.48	0.70	0.50	0.37	1.00	16.6
Gross income	0.33	0.50	0.85	1.23	2.09	1.00	100.0
Direct taxes	0.00	0.19	0.78	1.37	2.68	1.00	18.1
Disp. income	0.41	0.57	0.86	1.20	1.96	1.00	81.9
Indirect trsf.	0.93	0.94	0.96	1.06	1.09	1.00	14.7
Indirect taxes	0.37	0.64	0.93	1.23	1.82	1.00	20.8
Final income	0.52	0.62	0.86	1.17	1.83	1.00	75.6

a Source: Central Statistical Office: *Economic Trends*, Dec. 1985, p.99.
b Quintile groups of households by market income.
c Per cent of gross income.

The Counterfactual Problem

Standard method studies take the distribution of observed market income as the base line of comparison. There are good reasons for this. The distribution of market income shows, of course, how the market in the system in question distributes income and is, therefore, a relevant starting-point for the analysis. Also, market income is overwhelmingly the largest income component, in Table F1, for instance, contributing about 83 per cent to gross income for all households (and for the majority of households a great deal more). But this choice is not a theoretically obvious one and has an essential influence on the conclusions of standard method studies.

The distribution of market income is extremely inegalitarian. When the base line, against which the distributions of subsequent income concepts are compared, is as inegalitarian as in this case, hardly any other outcome is possible than to find less inequality in gross, disposable, or final income than in the base line market income. This is all the more so since most of the redistribution which has been identified in standard method studies is caused by direct transfers, which are precisely the policies which 'work on' market income and transform it into gross income.

This would be no problem if the distribution of market income could be taken as a theoretically meaningful counterfactual, reflecting either the distribution of income such as it would have been without a welfare state or the distribution under a different tax/transfer system. But this is not the case.

It is true that market income is made up of income components which are generated in the market, but since welfare state nations do not have free markets, this income distribution is not independent of political decisions. The market is heavily regulated through economic policies, incomes policies, labour market policies, and environmental policies. Government is itself a large employer. As we have seen in Chapter 5, individuals adjust their labour market behaviour to a considerable degree in response to transfer and tax policies and thereby bring about a secondary effect on the distribution of market income. Hence, standard method studies show that the tax/transfer system is redistributive compared to what is in a purely statistical meaning income before transfers and taxes, but since this is not a 'real' alternative income they do not show how much redistribution these policies cause compared to the distribution of income under a 'real' alternative system of transfers and taxes.

We cannot know what the distribution of income would have been if there were no welfare state, but it is fairly obvious that it would have been less inegalitarian than the observed distribution of market income in welfare state systems. Not even in a ruthless market economy would every extent of inequality be acceptable or possible. It is hard to believe that a mature economy would leave 20 or 30 per cent of the population with virtually no income, and even harder to believe that the poor could survive if this were attempted. Yet, this is the distribution of market income in the welfare state. For example, in Lindbeck's study for Sweden (Lindbeck, 1983:230) the poorest 30 per cent households have only about 2 per cent of total market income but 13 per cent of total disposable income. This shows that there are in Sweden a good many households who have almost no other income than public transfer income, but it does not show what income these households would have had if present public transfers had not been available. Clearly, however, they would have had more than 2 per cent. Had there been no public transfers, there would have had to be more private transfers; if private transfers were not sufficient, many of today's recipients of public tranfers would have had to have more market income, either from savings or earnings.

The comparisons by Ruggles and O'Higgins of income redistribution in the United States and Britain around 1970 shows the distribution of market income to be considerably more inegalitarian in Britain than in the United States. The two poorest deciles of households in the United States have average market incomes corresponding to 11 and 25 per cent of average market income for all households, as compared to only 1 and 14 per cent in Britain (Ruggles & O'Higgins, 1981:145; O'Higgins & Ruggles, 1981:304). This is not because there is more inequality in Britain than in the United States—in terms of gross income the poorest deciles are better off relatively in Britain than in the United States, which means that direct transfers more than compensate their disadvantage in market income—but should instead be understood as a result of, among other things, the relative inavailability of public transfers in the United States. (Public expenditure on income maintenance in per cent of GDP, 1970 — Britain 7.3, US 6.3. Saunders & Klau, 1985, Table 8.) The members of the lowest income deciles in the United States have to have more market income because less public transfers are available, whereas in Britain more households can afford to have less market income. The extremely inegalitarian distribution of market income in Britain compared to the US is probably in part a result of relatively more generous transfers.

The lack of a proper counterfactual is the most important methodological problem in the standard method. Observed market income under a system of high transfers and taxes must be assumed to be more inegalitarian than the potential distribution of disposable or final income under a system with lower (or no) transfers and taxes. Consequently, by comparing the actual distribution of disposable or final income to an unrealistically inegalitarian base line, the standard method tends to exaggerate the redistributive impact of transfers and taxes.

In addition to these theoretical problems with the concept of market income, there are a good many practical problems with recording it accurately and relevantly. For one thing, there is the eternal problem of good data. This applies to data about transfers and taxes as well, but is more serious for market income, because the recording of earnings, capital income, private transfers, and the like, requires more participation by the income earner, either through the process of taxation or for research purposes in surveys, and is, therefore, more susceptible to being misrecorded. Income data tend to be biased in that both low and high incomes are underestimated, for example because of problems of sample representativity and unreported or underreported income. Incomes which tend to be underreported are, for instance, income from wealth, income from household production, fringe benefits, income from the shadow economy, and, of course, tax evasions. Some unreported incomes may be more typical of high-income groups, for instance fringe benefits (see e.g. Royal Commission..., 1976) and, possibly, tax evasions; others may be more or less neutral—this has been suggested for income from the shadow economy—and others again may be more typical for low-income groups, for instance household production (Levekårsundersøkelsen, 1976). It is not clear what effects, if any, these problems may have on measured inequality.

More serious, probably, is the time period for which income is recorded, which is universally the year. This is done because there is no easy alternative, but that does not mean that yearly income is the theoretically most relevant income to consider in relation to redistribution. There may be considerable differences between individuals or families in yearly income for reasons which have nothing to do with inequality in a normative meaning. If one person has twice the income of another person because he has worked twice as many hours, most people would probably consider them equal, at least if they both had the same opportunity to choose their own working hours.

The alternatives to yearly income are income in relation to working time, for instance per hour, and life time income. Both working hours and the number of working years in the life time differ a great deal in the work force. Many employees work part time. Others work more than normal working hours, for example many of the self-employed. The distribution of yearly income is to a considerable degree influenced in the direction of inequality by differences in working time. According to Lindbeck (1983:223), '... whereas the Gini coefficient for factor incomes of all households is 0.50, of economically active households 0.33, and of individual employees 0.26, it is as low as 0.17 for the earnings of full-time employees'. (Swedish data, 1979. 60% of female and 20% of male employees work part time.) Workers with a long education usually have higher yearly incomes than other workers but fewer working years. It is, therefore, probable that the distribution of yearly income tends to be more inegalitarian than the distribution of life time income. Hence, to substitute any of these alternatives for yearly income would result in less observed inequality in the distribution of market income and consequently, again, temper the conclusions about redistribution through transfers and taxes which are based on standard method results.

The Treatment of Transfers and Taxes

There are three types of problems involved in determining how transfers and taxes are distributed among households: the problem of *coverage* (which public expenditures should be regarded as transfers and which revenues as taxes?), the problem of *allocation* (who benefits from the transfers and who bears the tax burden?), and the problem of *valuation* (what is the value of benefits received and taxes paid?). The assumptions in the standard method are that expenditures and revenues which are intuitively transfers and taxes within the household sector are covered, that transfers and taxes are allocated to those households who physically receive or pay, or who have members who physically receive or pay, and that taxes and direct transfers are evaluated according to their cash value and indirect transfers according to their public budget costs. Again, these are not the only possible answers. We need, therefore, to determine how other relevant assumptions might influence the conclusions about redistribution. The various types of transfers and taxes will be discussed in order of difficulty, starting with direct transfers, proceeding through direct and indirect taxes, and ending with indirect transfers.

Direct transfers

The treatment of direct transfers is fairly straightforward. Coverage is decided by their form, which is cash, the correct allocation is obviously to the recipient households (disregarding problems of distribution within households), and the value is the cash value. These transfers are, as we have seen, strongly redistributive.

The only difficulty here is with coverage. In the standard method only transfers to households are included while transfers to institutions are not taken into consideration, for instance agricultural support or support or subsidies to manufacturing. Such transfers are usually considered part of 'economic policy' and disregarded in the discussion of social policy issues such as redistribution. But since support to businesses often is, and must ultimately be, justified by their benefits to people, they ought ideally be included.

It is difficult to say for certain how the benefits of support to businesses are shifted further on to households. They are probably in some way divided between owners, in the form of higher profits (or lower losses), workers, in the form of higher wages (or wages instead of unemployment), and consumers, in the form of lower prices. But one thing can be said, namely that support to businesses can be regarded almost completely as a transfer to the economically active part of the population. How it is distributed within this group we cannot say, but it is clear enough that the non-active part of the population does not benefit much from such transfers, except possibly by lower prices. This is significant with regard to the findings of standard method studies. These show that direct transfers are strongly redistributive mainly because they redistribute income from the economically active part of the population to the non-active part. If transfers to businesses were included, a relatively smaller part of all transfers would go to the non-active part of the population and, consequently, the total redistributive impact of direct transfers would be more moderate than it appears to be when only transfers to households are included.

The redistributive impact of direct transfers is crucial for the general conclusion that the tax/transfer system redistributes income in favour of the poor. It is through direct transfers that most of this redistribution is found to take place. We have previously seen that this conclusion depends, to some extent, on the use of the unrealistically inegalitarian distribution of market income as the base line of comparison. We have now, in addition, found that the standard method probably exaggerates the redistributive impact of direct transfers because transfers outside of the household sector are not taken into consideration.

Direct taxes

Direct taxes are akin to direct transfers, but with the opposite direction. The standard method includes central and local household taxes on income and wealth, including payroll taxes (employees' social security contributions). The burden is allocated to the households who pay by the cash value of the tax paid.

Standard method studies typically show that direct taxes tend to be, at best, moderately progressive. This is one of the more surprising findings of these studies. There are two explanations why direct taxes may be less progressive than is widely believed to be the case. Not all direct taxes have progressive rates. Central income taxes are typically progressive, local taxes more or less flat, and payroll taxes flat or moderately regressive. The wealth tax is usually progressive but with a moderate rate so that it does not have much impact except for a small minority of wealthy households. In addition, even taxes which have progressive rates tend, in practice, to be less progressive than the formal rates suggest. This is because of the effects of income deductions before taxation and tax evasion. The first of these effects is captured in standard method studies since taxes paid are seen in relation to gross income and not taxable income. But the tax evasion effect is not captured since income tends to be underreported in the data used in these studies to the same extent as in taxation (the studies are often based on tax return data). If non-reported income has a pro-rich distribution, standard method studies may, therefore, show direct taxes as somewhat more progressive than they in fact are.

The standard method records the *vertical* distribution of taxes, and estimates their impact on the distribution between income groups. Here, the political goal is usually a progressive distribution of the tax burden. Another important principle of taxation is that of *horizontal* equity, which means that tax payers with the same income should bear the same tax burden. The individual's tax burden is determined not only by his income, but usually also to some extent by how he chooses to use his income. For example, the choice between owning or renting a home can have consequences for one's tax burden, as can the choice between financing large purchases by saving up for them in advance or by borrowing and paying down afterwards. Income tax systems have 'loopholes' and offer possibilities for deductions so that income earners can them-selves influence how much of their actual income is, in fact, taxed. This they can do by both legal and illegal means. The ability and willingness of income earners to make use of these possibilities must be expected to differ a great deal within income groups and so, consequently, will the tax burden.

No welfare state has even come close to achieving horizontal equity of taxation. This is relevant in the present context for two reasons. Horizontal equity is one of the criteria according to which the distributive profile of direct taxes should be evaluated. While there may be different views about whether a moderately pro-gressive system is a success in terms of vertical effects, there can be no question that horizontal inequity is a sign of failure in the tax system. The other reason is that these two aspects are related to each other. Income taxes are less progressive in reality than in formal rates mainly because loopholes are exploited more effi-ciently by higher income groups than lower income groups. In addition, it can be argued that loopholes are the 'bribe' that high-income groups have taken in return for accepting progressive tax rates, in which case the formal progression of income tax rates has contributed to causing the failure of the system in terms of horizon-tal equity.

As with direct transfers, there is with direct taxes some difficulty on coverage. In the same way that transfers to businesses ought ideally be included because there must ultimately be household benefits in such transfers, corporate taxes ought to be included because these burdens must ultimately be borne by households. Again, it is difficult to say how this burden is distributed except that it is probably divided between owners, workers, and consumers. The employers' social security contribution is a borderline case between household and non-household taxation, technically being paid by employers (and therefore generally not covered in standard method studies) but earmarked to finance social security transfers and other benefits to households. The consequences of incorporating employers' social security contributions are discussed in the section on mechanisms of redistribution in Chapter 8.

Indirect taxes

Indirect taxes are taxes on purchases, such as sales taxes, value added tax, and excise levies on alcohol, tobacco, gasoline, and other items. The standard method covers indirect taxes on household purchases and assumes these taxes to be borne by the consumer with a value corresponding to the tax rate. Indirect taxes are usually shown to be moderately regressive in relation to disposable income.

Indirect taxes have the effect of increasing the price of goods and services and thereby of lowering the real value of disposable income. What the consumer pays in indirect taxes is determined by tax rates and his level and pattern of consumption. The higher his level of consumption and the more he consumes of goods and services with excise levies, the more he will pay. Since the rich generally consume more than the poor, they also pay more in indirect taxes. In absolute terms, therefore, the distance between the rich and the poor is less after indirect taxes than in disposable income. But since the rich also tend to save more than the poor and consequently to use a smaller proportion of their disposable income for consumption, they pay less than the poor in indirect taxes relative to disposable income. A larger share of disposable income is absorbed by indirect taxes for the poor than for the rich. In relative terms, therefore, indirect taxes increase inequality. Excise levies on 'luxury items' may modify this pattern to the extent that the rich have a more 'luxurious' pattern of consumption than the poor. But not all excise levies are on 'luxury'. The tobacco tax is a heavy component in most countries and tobacco now tends to be consumed rather more by low-income groups than by high-income groups.

Since not all consumers with the same disposable income have the same level or pattern of consumption, they will not all pay the same indirect taxes. The spendthrift will be hit heavily while the miser will get away easily. The effect of behaviour on actual taxes paid may be stronger for indirect than for direct taxes, which is to say that there is possibly more horizontal inequity in indirect taxation than in direct taxation. While horizontal inequity of direct taxation is clearly a weakness of the system, this is not necessarily regarded in the same way for indirect taxes since these inequities can be seen as resulting from 'voluntary' consumer choices and hence as 'fair'.

It is slightly problematic with the standard method that indirect taxes outside of the household sector are not covered and that the burden of indirect taxes is assumed to be borne by the consumer alone. The first of these problems is of the same nature as the exclusion of non-household direct taxes. The meaning of the second problem is that producers and distributors do not necessarily pass on the entire indirect tax to consumers by increasing their prices by as much as the indirect tax, but may carry part of the burden themselves in the form of lower profits, or pass it on to their employees in the form of lower wages. If so, the indirect tax component may weigh too heavily in standard method estimates compared to other tax and transfer components.

Indirect transfers

Indirect transfers have the form of free goods and services, such as health care, education, and home-help services, and of subsidies, which can be defined broadly as partial exemptions from payments which one would otherwise have incurred for one's present consumption. Such benefits can reasonably be regarded as transfers since they must in some way be paid for over public budgets and since the consumption of goods and services without paying, or partial relief from payment, is as good as cash. While the main difficulty in the treatment of taxes and direct transfers has to do with coverage, there are, in the treatment of indirect transfers, difficulties with allocation and valuation as well as with coverage. The interpretation of the redistributive effects of indirect transfers is the most controversial issue in redistribution analysis.

Standard method studies tend to show that indirect transfers are, all in all, distributed moderately in favour of the poor, but some observers of social policy disagree. Brian Abel-Smith, in his essay 'Whose Welfare State?', which was published as early as 1958, argued that free social services were primarily to the benefit of the middle class, and Julien Le Grand has, in *The Strategy of Equality*, presented convincing evidence that the rich in most cases benefit more than the poor. An American commentator who visited Britain saw there a 'riot' against the Conservative government's plan to reduce public spending on higher education and observed that '...hell hath no fury like that of the middle class when its subsidies are at issue'. (George Will in *The International Herald Tribune*, 11 Dec. 1984.)

Consumer subsidies have the same general redistributional effects as indirect taxes, only with the opposite direction and with less weight because governments take in larger revenues through indirect taxation than the benefits they give out through subsidies. What has been said above about indirect taxes in principle applies equally to subsidies if only the direction of the effect is turned around. Since indirect taxes have been shown to be moderately regressive, one should expect subsidies to be moderately progressive, and this is what standard method studies tend to show. However, while indirect taxes, such as the value added tax, are to a large degree levied on (almost) all consumption, consumer subsidies are always itemized, for example, subsidies on food, on transportation, or on cultural consumption, such as opera, concerts, and the theatre. The effects of subsidies, therefore, depend completely on how the consumption of the subsidized items is distributed. To take the three types of subsidies mentioned, high-income groups use subsidized culture more than low-income groups and subsidies for such consumption is strongly regressive. Food subsidies are probably progressive since they benefit in particular families with (many) children, but food consumption does not depend all that much on income so these subsidies benefit high-income groups as well. Subsidies for transportation are often assumed to benefit low-income groups, who are more dependent on public transportation, but this assumption does not take into consideration the non-household subsidy of private motoring, such as free roads and 'generous' taxation of the private use of company cars, and probably underestimates the use of public transportation by high-income groups. According to Le Grand (1982:108), in Britain 'the richest fifth of the population spends nearly ten times as much on rail fares as the poorest fifth'. If the private benefits of rail subsidies are assumed distributed in proportion to what households spend on rail fares, it is shown that the rich benefit more than the poor not only in absolute sums but also relative to their income. The same, again according to Le Grand, holds true for what are in effect subsidies of private motoring.

An important form of 'hidden' subsidy is the benefit to certain households of not having to pay as much tax as they 'should have' paid, i.e. the distribution of the benefit from tax expenditures (see Owens, 1983; Surrey & McDaniel, 1985). The effects of such benefits are indirectly absorbed in the standard method in that only taxes actually paid are recorded (i.e. the tax which 'should have been' paid minus tax subsidies), but their distribution is not shown explicitly. An important form of tax subsidy, for which some information on distribution is available, is the implicit housing subsidy which owner-occupiers have in the form of tax reliefs, in particular the opportunity of tax deductions for mortgage interest. Estimates for both Britain (by Ray Robinson, quoted by Le Grand, 1982) and Sweden (Frykman, 1984) show that actual housing subsidies (in Britain on council housing and in Sweden in the form of a means-tested direct housing grant) is distributed in favour of the poor but that housing-related tax reliefs are distributed in favour of the rich. The net effect in both countries is that high-income households on average receive a larger total housing subsidy than low-income households. In Britain, the distribution of the total subsidy is still probably slightly progressive in that low-income groups, although their absolute subsidy is smaller, receive a larger subsidy relative to their income. In Sweden, however, the total subsidy is slightly regressive in that high-income groups receive more not only in absolute sums but also relative to their income.

The most important form of indirect transfers are social services, in particular education and health care. The standard method treats free services as in-kind income. Coverage is limited to the household sector, the services are allocated to the households who in fact consume them, and they are validated in accordance with the budget cost to government of providing them. This results in some redistribution in favour of the poor from indirect transfers, but with the exception that higher education is distributed in favour of the rich.

The limitation to the household sector is, as usual, problematic. Since all public expenditure is in the name of and, presumably, to the benefit of the population, why not include public expenditure on government administration, law and order, and defence? Even if one were to assume that everyone benefits equally from such expenditure, their inclusion would have consequences for measured redistribution. If the poor benefit more than the rich from direct transfers and if both benefit equally from defence expenditure, the poor would still benefit more than the rich from direct transfers and defence expenditure but less so than from direct transfers only. More about this in the final section of the appendix.

On the problem of valuation it can be argued that the cost to the producer does not necessarily reflect the value to the consumer. For one thing, government may be an inefficient producer, in which case valuation by cost will exaggerate the value since consumers could have had the same services at a lower cost (as discussed in Chapter 5). But more fundamentally, it may be that what consumers in fact consume is not services as such but some benefit which they derive from the services or their availability. (Following my discussion of the concept of welfare in Chapter 1, the term 'benefit' should not be confused with 'utility'.) If so, it is the benefit and not the service which needs to be evaluated. This raises difficult questions about allocation as well as valuation; the benefit is not necessarily limited to those who physically consume the service and the value is not necessarily derived from the service as such.

The standard method procedure is that the entire benefit falls on the households who physically consume the services, and no distinction is made between services as such, and benefits from services. This is unsatisfactory for several reasons.

As usual, we cannot know what the alternative is, but clearly it is not a society without health care or education. Had government chosen not to produce social services and let households pay correspondingly less tax, or increased direct transfers, the households would most likely have used at least some of their additional income to buy education, health care, and other services, either on their own or through some insurance system. It is not realistic to take all free education, health care and other services as redistribution, in the same way that it is not realistic to take all direct transfers as redistribution. In the absence of free services (as of direct transfers) there would have been at least some private provision of services (as there would have been private transfers). In consequence, the standard method exaggerates the redistributive effects of free services (as it does of direct transfers).

Both education and health care (as well as other social services) are, in part, public goods. The consumer benefits, of course, but non-consumers benefit too. Non-consumers of education benefit from the stock of education in society, and non-consumers of health care benefit from knowing that health care is available if they should need it in the future. In fact, the best one can do in relation to health care is to know it is there but never need to make use of it, which is to say that the benefit of free health care lies primarily in its availability and only secondarily in its consumption. The implication here would be to allocate services in part to consumers and in part to all households, instead of completely to consumers as is done in the standard method. The consequence would be that health care and primary education would be less pro-poor in their distribution, and higher education less pro-rich. Again, in the way it allocates in-kind income from social services, the standard method systematically exaggerates the redistributive effect.

The allocation of education and health care services to consumers has some strange consequences. Expenditures for primary education is allocated to the children's parent household, but the expenditure for higher education is allocated to the parent household only to the extent that students live with their parents, otherwise to student households. Since students for good reasons usually have little or no income, this has the consequence that a good deal of public expenditure on higher education is allocated to households that are classified as low-income households. This is in one way correct, since student households often are low-income households, but it still misrepresents the reality of which sections of the population benefit from higher education. Except for their transitory situation during student years, students of higher education typically belong to the economically privileged groups in society, both by virtue of their socio-economic background and their anticipated future standard of living (although this may have become somewhat more uncertain in recent years). Standard method studies therefore tend to underestimate the regressive distribution of public expenditure on higher education.

To allocate all health care to consumers is even more strange. Health care is overwhelmingly consumed by the elderly. Although the elderly on average have low incomes, to see this as a transfer in favour of low-income groups is to say that the elderly are better off than is reflected in their disposable income because they are ill. But, of course, between two elderly persons who both have low incomes, the one who is not ill and does not need health care is better off than the one who is ill, no matter how fine and expensive the health care he receives. On the other hand, the ill do receive these services. Had they not been free of charge they would either have had to make do without or in some way manage to pay, whereby they would in both cases be worse off. But, again, the alternative would hardly have been a situation where every consumer of health care would have had to pay out of his or her purse there and then.

The question raised through these comments is not merely the right way of evaluating and allocating in-kind income from public services, but the very relevance of regarding the consumption of social services as in-kind income and thereby as an issue of income redistribution. While direct transfers are unquestionably income and while there are good arguments for regarding consumer subsidies as a substitute for income—their effect is reflected in household purchasing power—it is more problematic to regard social services in the same way. Although they represent free consumption, their distribution cannot be meaningfully considered without bringing in some benefit which goes beyond the consumption of the service as such, and this benefit accrues to many more households than the ones who directly consume the services. It is true that public expenditure for social services has been thought of as a policy for advancing 'equality'—as documented e.g. by Le Grand (1982)—but this should not be understood as equality of final income as defined in standard method redistribution studies. Services are provided in relation to demands (e.g. for education) or needs (e.g. for health care). The redistributive goal with regard to social services should be seen as to promote equal access in relation to needs or demands, irrespective of for instance income or socio-economic background. Public expenditure for social services should make services available to low-income households, but free services are not simply a substitute for income. Rather than regarding free services as in-kind income, it is more to the point to see income as income and services as services and not to confuse the two. The access to education, health care, and other services, may improve our living conditions but it does not add to our income.

Whether services are regarded as in-kind income or simply as services makes all the difference in the world for how their distribution is interpreted. Studies of the consumption of free services have universally shown that high-income or high-status households on average consume more of free services than do low-income or low-status households (see e.g. Le Grand (1982) on the distribution of health care, education, subsidized housing, and transport in Britain; Townsend & Davidson (1982) on health care in Britain; Sociale en Cultureel Planbureau (1981) for the distribution of various free and subsidized services in Holland; and Statistics Sweden (1984) for the same in Sweden). This is not necessarily the case for all individual services but it does hold true when free services are seen as a whole. (Observe that this appears to be confirmed in Table F1 where the consumption of indirect transfers is in absolute terms higher in the upper than the lower quintiles. These estimates should, however, in the present discussion be interpreted with some caution since what is shown is the distribution of income per household without regard to differences in household size and since high-income households on average are larger than low-income households.)

Since it is only by regarding free services as in-kind income that it is relevant to evaluate the distributive effects of indirect transfers in relative terms and since this is a dubious understanding of free services, it is difficult to accept standard method results as evidence of a progressive effect of indirect transfers.

Non-household Transfers and Taxes

The effect of expanding coverage to non-household transfers and taxes is, as we have seen, that measured redistribution is less than if only transfers and taxes within the household sector are included. The degree to which this is the case has been demonstrated by O'Higgins and Ruggles (1981) in their study of redistribution in Britain in which all taxes and government expenditures are allocated to households. Some main results of this study are reproduced

Table F2 Income redistribution in Britain. 1971. Average quintile share in per cent of total.[a]

Quintile[b]	1	2	3	4	5	All
Market income	1.5	10.9	18.6	25.4	43.4	100
Gross income	5.9	12.0	18.0	24.0	40.0	100
Transfers:						
Standard method coverage[c]	29.1	20.4	16.6	17.3	16.4	100
Total coverage[d]	20.0	19.0	19.1	20.4	21.3	100
Taxes:						
Standard method coverage[e]	4.2	11.5	18.6	24.2	41.7	100
Total coverage[d]	4.9	12.1	18.2	23.5	41.4	100

a Source: O'Higgins & Ruggles (1981: 304).
b Quintile groups of households by market income.
c Covers 47% of total public expenditure, both direct and indirect tranfers. Indirect transfers include education, health care, housing, and welfare foods (same as in Table F1).
d Covers 100% of public (central and local) expenditure and revenue.
e Covers 79% of all taxes. Includes central and local direct and indirect household taxes (same as in Table F1).

in Table F2 and compared to the results of allocating only transfers and taxes in the household sector. These estimates show that public expenditures are in both cases redistributive in favour of the poor, but considerably less so when all expenditures are included compared to the inclusion of only expenditures within the household sector. In this table it is assumed that all households benefit equally from non-household expenditures (e.g. government administration, law and order, and defence). These expenditures are, therefore, allocated to households in proportion to household size. This results in a distribution of non-household expenditures in favour of the poor both in relation to market income and gross income, but much less so than the distribution of transfers within the household sector only. In the same study, non-household expenditures are, in addition, allocated to households in proportion to household income and household wealth, the argument being that households with higher incomes or wealth benefit more than poorer households from such expenditures. These assumptions result in a distribution of non-household expenditures more or less in proportion to gross income and thereby modify even further the standard method conclusion of a redistributive impact of public expenditures in favour of the poor.

As to the tax side, the incorporation of non-household taxes does not noticeably affect the distribution. Taxes are, all together in both cases, distributed roughly in proportion to gross income, although slightly progressively. This result is explained mainly by the treatment of employers' social security contributions. These are assumed to be carried in part by government, in part by capital, and in part by consumers. This results in a distribution of employers' contributions which is roughly proportional to gross income and to other taxes, hence the lack of effect.

Addendum

Other methodological problems discussed in the literature include ranking, i.e. how income units are assigned to income groups (e.g. quintiles), and the unit of analysis. In the standard method as exemplified in Table F1, ranking is by household market income. It might have been by any other income concept, or for example, as suggested by Gustafsson (1984b), by an index of income and wealth, or it might have been shifted so that income units were in each case ranked according to the income concept described. It has been shown that different methods of ranking make a great deal of difference for what income units are assigned to what income groups (O'Higgins, 1985b).

Several authors — e.g. Danziger & Taussig (1979); Gustafsson (1984b); Uusitalo (1985) — have suggested that the unit of analysis should always be the individual (even when the income unit is the household), since well-being must always be associated with individuals and in order to prevent patterns of household formation from influencing the results in irrelevant ways. There is as yet not much experience with the use of this method but estimates by Gustafsson (1984b) suggest that this may increase measured redistribution compared to the results of studies which use the household as the unit of analysis.

Appendix G International Comparisons of Income Distribution

Table G1 Selected income distribution statistics for seven nations. *Circa* 1980.

	Can.	Ger.	Isr.	Nor.	Swe.	UK	USA
Inequality[a]							
Market income	.398	.505	.459	.400	n.a.[k]	.414	.440
Gross income	.327	.363	.382	.289	.249	.297	.371
Disp. income	.299	.355	.333	.243	.205	.273	.326
Redistribution							
G.I. to M.I.[b]	.82	.72	.83	.72	n.a.	.72	.84
D.I. to G.I.[c]	.91	.98	.87	.84	.82	.92	.88
D.I. to M.I.[d]	.75	.70	.73	.61	n.a.	.66	.74
Level of							
Transfers	9.1	17.2	8.3	14.1	28.2	16.5	8.0
Taxes[e]	15.2	22.5	28.7	25.3	29.7	16.9	21.0
Elderly families[f]							
Inequality[g]	.291	.340	.429	.279	.126	.240	.355
Relative status[h]	.81	.77	.96	.79	.78	.67	.84
Incidence of							
poverty[i]	12.1	7.2	14.5	4.8	5.0	8.8	16.9
Low income, single							
parent families[j]	45.6	32.6	22.3	35.3	31.4	45.3	56.4

The source for Table G1 is the Luxembourg Income Study data bank. The data for Canada, West Germany, and Sweden are for 1981; for Israel, Norway, Britain, and the United States for 1979. All statistics are based on family equivalent income by the following equivalence scale:

No. of family members	1	2	3	4	. . . 10+
Equivalence factor		.50	.75	1.00	1.25 . . . 3.00

a Gini coefficients.
b Gross income gini relative to market income gini.
c Disposable income gini relative to gross income gini.
d Disposable income gini relative to market income gini.
e Per cent of gross income. Direct public transfers and direct taxes (including payroll taxes).
f Families with a head of family 75 years or older.
g Gini coefficient, family equivalent disposable income.
h Average family equivalent disposable income of elderly families in relation to the mean for all families.
i Per cent of persons belonging to families with family eqivalent disposable income below half of the median for all families.
j Per cent of non-elderly families with children below 18 years with family equivalent disposable income in the lowest quintile for all families.
k n.a. = not available.

Table G2 Redistribution of income in Norway and Sweden. 1982[a]

Quintile[b]	1	2	3	4	5	Total
Distribution[c]						
Norway						
Market income	0.7	7.5	18.1	27.9	45.9	100.0
Transfers	53.3	28.5	9.7	5.4	3.1	100.0
Gross income	8.2	10.5	16.9	24.6	39.8	100.0
Income tax	1.2	5.9	16.1	27.5	49.2	100.0
Disp. income	11.3	12.6	17.2	23.4	35.5	100.0
Sweden						
Market income	0.8	6.1	18.6	28.9	45.6	100.0
Transfers	47.9	33.5	10.3	4.6	3.7	100.0
Gross income	9.8	11.4	17.0	24.3	37.5	100.0
Income tax	3.5	7.6	16.5	26.6	45.7	100.0
Disp. income	14.8	14.3	17.3	22.5	31.1	100.0
Composition[d]						
Norway						
Market income	7.0	61.3	91.8	96.9	98.9	85.7
Transfers	93.0	38.7	8.2	3.1	1.1	14.3
Gross income	100.0	100.0	100.0	100.0	100.0	100.0
Income tax	4.7	17.4	29.6	34.7	38.4	31.0
Disp. income	95.3	82.6	70.4	65.3	61.6	69.0
Sweden						
Market income	6.1	43.3	88.4	96.4	98.1	80.8
Transfers	93.9	56.7	11.6	3.6	1.9	19.2
Gross income	100.0	100.0	100.0	100.0	100.0	100.0
Income tax	15.5	29.1	42.4	47.8	53.0	43.6
Disp. income	84.5	70.9	57.6	52.2	47.0	56.4
Simulated income[e]						
Norway						
Market income	0.7	7.5	18.1	27.9	45.9	100.0
Gross income	10.7	11.5	16.5	23.5	37.6	100.0
Disp. income	18.2	15.9	16.8	20.5	28.6	100.0
Sweden						
Market income	0.8	6.1	18.6	28.9	45.6	100.0
Gross income	10.8	10.4	16.9	24.4	37.5	100.0
Disp. income	18.3	13.9	17.5	22.1	28.3	100.0

a   Source: Ringen (1986). The distributions are of family equivalent income (equiv-
    alence scale: first adult = 1.0, second adult = 0.7, each child = 0.5).
b   Quintile groups of families by family equivalent market income.
c   Per cent of total.
d   Per cent of gross income.
e   Simulation for each country using the Swedish level of transfers and taxes and
    their Norwegian distributions, and assuming the distribution of market income
    remains unchanged.

Appendix H   A Note on Approach

> It is a general rule that when the grain of truth cannot be found,
> men will swallow great helpings of falsehood. Truth itself is often
> concealed in such a way that the harder you look for it, the harder
> it is to find.
>
>   Isaac Bashevis Singer (in 'Yentl the Yeshiva Boy')

Frame of References

This book takes its point of departure in the current critical debate,
academic and political, over the welfare state and over political
reform in general. The debate is, in part, a normative one of
whether we should seek equality, and, in part, a positive one of
whether the way this is done in the welfare state is effective. There is
nothing new in either question, but a shift in the balance of attention between them has created a new and more critical view of the
welfare state. Because of 'stagflation' and related problems, many
observers who, on normative grounds, belong to the pro-equality
camp have, on practical grounds, come to raise doubt about the
realism of the effort. This, I believe, and not the normative problem, is the core of the new debate. The issue of this study is not
desirability but that of doability: does the welfare state work?
Hence, I do not dismiss current criticisms of the welfare state as
'ideological'. I assume the criticism to be given in good faith and
have wanted to find out if it is well taken by confronting it with what
we now know. The frame of reference here, then, is that of the
critics of the welfare state more than of its closest friends.

Choice

Public policies are seen, ideally, as a choice on the part of the
citizenry. That is not to say that this is how things in fact work. But it
is how they should work in a democracy. This exceedingly simple
starting-point gives a criterion of success or failure in public policy:
Are policies formulated and enacted in the way we should expect
given that they were the rational choice of the citizenry?

The notion of rational choice implies action, intention, and anticipation. Action is successful if it produces the result that is intended and anticipated. It is a failure if something goes wrong so that either the intended action does not lead to the anticipated result or the action that is taken is different from what was intended. The perspective of choice leads us to look for things that go wrong.

There are several attractions in this understanding of public policy. It is faithful to the ideal of democratic politics, it has its theoretical basis in the principle of methodological individualism and thus avoids the fallacies of functional and related approaches, it squares with the notion that society is created by people and that people are active subjects and not mere passive objects, and it relieves us from having to start from any stated or tacit assumption of conspiracy or power abuse behind political failure. Democratic politics can obviously go wrong because of an inegalitarian distribution of power or if those who have been entrusted with authority ignore the rules of democracy, but it can also go wrong even if the structural conditions for democracy are satisfactory and there is no ill will in the political process, for instance because of bad management. To look for things that go wrong is not to assume harmony in politics, but merely to assume that a lack of harmony is not the only possible source of failure. The perspective of choice is not contrary to a perspective of conflict, but it is more general.

Narrowing Down

Three techniques are used to handle the broad issue of the analysis. The first is to break out of the strait-jacket of disciplinary confinement. The success of the welfare state is a political problem, an economic problem, and a sociological problem. It should be analysed not from the perspective of any single discipline but from several—political science, economics, sociology—or rather from a perspective where the division between disciplines is regarded as arbitrary and irrelevant. Our concern is with the welfare state, straight and simple, not with the sociology of the welfare state, the economics of the welfare state, or the politics of the welfare state— whatever the meaning of such jargon might be. If anything, our concern is with its anthropology; the welfare state as such, in pure form, abstracted from any of its specific manifestations.

The second technique is to select for detailed scrutiny a small number of sub-questions which represent the broader question without covering all its potential aspects, so to speak to draw a representative sample from a larger universe of relevant questions. The overriding question is brought down to earth in the three concepts of legitimacy, effectiveness, and side-effects, through the further operationalization of these concepts in six empirically formulated questions which are treated in Chapters 3 to 8, and by attempting in each chapter to develop something approaching 'strategic' rather than full answers. The core concepts of 'welfare' and 'welfare state' are defined narrowly, welfare being limited to objective conditions and the welfare state to the strategy of redistribution. The narrow definitions are argued and justified on theoretical grounds and are not used as a methodological convenience, but these choices nevertheless have the effect of limiting the questions which need to be raised in the analysis compared to what broader definitions might have suggested.

The third technique consists in a rigorous distinction between the problems which are addressed. Much effort is put into the categorization of problems and the sub-division of broader problems into their various components. The problem of legitimacy is separated from that of governability. The problem of economic inefficiency is sub-divided into internal and external inefficiencies. Behavioural responses which may give rise to economic inefficiencies (notably labour supply effects) are distinguished from other behavioural responses which are irrelevant for efficiency (although they may be problematic for other reasons, such as a switch from market activity to do-it-yourself work). The potential effects of the size of the public sector is distinguished from those of its structure. Activity in private life is treated separately from activity in economic life. In the analysis of effectiveness, a distinction is drawn between poverty and inequality.

Empirical Evidence

The question, Does the welfare state work?, although broad and general, is still a strictly empirical one. Its answer is a matter not of logic but of experience and observation. No theory, however powerful it is, can more than help us to formulate questions about empirical reality; it can itself provide no answers to such questions.

Much of the general literature on the welfare state has the form of argument more than of demonstration. The welfare state, however, is not a principle but a part of the empirical reality which surrounds us. The interpretation of this reality needs an empirical basis. If a social scientist is asked an empirical question, he should in his capacity of scientist say no more than can be substantiated by what is known.

It is, of course, no simple matter to establish what is known about a specific issue. Leaving aside the philosophical problem of positive knowledge, it is a matter of interpreting a (usually) overwhelming mass of information, of sorting out what is solid and important from what is speculative and peripheral, of knowing what is not known, of understanding on what terms things are known, and of being aware that information may appear to be factual although it is, in reality, evaluative. To insist on an empirically based interpretation of the welfare state is like wanting to describe the picture of a jigsaw puzzle from only half the pieces, some of which may possible belong to other puzzles. To aspire to say what is known, is not to pretend that one can find the final truth, but to establish a limit to what can be said. It is a commitment to caution.

Bibliography

AARON, H. J. (1982), *Economic Effects of Social Security*, Washington DC: Brookings
—— & M. J. BOSKIN, eds. (1980), *The Economics of Taxation*, Washington DC: Brookings
—— & J. A. PECHMAN, eds. (1981), *How Taxes Affect Economic Behaviour*, Washington DC: Brookings
ABEL-SMITH, B. (1958); 'Whose Welfare State?' in Mackenzie (1958)
—— (1980), 'The Welfare State: breaking the post-war consensus', *Political Quarterly* vol. 51
—— (1983), 'Economic efficiency in health care delivery', *International Social Security Review* 1983:2
—— & P. TOWNSEND (1965), *The Poor and the Poorest*, London: Bell
ÅBERG, R., J. SELÉN, & H. THAM (1984), 'Ekonomiska resurser', in Erickson & Åberg (1984)
ABRAMS, M. (1973), 'Subjective Social Indicators', *Social Trends* No. 4, London: Central Statistical Office
ALAPURO, R., M. ALESTALO, F. HAAVIO-MANNILA & R. VÄYRYNEN, eds. (1985), *Small States in Comparative Perspective*, Oslo: Norwegian University Press
ALBER, J. (1979). 'The Growth of Social Insurance in Western Europe: Has Social Democracy Made a Difference?' (mimeo)
ALESTALO, M. & H. UUSITALO (1985), 'Finland' in Flora (1985)
—— P. FLORA, & H. UUSITALO (1985), 'Structure and Politics in the Making of the Welfare State' in Alapuro *et al.* (1985)
ALLARDT, E. (1975), *Att Ha — Att Älska — Att Vara*, Lund: Argos
—— *et al.*, eds. (1981), *Nordic Democracy*, Copenhagen: Det Danske Selskab
ANCKAR, D., J. DAMGAARD & H. VALEN, eds. (1982), *Partier, ideologier, väljare*, Åbo: Åbo Akademi
ANDERSEN, J. G. (1982), 'Den folkelige tilslutning til social politikken — En krise for velfardsstaten?' in Anckar, Damgaard & Valen (1982)
ANDREWS, F. M. & S. B. WITHEY, (1976), *Social Indicators of Well-Being*, New York: Plenum
ARROW, K. J. (1963). *Social Choice and Individual Values*, 2nd edn, New York: Wiley
—— (1983), *Social Choice and Justice*, Cambridge, Mass.: Harvard University Press

ASHLINE, N., *et al.*, eds. (1976), *Education, Inequality, and National Policy*, Lexington: Heath

ATKINSON, B. A. (1970). 'On the Measurement of Inequality', *Journal of Economic Theory* vol. 2

—— (1972), *Unequal Shares. The Distribution of Wealth in Britain*, Harmondsworth: Penguin

—— ed. (1973), *Wealth, Income, and Inequality*, Harmondsworth: Penguin

—— (1975), *The Economics of Inequality*, Oxford: Oxford University Press

—— ed. (1976), *The Personal Distribution of Incomes*, London: Allen & Unwin

—— (1985), 'How Should We Measure Poverty?', London School of Economics: ERSC Programme on taxation, incentives and the distribution of income (Discussion Paper 85)

—— & A. J. HARRISON (1978), *Distribution of Personal Wealth in Britain*, London: Cambridge University Press

—— & J. E. STIGLITZ (1980), *Lectures in Public Economics*, London: McGraw-Hill

—— A. K. MAYNARD & C. G. TRINDER (1983), *Parents and Children. Income in Two Generations*, London: Heinemann

—— J. GOMULKA, J. MICKLEWRIGHT & N. RAU (1984), 'Unemployment Benefit, Duration and Incentives in Britain', *Journal of Public Economics* 1984: 1

AUSTIN, M. & J. POSNETT (1979), 'The Charity Sector in England and Wales — characteristics and public accountability', *National Westminster Bank Quarterly* 1979 (Aug.)

BACON, R. & W. ELTIS (1978), *Britain's Economic Problem: Too Few Producers*, 2nd ed., London: Macmillan

BALDWIN, R. W. (1966), *Social Justice*, Cambridge, Mass.: Harvard University Press

BALOGH, T. (1982), *The Irrelevance of Conventional Economics*, London: Weidenfeld & Nicolson

BANE, M. J. (1976), *Here to stay: American families in the twentieth century*, New York: Basic Books

—— (1983), 'Is the Welfare State Replacing the Family?', *The Public Interest* 1983 (Winter)

BARBER, W. J. (1967), *A History of Economic Thought*, Harmondsworth: Penguin

BARTH, F. (1981), *Process and Form in Social Life*, London: Routledge & Kegan Paul

BAUER, R. A., ed. (1966), *Social Indicators*, Cambridge, Mass.: MIT Press

BEAN, P., J. FERRIS & D. WHYNES, eds. (1985), *In Defence of Welfare*, London: Tavistock

―― & S. MacPHERSON, eds. (1983), *Approaches to Welfare*, London: Routledge & Kegan Paul

BECK, M. (1981), *Government Spending*, New York: Praeger

BECKER, G. S. (1976), *The Economic Approach to Human Behaviour*, Chicago: University of Chicago Press

BECKERMAN, W. (1978), *Measures of Leisure, Equality, and Welfare*, Paris: OECD

―― (1979a), *Poverty and the Impact of Income Maintenance Programmes*, Geneva: ILO

―― (1979b), 'The Impact of Income Maintenance Payments on Poverty in Britain', *Economic Journal* (June)

―― ed. (1979c), *Slow Growth in Britain*, Oxford: Clarendon Press

BENNETT, J. T. & M. H. JOHNSON (1979). 'Public versus Private Provision of Collective Goods and Services: Garbage Collection Revisited', *Public Choice* 34

―― (1980), 'Tax Reduction without Sacrifice: Private Sector Production of Public Services', *Public Finance Quarterly* 8

BENTZEL R. (1952), *Inkomstfördelningen i Sverige*, Stockholm: IUI

BERGER, P. L. & R. J. NEUHAUS (1977), *To Empower People. The Role of Mediating Structures in Public Policy*, Washington DC: American Enterprise Institute

BERTHOUD, R. *et al.* (1981), *Poverty and the Development of Anti-Poverty Policy in the UK*, London: Heinemann

BÉTEILLE, A., ed. (1969), *Social Inequality*, Harmondsworth, Penguin

BETSON D., D. GREENBERG & R. KASTEN (1982), 'A Simulation Analysis of the Economic Efficiency and Distributional Effects of Alternative Program Structures: The Negative Income Tax versus the Credit Income Tax', in Garfinkel (1982)

BEVERIDGE, W. H. (1942), *The Report on Social Insurance and Allied Services*, Command Paper to Parliament, Dec

BISHOP, J. H. (1980), 'Jobs, Cash Transfers, and Marital Instability', *Journal of Human Resources* 1980:3

BJERKE, K. & S. BRODERSEN (1978), 'Studies of Income Redistribution in Denmark', *Review of Income and Wealth* 1978: 2

BJERVE, P. J. (1959), *Planning in Norway 1947–1956*, Amsterdam: North-Holland

BJÖRKLUND, A. & B. HOLMLUND (1983), 'Arbetslöshetsersättningen i Sverige — motiv, regler och effekter', in Björklund *et al.* (1983)

―― *et al.* (1983), *Inför omprövningen: Alternativ till dagens socialförsäkringar*, Stockholm: Publica

BLADES, D. (1982), 'The Hidden Economy and the National Accounts', *OECD Economic Outlook—Occasional Studies*, Paris: OECD

BLOMQUIST, N. S. (1983), 'The Effect of Income Taxation on the Labour Supply of Married Men in Sweden', *Journal of Public Economics* 1983 (Nov)

—— (1985), *Skatter och arbetsutbud*, Stockholm: Ministry of Finance

BOLTHO, A., ed. (1982), *The European Economy: Growth and Crisis*, Oxford: Oxford University Press

BOOTH, C. (1903), *Life and Labour of the People in London*, London: Macmillan

BORCHERDING, T. E., ed. (1977), *Budgets and Bureaucrats: The Source of Governmental Growth*, Durham: Duke University Press

—— W. W. POMMEREHNE & F. SCHNEIDER (1982), 'Comparing the Efficiency of Private and Public Production: The Evidence from Five Countries', *Zeitschrift für Nationalökonomie/Journal of Economics* 1982, Supplementum 2

BOSWORTH, B. P. (1984), *Tax Incentives and Economic Growth*, Washington DC: Brookings

BOTT, E. (1971), *Family and Social Network*, 2nd edn., London: Tavistock

BOUDON, R. (1981), *The Logic of Social Action*, London: Routledge & Kegan Paul

—— (1984): *La place du désordre*, Paris: PUF

BOULDING, K. (1967), 'The Boundaries of Social Policy', *Social Work* 1967 (Jan.)

BOWLES, S., D. M. GORDON, & T. E. WEISSKOPF (1983), *Beyond the Waste Land*, New York: Doubleday

BRENNAN G. & J. M. BUCHANAN (1980), *The Power to Tax*, Cambridge: Cambridge University Press

—— (1985); *The Reason of Rules*, Cambridge: Cambridge University Press

BRIGGS, A. (1961), 'The Welfare State in Historical Perspective', *Archives européennes de sociologie* vol. ii

BRITAIN, S. (1975), 'The Economic Contradictions of Democracy', *British Journal of Political Science* vol. 5

BROWN, C. V. (1983), *Taxation and the Incentive to Work*, Oxford: Oxford University Press

—— BROWN, M. & S. BALDWIN, eds. (1980), *The Yearbook of Social Policy in Britain 1979*, London: Routledge & Kegan Paul

BROWNING, E. K. (1978), 'The Marginal Cost of Income Redistribution', *Southern Economic Journal* 1978 (July)

—— & W. R. JOHNSON (1984), 'The Trade-Off between Equality and Efficiency', *Journal of Political Economy* 1984: 2

BUCHANAN, A. (1985), *Ethics, Efficiency, and the Market*, Oxford: Clarendon Press

BUCHANAN, J. M. (1984), 'Victorian Budgetary Norms, Keynesian Advocacy, and Modern Fiscal Politics', Nobel Symposium on the Growth of Government, Stockholm

—— & G. TULLOCK (1962), *The Calculus of Consent*, Ann Arbor: University of Michigan Press

—— & G. TULLOCK (1977), 'The Expanding Public Sector: Wagner Squared', *Public Choice* 31: 147–50

—— & R. E. WAGNER (1977), *Democracy in Deficit*. New York: Academic Press

BURENSTAM LINDER, S. (1970), *The Harried Leisure Class*, New York: Columbia University Press

—— (1983), *Den hjärtlösa välfärdsstaten*, Stockholm: Timbro

BUXRUD, E. J., L. FORSÉN & II. K. OTTERSTAD (1985), *Hvordan de har det — hvordan de tar det*, Oslo: National Institute of Public Health

CAMERON, D. R. (1984), 'Social Democracy, Corporatism, Labour Quiescence and the Representation of Economic Interest in Advanced Capitalist Society', in Goldthorpe (1984)

—— (1985), 'Public Expenditure and Economic Performance in International Perspective', in Klein & O'Higgins (1985)

CAMPBELL, A., P. E. CONVERSE & W. L. RODGERS (1976), *The Quality of American Life*, New York: Russel Sage

CAMPBELL C. D., ed. (1977), *Income Redistribution*, Washington DC: American Enterprise Institute

CAPLOW, T., H. M. BAHR, B. A. CHADWICK, R. HILL & M. HOLMES-WILLIAMSON (1982), *Middletown Families*, Minneapolis: University of Minnesota Press

CAPLOVITZ, D. (1963), *The Poor Pay More*, New York: Free Press

CARSON, C. S. (1984), 'The Underground Economy: An Introduction', *Survey of Current Business* 1984:5,7

CARTER, C. & T. WILSON (1980), *Discussing the Welfare State*, London: Policy Studies Institute

CASTLES, F. G. (1978), *The Social Democratic Image of Society*, London: Routledge & Kegan Paul

—— (1981), 'The Influence of the Political Right on Public Income Maintenance, Expenditures and Equality', *Political Studies* 1981: 4

CAZES, B. (1981), 'The Welfare State: a Double Bind', in OECD (1981)

CENTRAL BUREAU OF STATISTICS (1954), *Det norske skattesystems virkninger på den personlige inntektsfordelning*, Oslo: Central Bureau of Statistics

—— (1965), *Progressiviteten i skattesystemet 1960*, Oslo: Central Bureau of Statistics

—— (1980), *Inntektsfordeling og levekår*, Oslo: Central Bureau of Statistics

CHENERY, I. H., ed. (1974), *Redistribution with Growth*, Oxford: Oxford University Press

CHILDS, M. (1936), *Sweden, The Middle Way*, New Haven: Yale University Press

CLARK, R. L. & J. J. SPENGLER (1980), *The Economics of Individual and Population Aging*, Cambridge: Cambridge University Press

CNOSSEN, S., ed. (1983), *Comparative Tax Studies*, Amsterdam: North-Holland

COATS, K. & R. SILBURN (1970), *Poverty: The Forgotten Englishmen*, Harmondsworth: Penguin

COLEMAN, J. (1971), *Resources for Social Change*, New York: Wiley

—— T. HOFFER & S. KILGORE (1982), *High School Achievement: Public, Catholic, and Private Schools Compared*, New York: Basic Books

COLLARD, D. (1978), *Altruism and Economy*, Oxford: Robertson

COMMISSION OF THE EUROPEAN COMMUNITIES (1981), *Final Report. First Programme to Combat Poverty*, Brussels (COM 81 769)

CONGRESSIONAL BUDGET OFFICE (1983), *Major Legislative Changes in Human Resources Programs since January 1981*, Washington DC

—— (1985), *The Economic and Budget Outlook: Fiscal Years 1986–1990*, Washington DC

COUGHLIN, R. M. (1979), 'Social Policy and Ideology: Public Opinion in Eight Rich Nations', *Comparative Social Research* vol. 2

—— (1980), *Ideology, Public Opinion and Welfare Policy: Attitudes Towards Taxes and Spending in Industrialized Societies*, Berkeley: Institute of International Studies

COVELLO, V., ed. (1980), *Poverty and Public Policy*, Boston: Hall

COWELL, F. A. (1984), 'The Structure of American Income Inequality', *Review of Income and Wealth* 30: 351–75

CROZIER, M. & E. FRIEDBERG (1977), *Actors and Systems*, Chicago: University of Chicago Press

CULYER, A. J. (1980), *The Political Economy of Social Policy*, Oxford: Robertson

DAHRENDORF, R. (1979), *Life Chances*, Chicago: Chicago University Press

DANZIGER, S. & P GOTTSCHALK (1985), 'The Poverty of Losing Ground', *Challenge* (May and June)

—— & R. PLOTNICK (1980), 'Has the War on Poverty Been Won?' University of Wisconsin-Madison, Institute for Research on Poverty (mimeo)

—— & E. SMOLENSKY (1983), 'Abrupt changes in Social Policy: The Redistributive Effects of Reagan's Budget and Tax Cuts', University of Wisconsin-Madison, Institute for Research on Poverty (mimeo)

—— & M. K. TAUSSIG (1979), 'The Income Unit and the Anatomy of Income Distribution', *Review of Income and Wealth* 25: 365–75

—— & D. H. WEINBERG, eds. (1986), *Fighting Poverty*, Cambridge, Mass: Harvard University Press

—— R. HAVEMAN & R. PLOTNICK (1981), 'How Income Transfer Programs Affect Work, Savings and the Income Distribution', *Journal of Economic Literature* 1981: 3

—— R. HAVEMAN & R. PLOTNICK (1986), 'Antipoverty Policy: Effects on the Poor and the Nonpoor', in Danziger & Weinberg (1986)

DEACON, A. & J. BRADSHAW (1983), *Reserved for the Poor: the means test in British social policy*, Oxford: Robertson

DEACON, R. T. (1979), 'The Expenditure Effects of Alternative Public Supply Institutions', *Public Choice* 1979: 3–4

DENISON, E. F. (1979), *Accounting for Slower Economic Growth. The United States in the 1970s*, Washington DC: Brookings

—— (1982), 'Is US Growth Understated Because of the Underground Economy? Employment Ratios Suggest Not', *Review of Income and Wealth* 1982: 1

—— (1984), 'Accounting for Slower Economic Growth: An Update', in Kendrick (1984)

DENITCH, B., ed. (1979), *Legitimation of Regimes*, Beverly Hills: Sage

DET ØKONOMISKE RÅD (1967), *Den personlige indkomstfordeling og indkomstutjaevningen over de offentlige finanser*, Copenhagen: Statens trykningskontor

DODGE, D. A. (1975), 'Impact of Tax, Transfer, and Expenditure Policies of Government on the Distribution of Personal Income In Canada', *Review of Income and Wealth* 21: 1–52

DOEL, H. v. d. (1979), *Democracy and Welfare Economics*, Cambridge: Cambridge University Press

DONATI, P. (1984), *Risposte alla crisi dello stato sociale*, Milano: Angeli

DONNISON, D. (1979), 'Social Policy since Titmuss', *Journal of Social Policy* vol. 8: 2

—— (1981), 'A radical strategy to help the poor?' *New Society* 29 Oct

—— (1982). *The Politics of Poverty*, Oxford: Robertson

DREWNOWSKI, J. (1968), *The Level of Living Index. New Version*, Geneva: UNRISD

—— (1970), *Studies in the Measurement of Levels of Living and Welfare*, Geneva: UNRISD

—— (1974), *On Measuring and Planning the Quality of Life*, Hague: Institute of Social Studies

DUNCAN, G. J., et al. (1983), *Years of Poverty, Years of Plenty: The Changing Economic Fortunes of American Workers and Families*, Ann Arbor: Institute for Social Research

—— M. HILL & W. RODGERS (1985), 'The Changing Economic Status of the Young and the Old', University of Michigan: Survey Research Centre (mimeo)

DWORKIN, R. (1981), 'What is Equality?' *Philosophy and Public Affairs* 1981:3,4

EDSALL, T. B. (1984), *The New Politics of Inequality*, New York: Norton

EFA (1984), *Arbetsmarknadspolitik under omprövning*, Stockholm (SOU 1984: 31)

EHRENBERG, R. ed. (1981), *Research in Labor Economics*, San Francisco: JAI Press

EINHORN, E. S. & J. LOGUE (1982), *Welfare States in Hard Times*, Kent: Kent Popular Press

EISENSTADT, S. N. & O. AHIMEIR, eds. (1985), *The Welfare State and its Aftermath*, London: Croom Helm

EISNER, R. & P. J. PIEPER (1984), 'A New View of the Federal Debt and Budget Deficit', *American Economic Review* (March)

ELLWOOD, D. & L. M. SUMMERS (1986), 'Poverty in America: Is Welfare the Answer or the Problem?', in Danziger & Weinberg (1986)

ELSTER, J. (1982), 'Marxism, Functionalism, and Game Theory', *Theory and Society* vol. 11: 453–82

—— (1983), *Sour Grapes*, Cambridge: Cambridge University Press

—— (1985), *Making Sense of Marx*, Cambridge: Cambridge University Press

ERIKSON, R. (1974), 'Welfare as a Planning Goal', *Acta Sociologica* 1974: 3

—— (1984), 'Passiviseras medborgarna i välfärdsstaten?' Stockholm: Swedish Institute for Social Research (mimeo)

—— & M. TÅHLIN (1984), 'Samgång mellan välfardsproblem', in Erikson & Åberg (1984)

—— & R. ÅBERG, eds. (1984), *Välfärd i förändring*, Stockholm: Prisma (Eng. tr., forthc., *Welfare in Transition*, Oxford: Oxford University Press)

—— & H. UUSITALO (1985), 'The Scandinavian Approach to Welfare Research', in Erikson, Hansen, Ringen & Uusitalo (1986)

—— E. J. HANSEN, S. RINGEN & H. UUSITALO, eds. (1986), *The Scandinavian Model: Welfare States and Welfare Research*, New York: Sharpe

ESO (1983), *Administrationskostnader för våra skatter*, Stockholm: Ministry of Finance

—— (1985a), *Produktions-, kostnads- och produktivitetsutveckling inom den sociala sektorn 1970–1980*, Stockholm: Ministry of Finance

—— (1985b), *Produktions-, kostnads- och produktivitetsutveckling inom offentligt bedriven hälso- och sjukvård 1960–1980*, Stockholm: Ministry of Finance

—— (1986), *Offentliga tjänster—sökarljus mot produktivitet och användare*, Stockholm: Ministry of Finance

ESPING-ANDERSEN, G. (1985), *Politics Against Markets*, Princeton: Princeton University Press
—— M. REIN & L. RAINWATER eds. forthc., *Staganation and Renewal in Social Policy*, New York: Sharpe
EUROPEAN CENTER FOR SOCIAL WELFARE TRAINING AND RESEARCH (1980), *Use and Abuse of Social Services and Benefits* (Recommendations of an Expert Group Meeting), Vienna
FALLERS, L. A. (1973), *Inequality: Social Stratification Reconsidered*, Chicago: University of Chicago Press
FEIGE, E. L. (1979), How Big Is the Irregular Economy?' *Challenge* (Nov. and Dec.)
—— (1980), 'Den dolda sektorns tillväxt', *Ekonomisk Dabatt* 1980: 8
FELDSTEIN, M. (1977), 'Social Insurance', in Campbell (1977)
FERBER, R. & W. Z. HIRSCH (1982), *Social Experimentation and Economic Policy*, Cambridge: Cambridge University Press
FERGE, Z. (1979), *A Society in the Making*, Harmondsworth: Penguin
FIEGEHEN, G. C., P. S. LANSLEY & A. D. SMITH (1977), *Poverty and Progress in Britain 1953–73*, Cambridge: Cambridge University Press
FLORA, P. (1985), 'On the History and Current Problems of the Welfare State', in Eisenstadt & Ahimeir (1985)
—— ed. forthc., *Growth to Limits*, Berlin &c
—— & J. ALBER (1981), 'Modernization, Democratization, and the Development of Welfare States in Western Europe', in Flora & Heidenheimer (1981)
—— & A. J. HEIDENHEIMER, eds. (1981), *The Development of Welfare States in Europe and America*, New Brunswick: Transaction Books
—— et al. (1983), *State, Economy, and Society in Western Europe 1951–1975* (vol. i), Frankfurt: Campus
FOULON, A. & G. HATCHUEL (1979), 'The Redistribution of Public Funds in France in 1965 and 1970', *Review of Income and Wealth* 25: 277–307
FRANTZÉN, T., K. LÖVGREN & J. ROSENBERG (1975), 'Redistributional Effects of Taxes and Public Expenditures in Sweden', *Swedish Journal of Economics* 1975: 1
FREE, L. & H. CANTRIL (1968), *The Political Beliefs of Americans*, New York: Simon & Schuster
FREY, B. S. (1983), *Democratic Economic Policy: A Theoretical Introduction*, Oxford: Robertson
—— & W. W. POMMEREHNE (1984), 'The Hidden Economy', *Review of Income and Wealth* 1984 (March)
FRIEDLAND, R. & J. SANDERS (1985), 'The Public Economy and Economic Growth in Western Market Economies', *American Sociological Review* 1985: 4

FRIEDMAN, M. (1962), *Capitalism and Freedom*, Chicago: University of Chicago Press

—— & R. (1979), *Free to Choose*, New York: Harcourt Brace Jovanovich

FRIIS, H. (1981), *Nederst ved bordet*, Copenhagen: Danish National Institute of Social Research

FRYKMAN, T. (1984), *Bostadssubventionernas fördelning år 1980*, Stockholm: Ministry of Housing

FUCHS, V. R. (1983), *How We Live*, Cambridge, Mass.: Harvard University Press

FURNISS, N. & T. TILTON (1977), *The Case for the Welfare State*, Bloomington: Indiana University Press

GALBRAITH, J. K. (1958), *The Affluent Society*, Harmondsworth: Penguin

GARFINKEL, I., ed. (1982), *Income-Tested Transfer Programs*, New York: Academic Press

GARTNER, W. & A. WENIG, eds. (1985), *The Economics of the Shadow Economy*, Berlin: Springer

GEIGER, T. & F. M. GEIGER (1979), *Welfare and Efficiency*, London Macmillan

GEORGE, V. (1968), *Social Security: Beveridge and After*, London: Routledge & Kegan Paul

—— & R. LAWSON, eds. (1980), *Poverty and Inequality in Common Market Countries*, London: Routledge & Kegan Paul

—— & P. WILDING (1984), *The Impact of Social Policy*, London: Routledge & Kegan Paul

GILBERT, N. (1983), *Capitalism and the Welfare State*, New Haven: Yale University Press

—— (1984), 'Welfare for Profit: Moral, Empirical and Theoretical Perspectives', *Journal of Social Policy* 1984 (Jan.)

GILDER, G. (1981), *Wealth and Poverty*, New York: Bantam

GILLESPIE, W. I. (1965), 'The Effects of Public Expenditures on the Distribution of Income', in Musgrave (1965)

—— (1978), *In Search of Robin Hood*, Montreal: C. D. Howe Research Institute

GLAZER, N. (1975), *Affirmative Discrimination: Ethnic Inequality and Public Policy*, New York: Basic Books

—— (1981), 'Roles and Responsibilities in Social Policy', in OECD (1981)

—— (1983), 'Towards a Self-Service Society?' *The Public Interest* 1983 (Winter)

—— (1984), 'Reagan's Social Policy—A Review', *The Public Interest* 1984 (Spring)

GLENNERSTER, H. ed. (1983), *The Future of the Welfare State: Remaking Social Policy*, London: Heinemann

GODFREY, L. (1975), *Theoretical and Empirical Aspects of the Effects of Taxation on the Supply of Labour*, Paris: OECD

GOLDTHORPE, J. ed. (1984), *Order and Conflict in Contemporary Capitalism*, Oxford: Clarendon Press

—— *et al.* (1980), *Social Mobility and Class Structure in Modern Britain*, Oxford: Clarendon Press

GOUDSWAARD, K. & P. de JONG (1985), 'The Distributional Impact of Current Income Transfer Policies in the Netherlands', *Journal of Social Policy* 1985: 3

GOUGH, I. (1979), *The Political Economy of the Welfare State*, London: Macmillan

GOUL ANDERSEN, J., F. K. HANSEN & O. BORRE (1984), *Konflikt og tilpasning*, Copenhagen: Aschehoug

GOULD, F. (1983), 'The Development of Public Expenditures in Western Countries: A Comparative Analysis', *Public Finance* 1983: 1

GRAAFF, J. de V. (1971). *Theoretical Welfare Economics*, Cambridge: Cambridge University Press

GREEN, P. (1981), *The Pursuit of Inequality*, Oxford: Robertson

GRESS, D. (1982), 'Daily Life in the Danish Welfare State', *The Public Interest* 1982 (Fall)

GREYCAR, A., ed. (1983), *Retreat from the Welfare State*, Sydney: Allen & Unwin

GROSS, B. M. (1966), *The State of the Nation. Social Systems Accounting*, London: Tavistock

GUSTAFSSON, Bj. (1984a), *En bok om fattigdom*, Gothenburg: Studentlitteratur

—— (1984b), *Transfereringar och inkomstskatt samt hushållens materiella standard*, Stockholm: Ministry of Finance

GUSTAFSSON, Bo., ed. (1977), *Den offentliga sektorns expansion*, Uppsala: Uppsala Studies in Economic History 16

GUSTAFSSON, S. & R. JACOBSSON (1983), *Trends in Female Labour Force Participation in Sweden*, Stockholm: Arbetslivscentrum

GUTMAN, P. M. (1977), 'The Subterranean Economy', *Financial Analysts Journal* (Nov. and Dec.)

GUTMANN, A. (1980), *Liberal Equality*, Cambridge: Cambridge University Press

HABERMAS, J. (1975), *Legitimation Crisis*, Boston: Beacon Press

HACKER, A. (1985), 'Welfare. The Future of an Illusion', *The New York Review of Books* 28 Feb

HALEY, B. F. (1968), 'Changes in the distribution of Income in the United States', in Marchal & Ducros (1968)

HANSEN, E. J. (1982), *The Distribution of the Living Conditions in Denmark*, Copenhagen: The Danish National Institute of Social Research

—— *et al.* (1978), *Fordelingen af levekårene* (vols. i–v), Copenhagen: The Danish National Institute of Social Research

HANSEN, F. K. (1985), *Fordelingspolitikken og deres virkninger*, Copenhagen: Danish National Institute of Social Research

—— (1968), 'Redistribution of Income in Denmark', in Erikson, Hansen, Ringen & Uusitalo (1986)

HANSSON, I. (1984a), *Sveriges svata sektor*, Stockholm: Riksskatteverket

—— (1984b), 'Marginal Cost of Public Funds for Different Tax Instruments and Government Expenditures', *Scandinavian Journal of Economics* 1984: 2

HARRINGTON, M. (1962), *The Other America*, Harmondsworth: Penguin

—— (1984), *The New American Poverty*, New York: Holt, Rinehart & Winston

HARRIS, J. (1975), 'Social Planning in war-time: some aspects of the Beveridge Report', in Winter (1975)

HARRIS, R. &. A. SELDON (1978), *Over-ruled on Welfare*, London: Institute of Economic Affairs

HARRISON, A. J. (1979), *The Distribution of Wealth in The Countries*, London: Royal Commission on the Distribution of Income and Wealth, Background Paper No. 7, London: HMSO

HATLAND, A. (1984), *Folketrygdens framtid*, Oslo: Universitetsforlaget

HAUSMAN, J. A. (1981a), 'Income and Payroll Tax Policy and Labour Supply', in Meyer (1981)

—— (1981b), 'Labour Supply', in Aaron & Pechman (1981)

—— & D. A. WISE, eds. (1985), *Social Experimentation*, Chicago: University of Chicago Press

HAVEMAN, R. M. (1986), 'What Antipoverty Policies Cost the Nonpoor', *Challenge* (Jan. and Feb.)

—— V. HALBERSTADT & R. V. BURKHAUSER, eds. (1984), *Public Policy Toward Disabled Workers*, Ithaca: Cornell University Press

HAYEK, F. A. (1944), *The Road to Serfdom*, London

HEALD, D. (1983), *Public Expenditure*, Oxford: Robertson

HEALTH AND WELFARE CANADA (1977), 'The Distribution of Income in Canada: Concepts, Measures, and Issues', Social Security Research Report No. 4

HECHSCHER, G. (1984), *The Welfare State and Beyond*, Minneapolis: University of Minnesota Press

HECKMAN, J. J., & M. R. KILLINGSWORTH & T. MACURDY (1981), 'Empirical Evicende on Static Labour Supply Models: A Survey of Recent Developments', in Hornstein, Grice & Webb (1981)

HECLO, H. (1974), *Modern Social Politics in Britain and Sweden*, New Haven: Yale University Press

—— (1981), 'Toward a New Welfare State?' in Flora & Heidenheimer (1981)

HEDSTRÖM, P. (1981), 'Poverty and Low Income in the United States and Sweden', Cambridge: Joint Center for Urban Studies (mimeo)

—— & S. RINGEN (1985), 'Age and Income in Contemporary Society', Stockholm: The Swedish Institute for Social Research (mimeo)

HELD, D. (1982), 'Crisis Tendencies, Legitimation and the State', in Thompson & Held (1982)

HELPMAN E. *et al.* (1983), *Social Policy Evaluation*, New York: Academic Press

HEIDENHEIMER, A., H. HECLO & C. ADAMS (1975), *Comparative Social Policy*, London: Macmillan

—— (1975), *Comparative Public Policy*, New York: St Martin's Press

HEMMING, R. (1984), *Poverty and Incentives. The Economics of Social Security*, Oxford: Oxford University Press

HENDERSON, R. F., A. HARCOURT & R. J. A. HARPER (1970), *People in Poverty*, Melbourne: Cheshire

HERNES, G. (1977), 'Mot en institusjonell økonomi', *Statsøkonomisk Tidsskrift* 1977: 2

—— red. (1978), *Forhandlingsøkonomi og blandingsadministrasjon*, Bergen: Universitetsforlaget

—— (1979), 'Marked og hierarki—entreprenør og byråkrat', *Sosialøkonomen* 1979: 10

—— & K. KNUDSEN (1976),' *Utdanning og ulikhet*, Oslo: Universitetsforlaget (NOU)

HERNES, H. (1982), *Staten: Kvinner ingen adgang*, Oslo: Universitetsforlaget

—— (1984), 'Women and the Welfare State. The Transition from Private to Public Dependence', in Holter (1984)

HEW (1969), *Toward a Social Report*, Washington DC: Department of Health, Education and Welfare

—— (1976), *The Measure of Poverty*, Washington DC: Department of Health, Education and Welfare

—— (1978), *Summary Report: Seattle-Denver Income Maintenance Experiment*, Washington DC: Department of Health, Education and Welfare

HIGGINS, J. (1981), *States of Welfare*, Oxford: Blackwell

HILL, M. (1980), *Understanding Social Policy*, Oxford: Robertson

HIRSCH, F. (1977), *Social Limits to Growth*. London: Routledge & Kegan Paul

—— & J. H. GOLDTHORPE, eds. (1978), *The Political Economy of Inflation*, Oxford: Robertson

HIRSCHMAN, A. O. (1970), *Exit, Voice, and Loyalty*, Cambridge: Harvard University Press

HOBSBAWM, E. J. (1968), 'Poverty', *New International Encyclopedia of the Social Sciencies*, London: Macmillan

HOCHMAN, H. M. (1983), 'Contractarian Theories of Income Redistribution', in Helpman (1983)
—— & G. E. PETERS, eds. (1974), *Redistribution through Public Choice*, New York: Columbia University Press
HOLMBERG, S. (1982), *Svenska väljare*, Stockholm: Publica
—— (1984), *Väljare i förändring*, Stockholm: Publica
HOLMUND, B. (1983), 'Payroll Taxes and Wage Inflation', *Scandinavian Journal of Economics* 1983: 1
HOLTER, H., ed. (1984), *Patriarchy in a Welfare Society*, Oslo: Universitetsforlaget
HÖÖK, E. (1962), *Den offentliga sektorns expansion*, Stockholm: IUI
HORNSTEIN, Z., J. GRICE & A. WEBB, eds. (1981), *The Economics of Labour Markets*, London: HMSO
HOWE, J. ed. (1982), *Beyond the Welfare State*, New York: Schocken
HOVEN, F. H. (1981), 'Forskning om vanskeligstiltes forhold til det offentlige velferdsbyråkrati', *Sosial Trygd* 1981: 1
INGLEHART, R. (1977), *The Silent Revolution*, Princeton: Princeton University Press
IRS (1983), *Income Tax Compliance Research*, Washington DC: Internal Revenue Service
ISACHSEN, A. J., J. T. KLOVLAND & S. STRØM (1982), 'The Hidden Economy in Norway', in Tanzi (1982)
—— & S. STRØM (1985), 'The Size and Growth of the Hidden Economy in Norway', *Review of Income and Wealth* 1985: 1
JANOWITZ M. (1976), *Social Control of the Welfare State*, New York: Elsevier
JENCKS, C. (1979), *Who Gets Ahead?* New York: Basic Books
—— (1984), 'The Hidden Prosperity of the 1970's', *The Public Interest* (Fall)
—— (1985), 'How Poor are the Poor?', *New York Review of Books* 9 May
—— *et al.*, (1972), *Inequality*, New York: Basic Books
—— L. PERMAN & L. RAINWATER (1985), 'What is a Good Job? A New Measure of Labour Market Success', (mimeo)
JOHANSEN, L. (1977), *Lectures in Macroeconomic Planning* (vols. i–ii: 1977, 1978), Amsterdam: North-Holland
JOHANSSON, S. (1970), *Om levnadsnivåundersökningen*, Stockholm: Allmänna Förlaget
—— (1973), 'The Level of Living Survey: A Presentation', *Acta Sociologica* 1970: 3
—— (1979), *Mot en teori för social rapportering*, Stockholm: Swedish Institute for Social Research
—— (1981), *Välfärdsförändringar vid sidan av inkomsten 1968-1974-1981*, Stockholm: Swedish Institute for Social Research

JONES, M. A. (1983), *The Australian Welfare State*, Sydney: Allen & Unwin

JÖNSSON, B. (1984), 'Produktivitet i privat och offentlig tandvård', *Ekonomisk Debatt* 1984: 1

JUDGE, K. (1978), *Rationing Social Services*, London: Heinemann

—— & M. KNAPP (1985), 'Efficiency in the Production of Welfare: The Public and Private Sectors Compared', in Klein & O'Higgins (1985)

JUSTER, F. T. & F. STAFFORD, eds. (1984), *Times, Goods and Well-Being*, Ann Arbor: Institute for Social Research

KAHN, A. J. & S. B. KAMERMAN (1978), *Social Services in International Perspective*, Washington DC: Department of Health, Education and Welfare

KATZ, C. J., V. A. MAHLER & M. G. FRANZ (1983), 'The Impact of Taxes on Growth and Distribution in Developed Capitalist Countries: A Cross-National Study', *American Political Science Review* (Dec.)

KENDRICK, J. W., ed. (1984), *International Comparisons of Productivity and Causes of the Slowdown*, Cambridge: Ballinger

KESSLER, D. & A. MASSON (1985), 'What are the Distributional Consequences of the Socialist Government Policy in France?' *Journal of Social Policy* 1985: 3

KILLINGSWORTH, M. R. (1983), *Labour Supply*, Cambridge: Cambridge University Press

KINCAID, J. C. (1973), *Poverty and Inequality in Britain*, Harmondsworth: Penguin

KLEIN, R. (1974), 'The case for elitism', *Political Quarterly* vol. 45

—— (1980), 'The welfare state: a self-inflicted crisis?', *Political Quarterly* 1980:1

—— (1981), 'Values, Power and Policies', in OECD (1981)

—— & M. O'HIGGINS, eds. (1985), *The Future of Welfare*, Oxford: Blackwell

KNAPP, M. (1984), *The Economics of Social Care*, London: Macmillan

KNUDSEN., K. (1980), *Ulikhet i grunnskolen*, Bergen: Universitetsforlaget

KÖHLER, P. A. & H. F. ZACHER, Hrsg. (1983), *Beitrage zur Geschichte und aktuelle Situation der Sozialversicherung*, Berlin: Duncker & Humblot

KOLBERG, J. E. (1983a), *Farvel til velferdsstaten?* Oslo: Cappelen

—— (1983), *Utviklningen av de skandinaviske velferdsstater fra 1970 til 1980*, Oslo: FAFO

—— (1984), 'Private og offentlige velferdskomponenter', in *Norsk Årbok for Sosialpolitisk Forskning*

—— & P. A. PETTERSEN (1981), 'Om velferdsstatens politiske basis', *Tidsskrift for samfunnsforskning* 1981:2–3

KORPI, W. (1978), *The Working Class in Welfare Capitalism*, London: Routledge & Kegan Paul

—— (1980), 'Social Policy and Distributional Conflict in the Capitalist Democracies', *West European Politics* (Oct.)

—— (1982), *Från undersåte till medborgare*, Stockholm: Tiden

—— (1983), *The Democratic Class Struggle*, London: Routledge & Kegan Paul

—— (1985), 'Economic Growth and the Welfare State: Leaky Bucket or Irrigation System?' *European Sociological Review* 1985: 2

KRAMER, R. M. (1981), *Voluntary Agencies in the Welfare State*, Berkeley: University of California Press

KRISTENSEN, O. P. (1982), 'Privat eller offentlig produktion af offentlige serviceydelser: Dansk brandvæsen som eksempel', *Nordisk Administrativt Tidsskrift* 1982:3

KRISTOL, I. (1975), 'The High Cost of Equality', *Fortune* (Nov.)

—— (1977), 'Thoughts on Equality and Egalitarianism', in Campbell (1977)

—— (1978), *Two Cheers for Capitalism*, New York: Basic Books

KRUSE, A. (1983), *Den offentliga sektorns sysselsättningsutveckling i Norden under 1970-talet*, Oslo: Nordic Council

KUHNLE, S. (1983), *Velferdsstatens utvikling: Norge i komparativt perspektiv*, Bergen: Universitetsforlaget

—— & S. ROKKAN (1979), 'Thomas Humphrey Marshall', *International Encyclopedia of the Social Sciences* vol. 18 (Biographical Supplement)

KUTTNER, R. (1984), *The Economic Illusion*, Boston: Houghton Mifflin

KUUSI, P. (1964), *Social Policy for the Sixties. A Plan for Finland*, Helsinki: The Finnish Social Policy Association

LADD, E. C. (1979), 'The Riddle of the "Tax Revolt" ', *Economic Impact* 1979: 3

LADD H. & N. TIDEMAN, eds. (1981), *Taxable Expenditure Limitations*, Washington DC: Urban Institute

LAMPMAN, R. J. (1984), *Social Welfare Spending*, New York: Academic Press

LANE, R. E. (1979), 'The Legitimacy Bias', in Denitch (1979)

LANSLEY, S. & S. WEIR (1983), 'Towards a popular view of poverty', *New Society* 25 Aug

LAVINDKOMSTKOMMISSIONEN (1981), *Betaenkning*, Copenhagen: Ministry of Labour

LE GRAND, J. (1982), *The Strategy of Equality*, London: Allen & Unwin

—— (1983), 'On Measuring the Distributional Impact of Public Expenditures: Some Methodological Problems', London School of Economics (mimeo)

—— (1984), 'Equity as an Economic Objective', *Journal of Applied Philosophy* 1984:1

—— & R. ROBINSON (1976), *The Economics of Social Problems*, London: Macmillan

LEIN, L. (1984), *Families without Villains*, Lexington: Lexington Books

LEU, R. E., R. L. FREY & B. BUHMANN (1985), 'Taxes, Expenditures and Income Distribution in Switzerland', *Journal of Social Policy* 1985: 3

LEVEKÅRSUNDERSØKELSEN (1976), *Slutrapport*, Oslo: Universitetsforlaget (NOU)

LEWIN, L. (1984), *Ideologi och strategi*, Stockholm: Norstedts

LINDBECK, A. (1981a), *Disincentive Problems in Developed Countries*, International Chamber of Commerce

—— (1981b), 'Work Disincentives in the Welfare State', in *Nationalökonomische Gesellschaft Lectures 79–80*, Vienna: Manz

—— (1983), 'Interpreting Income Distributions in a Welfare State', *European Economic Review* (May)

—— (1985), 'Redistribution Policy and the Expansion of the Public Sector', *Journal of Public Economics* 1985: 3

—— (1986), 'Limits to the Welfare State', *Challenge* (Jan. and Feb.)

LINDENJÖ, B. (1978), 'Effektivitet, legitimitet och kris', *Häften för Kritiska Studier* 1978: 5

LINGSOM, S. (1984), 'Omsorg for ektefellen', *Tidsskrift for samfunnsforskning* 1984: 3

LINGÅS, L. G., red. (1970), *Myten om velferdsstaten*, Oslo: Pax

LIPSET, S. M. & E. RAAB (1978), 'The Message of Proposition 13', *Commentary* (Sept.)

—— & W. SCHNEIDER (1983), *The Confidence Gap*, New York: Free Press

LITTLE, I. M. D. (1960), *A Critique of Welfare Economics*, Oxford: Oxford University Press

LODIN, S. O. (1977), 'Swedish Tax Reforms 1971–1977. Why so Many?' *Scandinavian Studies in Law* vol. 21

LOGUE, J. (1979), 'The Welfare State: Victim of its own Success', *Daedalus* (Fall)

LONEY, M., D. BOSWELL & J. CLARKE, eds. (1983), *Social Policy and Social Welfare*, Milton Keynes: Open University Press

LOWI, T. J. (1972), 'Four Systems of Policy, Politics, and Choice', *Public Administration Review* 1972 (July and Aug.)

LYBECK, J. A. (1984), 'Hur stor är den offentliga sektorn?' *Ekonomisk Debatt* 1984: 2

MCDANIEL, P. R. & S. S. SURREY (1985), *International Aspects of Tax Expenditures: A Comparative Study*, Amsterdam: North-Holland

MCGREGOR, D. (1960), *The Human Side of Enterprise*, New York: McGraw Hill

MCGREGOR, S. (1981), *The Politics of Poverty*, London: Longman

MACK, J. & S. LANSLEY (1985), *Poor Britain*, London: Allen & Unwin

MACKENZIE, N., ed. (1958), *Conviction*, London: MacGibbon & Kee
McKEOWN , T. (1965), *Medicine in Modern Society*, London: Allen & Unwin
—— (1979), *The Role of Medicine*, Oxford: Blackwell
MAGNUSSON, D. (1980), 'Learned Helplessness', *Skandinaviska Banken Quarterly Review* 1980: 3–4
MAKTUTREDNINGEN (1982), *Sluttrapport*, Oslo: Universitetsforlaget (NOU)
MARCHAL, J. & B. DUCROS, eds. (1968), *The Distribution of National Income*, New York & London: International Economic Association
MARKLUND, S. & S. SVALLFORS (1985), 'Dual Welfare: Segmentation and Work Enforcement in the Swedish Welfare System', University of Umeå (mimeo)
MARSH, D. (1980), *The Welfare State: Concept and Development*, London: Longman
MARSHALL, A. (1949), *Principles of Economics*, 8th edn., London: Macmillan
MARSHALL, T. H. (1961), 'The Welfare State: A Sociological Interpretation', *Archives européennes de sociologie* 1961:2
—— (1964), *Class, Citizenship, and Social Development*, New York: Doubleday
—— (1972), 'Value Problems and Welfare-Capitalism', *Journal of Social Policy* 1972: 1
—— (1977), *Social Policy in the Twentieth Century*, London: Hutchinson
MARTIN E. (1982), 'Public Opinion on Welfare and Related Issues', Washington DC: National Academy of Sciences/Committee on National Statistics (mimeo)
MARTINUSSEN, W. (1981), 'Høyrebølgens understrømmer', *Tidsskrift for samfunnsforskning* 1981:2–3
MATTHEWS, R. C. O., ed. (1982), *Slower Growth in the Western World*, London: Heineman
MATZNER, E. (1982), *Der Wohlfahrtsstaat von morgen*, Frankfurt: Campus
MEAD, L. M. (1982), 'Social programs and social obligations', *The Public Interest* (Fall)
MEYER, L. M., ed. (1981), *The Supply Side Effects of Economic Policy*, Boston: Kluwer-Nijhoff
MIESZKOWSKI, P. (1969), 'Tax Incidence Theory: The Effects of Taxes on the Distribution of Income', *Journal of Economic Literature* 7: 1103–24
MILLER, A. H. (1981), 'Policy and Performance in the 1980 Election', Ann Arbor: Center for Political Studies (mimeo)
MILLER, S. M. (1976), 'Types of Equality: Sorting, Rewarding, Performing', in Ashline (1976)
—— & M. REIN (1975), 'Can Income Redistribution Work?' *Social Policy* (May and June)

—— & P. ROBY (1970), 'Poverty: Changing Social Stratification', in Townsend (1970)

MILLWARD, R. (1982), 'The comparative performance of public and private ownership', in Roll (1982)

MISHAN, E. J. (1967), *The Costs of Economic Growth*, Harmondsworth: Penguin

—— (1982), *Introduction to Political Economy*, London: Hutchinson

MISHRA, R. (1977), *Society and Social Policy*, London: Macmillan

—— (1984), *The Welfare State in Crisis*, Bristol: Wheatsheaf

MOFFITT, R. A. (1981), 'The negative income tax: would it discourage work?' *Monthly Labor Review* (April)

—— & K. C. KEHRER, (1981), 'The Effects of Tax and Transfer Programs on Labor Supply', in Ehrenberg (1981)

MOGENSEN, G. V. (1985), 'Forskning i sort økonomi—en oversigt', *Nationaløkonomisk Tidsskrift* 1985: 1

MOMMSEN, W. S., ed. (1981), *The Emergence of the Welfare State in Britain and Germany*, London: Croom Helm

MORONEY, J. R., ed. (1979), *Income Inequality: Trends and International Comparisons*, Lexington: Lexington Books

MOSS, M., ed. (1973), *The Measurement of Economic and Social Performance*, New York: Columbia University Press

MOYNIHAN, D. P., ed. (1968), *On Understanding Poverty*, New York: Basic Books

MURNANE, R. J. (1984), 'Comparisons of Public and Private Schools: Lessons from the Uproar', *Journal of Human Resources* 1984: 2

MUSGRAVE, R. A., ed. (1965), *Essays in Fiscal Federalism*, Washington DC: Brookings

—— (1981) 'Leviathan Cometh—Or Does He?' in Ladd & Tideman (1981)

—— (1984) 'Excess Budget: Norms, Hypotheses, and Performance', Nobel Symposium on the Growth of Government, Stockholm

—— & P. B. MUSGRAVE (1976), *Public Finance in Theory and Practice*, New York: McGraw-Hill

—— K. E. CASE & H. LEONARD (1974), 'The Distribution of Fiscal Burdens and Benefits', *Public Finance Quarterly* (July)

MYRDAL, G. (1953), *The Political Element in the Development of Economic Theory*, London: Routledge & Kegan Paul

—— (1959), *Value in Social Theory*, New York: Harper

—— (1960), *Beyond the Welfare State*, New Haven: Yale University Press

—— (1968), *Asian Drama*, New York: Pantheon

NATH, S. K. (1973), *A Prespective of Welfare Economics*, London: Macmillan

NICHOLSON, J. L. (1964), *Redistribution of Income in the United Kingdom in 1959, 1957, and 1953*, London: Bowes & Bowes

—— (1979), *The Changing Impact of Taxes and Benefits on Household Incomes in the United Kingdom, 1957–1976*, London: Policy Studies Institute

—— & A. J. C. BRITTON (1976), 'The Redistribution of Income', in Atkinson (1976)

NISBET, R. (1977), 'Where do we go from here?' in Campbell (1977)

NORDHAUS, W. & J. TOBIN (1972), *Is Economic Growth Obsolete?* New York: National Bureau of Economic Research

NOZICK, R. (1974), *Anarchy, State and Utopia*, New York: Basic Books

NSI (1981), *Människan och myndigheterna*, Stockholm: Nämnden för samhällsinformation

NYGÅRD, F. (1984), 'Inkomstbildningen och inkomstfördelningen i Finland och Sverige under 1970-talet', *Statistisk analys av inkomstfördelningar*, Åbo: Åbo Akademi

O'CONNOR, J. (1973), *The Fiscal Crisis of the State*, New York: St Martin's Press

OECD (1976), *Public Expenditure on Income Maintenance Programmes*, Paris

—— (1978), *Public Expenditure Trends*, Paris

—— (1981), *The Welfare State in Crisis*, Paris

—— (1984), *Tax Expenditures*, Paris

—— (1985), *Social Expenditure 1960–1990*, Paris

OFFE, C. (1984), *Contradictions of the Welfare State*. London: Hutchinson

O'HIGGINS, M. (1980a). 'The Distributive Effects of Public Expenditure and Taxation: An Agnostic View of the CSO Analyses', in Sandford, Pond & Walker (1980)

—— (1980b), 'Income Distribution and Social Policy: an Assessment after the Royal Commission on the Distribution of Income and Wealth', in Brown & Baldwin (1980)

—— (1983), 'Issues of Redistribution in State Welfare Spending', in Loney, Boswell & Clarke (1983)

—— (1985a), 'Inequality, Redistribution and Recession: The British Experience', *Journal of Social Policy* 1985: 3

—— (1985b), 'Welfare, redistribution and inequality—disillusion, illusion and reality', in Bean, Ferris & Whynes (1985)

—— & P. RUGGLES (1981), 'The distribution of Public Expenditures and Taxes among Households in the United Kingdom', *Review of Income and Wealth* 1981: 3

OKUN, A. M. (1975), *Equality and Efficiency. The Big Tradeoff*, Washington DC: Brookings

—— (1977), 'Further Thoughts on Equality and Efficiency', in Campbell (1977)

OLAVSSON, S. (1984), *Islenska velferðarrikit: Livskjør og stjórnmal.* Reykjavik: University of Iceland

OLSON, M. (1982), *The Rise and Decline of Nations*, New Haven: Yale University Press

OLSSON, S. E. (1985), *Welfare Programs in Sweden*, Stockholm: Institute for Social Research

ORCUTT, G., S. CALDWELL & R. WERTHEIMER (1976), *Policy Exploration through Microanalytic Simulation*, Washington DC: Urban Institute

ORSHANSKY, M. (1965), 'Counting the Poor: Another Look at the Poverty Profile', *Social Security Bulletin* vol. 28

—— (1969), 'How Poverty is Measured', *Monthly Labor Review* (Feb.)

OTTER, C. von (1983), *Mätning, management och mobilisering i offentlig verksamhet*, Stockholm: Arbetslivscentrum

OWENS, J. P. (1983), 'Tax expenditures and direct expenditures as instruments of social policy', in Cnossen (1983)

PALMER, J. L. & J. W. SAWHILL, eds. (1982), *The Reagan Experiment*, Washington DC: Urban Institute

PEACOCK, A. (1974), 'The Treatment of Government Expenditure in Studies of Income Redistribution', in Smith & Culbertson (1974)

—— & M. RICKETS (1978), 'The Growth of the Public Sector and Inflation', in Hirsch & Goldthorpe (1978)

PECHMAN, J. A. (1973), *International Trends in the Distribution of Tax Burdens: Implications for Tax Policy*, London: Institute for Fiscal Studies

—— (1983a), *Federal Tax Policy*, 4th edn., Washington DC: Brookings

—— (1983b), 'Anatomy of the US individual income tax', in Cnossen (1983)

—— & M. J. MAZUR (1984), 'The Rich, the Poor and the Taxes They Pay: An Update', *The Public Interest* (Fall)

—— & B. A. OKNER (1974), *Who Bears the Tax Burden?* Washington DC: Brookings

PEN, J. (1979), 'A Clear Case of Leveling: Income Equalization in the Netherlands', *Social Research* No. 4

PETTERSEN, P. A. (1982), *Lenjer i norsk sosialpolitikk*, Oslo: Universitetsforlaget

PIACHAUD, D. (1981), 'Peter Townsend and the Holy Grail', *New Society* 10 Sept

PIGOU, A. C. (1929), *The Economics of Welfare*, 3rd edn., London: Macmillan

PINKER, R. (1971), *Social Policy and Social Theory*, London: Heinemann

—— (1979), *The Idea of Welfare*, London: Heinemann

PIVEN, F. F. & R. A. CLOWARD (1972), *Regulating the Poor: The Functions of Public Welfare*, London: Tavistock

—— (1982), *The New Class War*, New York: Pantheon

POPPER, K. R. (1947), *The Open Society and its Enemies*, London

—— (1957), *Poverty of Historicism*, London: Routledge

PORTER, R. D. & A. S. BAYER (1984), 'A Monetary Perspective on the Underground Economic Activity in the United States', *Federal Reserve Bulltin* (March)

PRAAG, B. M. S. van, A. J. M. HAGENAARS & H. van WEEREN (1982), 'Poverty in Europe', *Review of Income and Wealth* vol. 28: 345–59

PRYOR, F. L. (1968), *Public Expenditures in Communist and Capitalist Nations*, Irwin: Homewood

PÖNTINEN, S. & H. UUSITALO (1986), *The Legitimacy of the Welfare State in Finland*, Helsinki: Suomen Gallup

RAINWATER, L. (1982), 'Stigma and Income-Tested Programs', in Garfinkel (1982)

RAWLS, J. (1971), *A Theory of Justice*, Cambridge: Harvard University Press

REIN, M. (1970a), *Social Policy. Issues of Choice and Change*, New York: Random House

—— (1970b), 'Problems in the Definition and Measurement of Poverty', in Townsend (1970)

—— (1976), *Social Science and Public Policy*, Harmondsworth: Penguin

—— (1985a), 'The Social Welfare Labour Market', in Eisenstadt & Ahimeir (1985)

—— (1985b), 'Women, Employment and Social Welfare', in Klein & O'Higgins (1985)

—— & L. RAINWATER (1981), 'From Welfare State to Welfare Society: Some Unresolved Issues in Assessment', Berlin: IIVG Papers

REYNOLDS, M. & E. SMOLENSKY (1977), *Public Expenditures, Taxes, and the Distribution of Income*, New York: Academic Press

RIMLINGER, G. (1971), *Welfare Policy and Industrialization in Europe, America and Russia*, New York: Wiley

RINGEN, A. red. (1975), *Velferdsforsforskning og sosialpolitikk*, Oslo: Institute for Applied Social Research

RINGEN, K. (1977), *The Development of Health Policy: Norway, England and Germany*, The Johns Hopkins University: School of Hygiene and Public Health

RINGEN, S. (1974), 'Welfare Studies in Scandinavia, *Scandinavian Political Studies* vol. 9

—— (1980), 'Utviklingen av den personlige inntektsfordeling', *Statsøkonomisk Tidskrift* 1980: 2

—— (1981a), *Hvor går velferdsstaten?* Oslo: Gyldendal

—— (1981b), *Levekår og samfunnsplanlegging*, Oslo: Ministry of Consumer Affairs and Government Administration

—— (1982), *Inntekt og forbruk i Norge 1950–1980*, Oslo: Ministry of Consumer Affairs and Government Administration

—— (1985), 'Toward a Third Stage in the Measurement of Poverty', *Acta Sociologica* 1985: 2

—— (1986), *Difference and Similarity: Two Studies in Comparative Income Distribution*, Stockholm: Swedish Institute for Social Research

—— & K. WÆRNESS, red. (1982), *Sosialpolitikk for 1980-åra*, Oslo: Gyldendal

RIVLIN, A. M. (1971), *Systematic Thinking for Social Action*, Washington DC: Brookings

ROBBINS, L. (1935), *An Essay on the Nature and Significance of Economic Science*, 2nd edn., London: Macmillan

ROBERTSON, J. (1982), 'What Comes After the Welfare State?', *Futures* (Feb.)

ROBINS, P. K. (1985), 'A Comparison of the Labor Supply Findings from the Four Negative Income Tax Experiments', *Journal of Human Resources* 1985: 4

ROBINSON, J. (1964), *Economic Philosophy*, Harmondsworth: Penguin

ROBSON, W. A. (1976), *Welfare State and Welfare Society*, London: Allen & Unwin

RØDSETH, T. (1977), *Inntektsfordeling i Norge*, Oslo: Universitetsforlaget, (NOU)

ROGERS, H. R. (1982), *The Costs of Human Neglect*, New York: Sharpe

ROGERS, J. D. (1974), 'Explaining Income Redistribution', in Hochman & Peterson (1974)

ROGOFF RAMSØY, N. (1977), *Sosial Mobilitet i Norge*, Oslo: Tiden

ROKKAN, S. (1970), *Citizens, Elections, Parties*, Oslo: Universitetsforlaget

ROLD ANDERSEN, B. (1984), 'Rationality and Irrationality of the Nordic Welfare State', *Daedalus* (Winter)

ROLL (Lord), ed. (1982), *The Mixed Economy*, London: Macmillan

ROOM, G. (1979), *The Sociology of Welfare*, Oxford: Robertson

ROSANVALLON, P. (1981), *La crise de l'État-providence*, Paris: Seuil

ROSE, R. & G. PETERS (1978), *Can Government Go Bankrupt?* London: Macmillan

ROWNTREE, S. (1901), *Poverty: A Study of Town Life*, London: Macmillan

—— (1941), *Poverty and Progress*, London: Longmans

—— & G. R. LAVERS (1951), *Poverty and the Welfare State*, London: Longmans

ROYAL COMMISSION ON THE DISTRIBUTION OF INCOME AND WEALTH (1976), *Higher Incomes from Employment*, Report No. 3, London: HMSO

RUGGLES, P. & M. O'HIGGINS (1981), 'The Distribution of Public Expenditure among Households in the United States', *Review of Income and Wealth* 1981:2

SANDFORD, C. T., C. POND & R. WALKER, eds. (1980), *Taxation and Social Policy*, London: Heinemann

SAUNDERS, P. (1984), 'Evidence on Income Redistribution by Governments', *Economics and Statistics Department. Working Papers No. 11*, Paris: OECD

—— (1985), 'Public Expenditure and Economic Performance in OECD Countries', *Journal of Public Policy* 1985: 1

—— (1986), 'What Can We Learn from International Comparisons of Public Sector Size and Economic Performance?' *European Sociological Review* 1986: 1

—— & F. KLAU (1985), *The Role of the Public Sector*, Paris: OECD

SAWYER, M. (1976), 'Income Distribution in OECD Countries', *OECD Economic Outlook—Occasional Studies*, Paris: OECD

—— (1982), 'Income Distribution and the Welfare State', in Botho (1982)

SCHMID, G. (1984), 'Krise des Wohlfahrsstaates: Alternativen zur staatlichen Finanzierung und Bereitstellung Kollektiver Güter', *Politische Vierteljahrschrift* 1984: 1

SCHOTTLAND, C. I., ed. (1967), *The Welfare State: Selected Essays*, New York: Harper & Row

SCHULTZ, J. (1974), 'The Economics of Mandatory Retirement', *Industrial Gerontology* (Winter)

SCHULTZ, T. W. (1981), *Investing in People*, California: University of California Press

SCHULTZE, C. P. (1977), *The Public Use of Private Interests*, Washington DC: Brookings

SEIP, A.-L. (1981), *Om velferdsstatens framvekst*, Oslo: Universitetsforlaget

—— (1984), *Sosialhjelpstaten blir til*, Oslo: Gyldendal

SEJERSTED, F. (1984), *Demokrati og rettsstat*, Oslo: Universitetsforlaget

SELDON, A. (1981), *Wither the Welfare State*, London: Institute of Economic Affairs

—— ed. (1983), *Agenda for Social Democracy*, London: Institute of Economic Affairs

SEN, A. K. (1970), *Collective Choice and Social Welfare*, London: Holden-Day

—— (1973), *On Economic Inequality*, Oxford: Oxford University Press

—— (1979a), 'Personal Utilities and Public Judgements: or What's Wrong with Welfare Economies?' *Economic Journal* (Sept.)

—— (1979b), 'Issues in the Measurement of Poverty', *Scandinavian Journal of Economics* 1979: 285–307

—— (1980), 'Equality of What?' *The Tanner Lectures on Human Values* vol. i, Cambridge: Cambridge University Press

—— (1981), *Poverty and Famines*, Oxford: Oxford University Press
—— (1982), *Choice, Welfare and Measurement*, Oxford: Blackwell
—— (1983), 'Poor, Relatively Speaking', *Oxford Economic Papers* 35: 153–69
—— (1984), *Resource, Values and Development*, Oxford: Blackwell
—— (1985a), 'Social Choice and Justice: A Review Article', *Journal of Economic Literature* XXIII: 1764–76
—— (1985b), 'A Sociological Approach to the Measurement of Poverty: A Reply to Professor Peter Townsend', *Oxford Economic Papers* 1985: 4
—— (1985c), *Commodities and Capabilities*, Amsterdam: North-Holland
—— & B. WILLIAMS, eds. (1982), *Utilitarianism and Beyond*, Cambridge: Cambridge University Press
SHALEV, M. (1983), 'Class Politics and the Western Welfare State', in Spiro & Yuchtman-Yaar (1983)
SIDGWICK, H. (1983), *The Principles of Political Economy*, London: Macmillan
SIMON, H. A. (1983), *Reason in Human Affairs*, Stanford: Stanford University Press
SIMONS, H. (1948), *Economic Policy for a Free Society*, Chicago: University of Chicago Press
SKOCPOL, T., forthc., 'America's Incomplete Welfare State', in Esping-Andersen, Rein & Rainwater, forthc.
SMEEDING, T. *et al.* (1985), 'Poverty in Major Industrialized Countries', Luxembourg Income Study (Working Paper No. 2)
—— M. O'HIGGINS & L. RAINWATER, eds., forthc., *Poverty, Inequality and the Distribution of Income*, Brighton: Wheatsheaf
SMITH, D. (1975), 'Public Consumption and Economic Performance', *National Westminster Bank Quarterly* (Nov.)
SMITH, W. L. & J. M. CULBERTSON, eds. (1974), *Public Finance and Stabilization Policy*, Amsterdam: North-Holland
SMOLENSKY, F., W. POMMEREHNE & R. DALRYMPLE (1979), 'Postfisc Income Inequality: A Comparison of the United States and West Germany', in Moroney (1979)
SOCIALE EN CULTUREEL PLANBUREAU (1981), *Profijt van de overheid in 1977*, s-Gravenhage: Staatsnitgeverij
SOLTOW, L., ed. (1969), *Six Papers on the Size Distribution of Wealth and Income*, New York: Colombia University Press (NBER)
SPANN R. M. (1977), 'Public versus Private Provision of Governmental Services', in Borcherding (1977)
SPÅNT, R. (1979a), *Den svenska förmögenhetsfördelningens utveckling*, Uppsala: Acta Universitatis Upsaliensis
—— (1979b), *Den svenska inkomstfördelningens utveckling 1920–1976*, Stockholm: Liber

—— (1983), 'Wealth Distribution in Sweden 1920–1983', Stockholm: TCO (mimeo)

SPIRO, S. H. & E. YUCHTMAN-YAAR, eds. (1983), *Evaluating the Welfare state*, New York: Academic Press

STAFFORD, F. P. (1985), 'Income-Maintenance Policy and Work Effort', in Hausman & Wise (1985)

STARK, T. (1977), *The Distribution of Income in Eight Countries*, Royal Commission on the Distribution of Income and Wealth, Background paper No. 4, London: HMSO

STATISTICS SWEDEN (1984), *Vem utnyttjar den offentliga sektorns tjänster?* Stockholm: Statistics Sweden

STATSKONTORET (1985), *Statlig tjänsteproduktion. Produktivitetsutvecklingen 1960-1980. Huvudrapport*, Stockholm: Statskontoret

STÅHL, J. (1983), 'Sjukdom och socialförsäkringar', in Björklund *et al.* (1983)

STÅHLBERG, A.-C. (1983), 'Ålderspensionen i ATP', in Björklund *et al.* (1983)

STEPHENSON G, (1980), 'Taxes, Benefits and the Redistribution of Income', in Sandford, Pond & Walker (1980)

STEUERLE, E. & M. HARTZMARK (1981), 'Individual Income Taxation, 1947–79', *National Tax Journal* (June)

STJERNØ, S. (1985), *Den moderne fattigdommen*, Oslo: Universitetsforlaget

SUNDSTRÖM, G. (1983), *Caring for the Aged in Welfare Society*, University of Stockholm: School of Social Work

—— (1984), *De gamla, deras anhöriga och hemtjänsten*, University of Stockholm: School of Social Work

SURREY, S. S. & P. R. MCDANIEL (1985), *Tax Expenditures*, Cambridge, Mass.: Harvard University Press

TANZI, V., ed. (1982), *The Underground Economy in the United States and Abroad*, Lexington: Lexington Books

TARSCHYS, D. (1975), 'The Growth of Public Expenditures: Nine Modes of Explanation', *Scandinavian Political Studies* vol. 10

TAWNEY, R. H. (1964), *Equality*, London: Allen & Unwin

TAYLOR-GOOBY, P. (1982), 'Two Cheers for the Welfare State: Public Opinion and Private Welfare', *Journal of Public Policy* 1982: 4

—— (1983), 'Legitimation Deficit, Public Opinion and the Welfare State', *Sociology* vol. 17: 2

—— (1985a), 'The Politics of Welfare: Public Attitudes and Behaviour', in Klein & O'Higgins (1985)

—— (1985b), 'Attitudes to Welfare', *Journal of Social Policy* 1985: 1

—— (1985c), *Public Opinion, Ideology and State Welfare*. London: Routledge & Kegan Paul

—— (1985d), 'The Attitudes to Welfare Project: Final Report', London: ESRC (mimeo)

THOMPSON, J. B. & D. HELD, eds. (1982), *Habermas—Critical Debates*, London: Macmillan

THUROW, L. C. (1971), 'The income distribution as a pure public good', *Quarterly Journal of Economics* 85: 327–36

—— (1975), *Generating Inequality*, New York: Basic Books

—— (1981), 'Equity, Efficiency, Social Justice, and Redistribution', in OECD (1981)

TINBERGEN, J. (1952), *On the Theory of Economic Policy*, Amsterdam: North-Holland

TITMUSS, R. M. (1958), *Essays on 'The Welfare State'*, London: Allen & Unwin

—— (1962), *Income Distribution and Social Change*, London: Allen & Unwin

—— (1963), 'The Welfare State: Images and Realities', *Social Service Review* (March)

—— (1968), *Commitment to Welfare*, London: Allen & Unwin

—— (1970), *The Gift Relationship*, London: Allen & Unwin

—— (1974), *Social Policy*, London: Allen & Unwin

—— (1976), *Commitment to Welfare*, London: Allen & Unwin

TOBIN, J. (1970), 'On Limiting the Domain of Inequality', *Journal of Law and Economics* vol. 13 (Oct.)

—— (1983), 'Keynes' Policies in Theory and Practice', *Challenge* (Nov. and Dec.)

—— (1985), 'The Fiscal Revolution: Disturbing Prospects', *Challenge* (Jan. and Feb.)

TOLLEY, G. S. & W. B. SHEAR (1984), 'International Comparison of Tax Rates and Their Effects on National Incomes', in Kendrick (1984)

TOWNSEND, P., ed. (1970), *The Concept of Poverty*, London: Heinemann

—— (1979), *Poverty in the United Kingdom*, London: Penguin

—— (1985), 'A Sociological Approach to the Measurement of Poverty: A Rejoinder to Professor Amartya Sen', *Oxford Economic Papers* 1985: 4

—— & N. DAVIDSON, eds. (1982), *Inequalities in Health. The Black Report*, Harmondsworth: Penguin

TÅHALIN, M. (1984), 'Fritid och rekreation', in Erikson & Åberg (1984)

USHER, D. (1981), *The Economic Prerequisite to Democracy*, Oxford: Blackwell

UUSITALO, H. (1975), *Income and Welfare*, University of Helsinki: Research Group for Comparative Sociology

—— (1984), 'Comparative Research on the Determinants of the Welfare State: the State of the Art', *European Journal of Political Research* vol. 12: 403–22

—— (1985), 'Redistribution and Equality in the Welfare State', *European Sociological Review* 1985: 2

WADENSJÖ, E. (1984), 'Disability Policy in Sweden', in Haveman, Halberstadt & Burkhauser (1984)

—— (1985), *Disability Pensioning of Older Workers in Sweden*, Stockholm: Swedish Institute for Social Research

WÆRNESS, K. (1975), 'Kvinners omsorgsarbeid i den ulønnete produksjon', Bergen: Levekårsundersøkelsen

—— (1978), 'The Invisible Welfare State: Women's Work at Home', *Acta Sociologica* vol. 21, Supplement

—— (1982), *Kvinneperspektiver på sosialpolitikken*, Oslo: Universitetsforlaget

—— (1983), 'On the Rationality of Caring', University of Bergen: Department of Sociology (mimeo)

—— & S. RINGEN (1986), 'Women in the Welfare State: The case of Formal and Informal Old-Age Care', in Erikson, Hansen, Ringen & Uusitalo (1986)

WALKER, A., ed. (1982), *Public Expenditure and Social Policy*, London: Heinemann

WALZER, M. (1983), *Spheres of Justice*, New York: Basic Books

WATTS, H. (1968), 'An Economic Definition of Poverty', in Moynihan (1968)

WEALE, A. (1978), *Equality and Social Policy*, London: Routledge & Kegan Paul

—— (1983), *Political Theory and Social Policy*, London: Macmillan

WEDDERBURN, D., ed. (1974), *Poverty, Inequality, and Class Structure*, Cambridge: Cambridge University Press

—— (1980), 'Some Reflections on Inequality and Class Structure' (Stamp Memorial Lecture 1979), London: University of London

WESTERGAARD, J. & H. RESLER, (1976), *Class in a Capitalist Society*, London: Heinemann

WILENSKY, H. (1975), *The Welfare State and Equality*, Berkeley: University of California Press

—— (1981), 'Democratic Corporation, Consensus and Social Policy', in OECD (1981)

—— & G. M. LUEBBERT, S. R. HAHN & A. M. JAMIESON (1985), *Comparative Social Policy: Theories, Methods, Findings*, Berkeley: Institute of International Studies

WILLIAMSON, J. G. & P. H. LINDERT (1980), *American Inequality*, New York: Academic Press

WILSON, D. (1979), *The Welfare State in Sweden*, London: Heinemann

WILSON, T. & D. J. WILSON (1982), *The Political Economy of the Welfare State*, London: Allen & Unwin

WINTER, M., ed. (1975), *War and Economic Development*, Cambridge: Cambridge University Press.

WOLFE, B. L., P. R. de JONG, R. H. HAVEMAN, V. HALBERSTADT & K. P. GOUDSWAARD (1983), 'The Contribution of Income Transfers to Lagging Economic Performance: The United States and the Netherlands in the 1970s' (mimeo)

WORCESTER, D. A. (1980), 'Blueprint for a Welfare State That Contributes to Economic Efficiency', *Social Service Review* (June)

YANKELOVICH, D., *et al.* (1983), *Work and Human Values*, New York: Aspen Institute

YUCHTMAN-YAAR, E. (1983), 'Expectations, Entitlements, and Subjective Welfare', in Spiro & Yuchtman-Yaar (1983)

ZAPF, W. (1984), 'Welfare Production: Public versus Private', *Social Indicators Research* (Apr.)

ZETTERBERG, H. L. (1979), 'The Public's View of Social Welfare Policy in Sweden', Stockholm: SIFO (mimeo)

Index